THIS BOOK BELONGS TO

_____

D1010864

She speaks with wisdom,

and faithful instruction is on her tongue.

She watches over the affairs of her household

and does not eat the bread of idleness.

Her children arise and call her blessed.

PROVERBS 31:26-28 NIV

# INTRODUCTION

There are moments in motherhood where life feels like one endless task. Where nothing seems to get done even though you've been working at it (what was "it" again?) all day. The dishes, the diapers, the homework assignments, the grocery shopping, the sporting events, the music lessons—and those all have to happen before five. Then it's time for the evening cycle. Dinner, laundry, baths, story time, and the age-old, half-hour "but I don't want to go to bed" drama. It's enough to exhaust the most energetic person on earth. And tomorrow you get to do it all again.

Finding time to be still in the chaos of motherhood is no simple task. Yet, when we do make time to quiet ourselves before God, something powerful happens. He gives us supernatural rest. He floods our minds with peace. He restores our joy. And he whispers to the deepest part of our hearts that it all matters. That *we* matter.

As you reflect on these devotions, Scriptures, and prayers, be reminded that God sees every effort you make and he is deeply pleased with your sacrifice. Sit quietly with him and let his love flow into every part of you. He has called you, and he will equip you with everything you need. Be still and be blessed.

# JANUARY

"So do not fear, for I am with you;
do not be dismayed, for I am your God.
I will strengthen you and help you;
I will uphold you with
my righteous right hand."

ISAIAH 41:10 NIV

# NOT HIDING

*He has done this so that every person would long for God,*
*feel their way to him, and find him—*
*for he is the God who is easy to discover!*
ACTS 17:27 TPT

There are plenty of times as a mother when even your best doesn't seem good enough. There are problems you cannot solve, and you certainly don't have all of the answers. You can't always heal broken hearts or find what is lost. It might be tempting to focus on what you cannot do, to keep your eyes fixated on the areas you are lacking. Instead, today turn your eyes to what is infinitely and consistently possible.

Seeking God is not a not an unsolvable problem. He is not hiding behind closed doors, waiting for you to crack the code. He is the knowable God. He longs to be known by you, his child. Amidst uncertainty, failure, frustration, and stress, abiding in him is a sweet rush of fresh air, as natural as breathing and as simple as asking. Your relationship with him need not be a burden or another thing you can't accomplish. He is the God who is easy to discover.

Thank you, God, that you are not difficult to discover. In my weakness, I can have confidence that you are easy to find. When I am overwhelmed by my inadequacies, give me the grace to choose you. Help me develop quick reflexes when it comes to seeking you. You are not complicated or overwhelming. Today, as I turn my eyes to you, teach me to depend on you more fully.

# UNDER HIS CARE

*"I tell you, do not worry about your life, what you will eat or drink;
or about your body, what you will wear. Is not life more than food,
and the body more than clothes? Look at the birds of the air;
they do not sow or reap or store away in barns, and yet your heavenly
Father feeds them. Are you not much more valuable than they?
Can any one of you by worrying add a single hour to your life?"*

MATTHEW 6:25-27 NIV

The nurturing of a family often falls to the mother. It might feel as
though the weight of your family is carried on your shoulders. You
schedule appointments, plan the meals, bandage skinned knees,
and help with math homework. Beyond the level that you pour
yourself out in caring for your family, you are cared for even more.
You are of utmost importance on God's list. He clothes the lilies and
he will clothe you as well. He will care for your needs just as you
care for you family, tirelessly and sometimes alone.

Take heart in knowing that while your responsibilities might feel
overwhelming, God's ability to care for you individually is more
than sufficient. If his eyes are on the sparrow, you can be confident
that he will be consistent in providing for you and your family.

Change my perspective today, God. Show me the ways you have
provided for me. Renew my trust in your faithfulness. Where I
have been anxious about my needs, bring peace. Where I have
felt worn out in managing my family's needs, bring rest. You are
a good father who cares for his children. Remind me of your
goodness. You are a kind father who is attentive to his children.
Remind me of your kindness. You are a capable father whose
resources are never limited. Remind me of your provision.

# DON'T BE TROUBLED

*"Don't let your hearts be troubled. Trust in God, and trust also in me. There is more than enough room in my Father's home. If this were not so, would I have told you that I am going to prepare a place for you? When everything is ready, I will come and get you, so that you will always be with me where I am."*

JOHN 14:1-3 NLT

God knows your afflictions. He knows the pain you've experienced and the struggles you face in your daily life. He sees you and he is intricately aware of what troubles your heart at any given time. You are fully known. But there's more. He not only knows your afflictions, he comforts you in them, provides a solution, and then gives you a great hope to hold onto. His awareness brings comfort, his reminder to trust brings a solution, and his promise of returning cements that our hope is not in our problems dissolving but in the promise that he is coming back for us.

Today, as the mundane details of motherhood overwhelm you, set your eyes on this great hope. As you cultivate your home to be a safe and peaceful place for your children, remember that Jesus too is preparing a place for you in his Father's house. As today's afflictions threaten to capsize you, remember that a day is coming when everything will be made right. Don't let your heart be troubled. Trust in the promise that in his perfect timing, when everything is ready, he will come back for you.

Thank you, God, that you have not left me hopeless. I am known; I can trust in you. When I am overwhelmed, remind me that the hope of what's to come is greater than today's afflictions. Help me to teach my children that you are faithful. May my actions reflect the steadiness that comes from a faith rooted and established in you.

# FORGIVE YOUR CHILDREN

*"If you forgive those who sin against you,*
*your heavenly Father will forgive you.*
*But if you refuse to forgive others,*
*your Father will not forgive your sins."*
MATTHEW 6:14-15 NLT

Sometimes we forget the humanity of our children. It's so easy to see them as an extension of ourselves that we forget that are fully individual. They will make the wrong choices and will likely hurt you at some point. You are the safest place for their developing minds, social skills, and behaviors. As they sin in their youth, you are a soft place to land. As mothers, we are often on the receiving end of raging emotions and loud tantrums as they muddle through development.

In this place, forgiveness will abound. Forgive your children quickly as Christ has forgiven you. Remember that you are the model they have for who Jesus is. When we think of forgiveness, we often think of those who have deliberately wronged us, or of our enemies. Today, remember that your children are just as in need of soft-hearted forgiveness as anyone else. Walk with them in compassion just as the Father walks with you.

Father, soften my heart toward my children. Teach me how to forgive quickly and to model compassion to them. When their emotions feel out of control, teach me to be steady. Forgive me for the times I have acted in frustration and have held onto hurts from my family. If there are places in my heart that unforgiveness has hardened, show them to me so I can confess them to you and seek forgiveness. As a leader of my family, show me ways to model Christlike forgiveness in my home.

# IN EVERY SEASON

*The day is yours, and yours also the night;*
*you established the sun and moon.*
*It was you who set all the boundaries of the earth;*
*you made both summer and winter.*

PSALM 74:16-17 NIV

Nothing earthly lasts forever. God has designed it this way. He has made the boundaries of the earth; he has made both summer and winter. The seasons are his personal design. In motherhood, you will encounter summers and winters. You will walk through countless different seasons with your children. Learn to recognize where you and then you can plan and react accordingly. Just as you plan for the weather, equip yourself in motherhood.

Maybe you are in a season of little sleep; give yourself margin and recognize that it won't last forever. Maybe you're in a season of busy schedules and endless appointments; prepare by asking God for increased patience and endurance when you want to quit. If you're in a season of increased conflict, equip yourself by safeguarding your time with God and refueling when your emotions feel fried. Relish in the summers of motherhood and shelter in the winters. Soak up the sun and take shelter from the rain and storm. God, the designer of seasons, will see you through both.

Thank you, God, that you know which season I am in. You see me clearly and you know exactly what I need to get through the summers and the winters. Help me to turn my eyes to you. I praise you, the Creator of the sun and the moon. Nothing is beyond you. As I walk through my current season, equip me with endurance and remind me of the hope that comes from knowing that it won't last forever. No matter which season I am in, you are worthy of praise.

# WORK UNTO GOD

*Whatever you do, do your work heartily,*
*as for the Lord rather than for men.*
COLOSSIANS 3:23 NASB

Each day, you pour yourself out for your family. You are constantly serving whether your days are filled with daycare pick-ups, work schedules, homeschooling, or diaper changes. Your work as a mother ranges from the miniscule to the monumental. Remember that each task you complete as a mother is not simply for the wellbeing of your family. It is also work that is done unto the Lord.

When you repeat a direction for the millionth time, do it unto the Lord. When you wake up for the second and third time to settle the fussy baby, do it unto the Lord. When you drive back to school to pick up the forgotten backpack, do it unto the Lord. Working for people, even those you love most, will in the end be a fruitless work. Working unto the Lord brings lasting rewards in age the come. He promises us that he sees each of our actions. No matter how big or small, your work counts.

God, when I am worn out, remind me that my work is unto you and that you count it as valuable. When I feel less than appreciated, show me how you see me. When I feel like giving up, or serving my family half-heartedly, remind me that what I do now has lasting impact in your kingdom. Thank you, God, that you have equipped me well. If I am lacking, I can turn to you and ask for help. As I commit my work to you, thank you for being an ever-present help in my time of need.

# PATIENTLY ENDURE

*May the Lord lead your hearts into a full understanding and expression of the love of God and the patient endurance that comes from Christ.*

2 Thessalonians 3:5 NLT

From Christ we can learn patient endurance. Is there a quality that is more needed as a mother? Your job of caring, nurturing, and guiding your children is not a sprint but a marathon. From the moment you became a mother, you took on a job that never ends. You will always be a mother. Your job won't end when your child sleeps through the night, or starts kindergarten, or graduates college. It is continuous, and endurance is necessary.

As you move through your day today, may the Lord bless you with the patient endurance that comes from Christ. You don't need to muster it up. If you feel like quitting, you don't need to grit your teeth to get through your day. The love of God produces in you the endurance that you need. Keep your eyes on Christ, lean on him for understanding, and joyfully await his return.

God, thank you that you will see me through. Though my job is never-ending, you have equipped me with the patient endurance that comes from Christ. Teach me how to further lean on you for understanding. Thank you for your guidance and that you see each of the days laid out before me. Today, help me to grow in your love as I pour myself out for my children. May patience bear fruit as I abide in you.

# WISDOM FROM CHRIST

*The Spirit of the LORD will rest on him—*
*the Spirit of wisdom and understanding.*

ISAIAH 11:2 NLT

Parenting is full of questions and not very many answers. There isn't a manual that perfectly explains each of your children. While we can seek resources and educate ourselves as much as possible, we will still find ourselves wanting in the vast task of caring for growing children.

Thankfully, there is a storehouse of wisdom that comes from the Lord. Isaiah 11 is a description of Jesus. He has been given the spirit of wisdom and understanding. As such, you can depend on him for those things. What has been given to Christ has also been given to you through the Holy Spirit. Today, as you might find yourself with problems you cannot solve, lean on Jesus, the one with true wisdom. When you have many questions and few answers, turn your eyes to Christ.

God, thank you that you promise wisdom and understanding. I am not alone as a mother and I can turn to you when I'm unsure of what to do. I praise you for making a way for me. Jesus' death means that I can come to you and receive what I need. When I lack wisdom and understanding, help me to turn to you first. Forgive me for the times that I have sought counsel apart from you. Teach me how to lean on you and receive from you.

# FEARING GOD

*In the fear of the LORD there is strong confidence,*
*And his children will have refuge.*
PROVERBS 14:26 NASB

Where do you place your confidence? Do you feel secure because of a consistent paycheck or a particular set of skills that you have? Does your security come from your home or your relationships with loved ones? Instead of placing your confidence in what is fleeting, seek to glean confidence from your fear of the Lord. He is the one who sustains you. Your job, home, or bank account are never guaranteed.

Instead of placing your trust in sinking sand, stand upon the solid rock of Christ. Fear the Lord your God and depend on him alone. As a mother, you have the unique opportunity to teach your children where true confidence comes from. As you seek refuge in God, they will learn to do the same. When storms come and your circumstances change, you can give your children the steady and great gift of leaning firmly upon the Lord.

Lord, you are great! You are a safe refuge and my truest source of confidence. Forgive me for placing my security in areas other than you. Help me to turn to you when life is rocky and to then teach my children to do the same. I am thankful that I can trust in you no matter my circumstances. As I look to you, I know that you will strengthen me from the inside out. Today, teach me how to fear you.

# UNFATHOMABLE WAYS

*Oh, the depth of the riches both of the wisdom and knowledge of God!*
*How unsearchable are His judgments and unfathomable His ways!*
ROMANS 11:33 NASB

Paul wrote this portion of Scripture after detailing the gospel. He explains thoroughly all that God has done through Jesus Christ. Then, he goes on to exclaim how marvelous God is. It's as if he's done all of the hard work of hiking up a mountain so that he can look back and watch the sunset from the best possible vantage point.

God has done incredible things for you! He has carried you through your life with abundant grace and kindness. It can be easy to get lost in the hard work of mothering. The days stretch on, sleep may be fleeting, and your task list can be unending. Take a moment to look back and declare the goodness of God. His riches are deep, and his ways are unfathomable!

Thank you, God, for how far you have brought me! I praise you for all that you have done in my life. When I feel lost in tasks that feel mundane, help me to see all you have done and all you are doing. Thank you for leading me as a mother. You are great and your ways are unfathomable!

# BURDEN PASSER

*Give your burdens to the LORD,*
*and he will take care of you.*
PSALM 55:22 NLT

No matter the task you face today, you are not left helpless. You are invited to openly cast your burdens upon the Lord. You can confidently and continuously submit your problems to God. What a blessing you have been given to be able to fearlessly commune with a God who can handle your complaints, grievances, and cries.

Today, seek to be a burden passer. As a mother, it can feel like second nature to carry the burdens of your children. You don't need to shoulder their troubles. Instead, pass them on to the one who is able to effortlessly bear all of them. Let God's ability to bear burdens be lifegiving to you today. Where you have been holding onto heaviness, surrender it to the Lord. Let him carry what you cannot. He invites you to come to him in the same way that you invite your children to come to you.

Thank you, God, that I am not required to bear my children's burdens. You are a good father who cares for me. Forgive me for the times that I have attempted to do this on my own. Teach me how to cast my cares upon you when I am heavy laden. Help me to depend on you and to lead my children to do the same.

# IN YOUR MIDST

*God is in the midst of her;*
*she shall not be moved;*
*God will help her when morning dawns.*

PSALM 46:5 ESV

God is with you. He's not just beside you, all around you, or somewhere far off observing you. He is in the midst of you. He is enduring with you individually and also collectively with the body of Christ. You are not alone. Mothering can feel lonely. At times you might feel disconnected from friends and community as you devote yourself to mothering. Perhaps you're the only one with children, or maybe your busy schedule leaves you missing a time when you could more easily connect with those around you.

To whatever degree you might be feeling lonely, God is with you. He is your constant help and companion. He is your faithful deliverer in times of need. No matter how isolated you may feel as you pour yourself out for your children, you are never alone, and you are never left helpless.

Thank you, God, that you are an intimate God. You are not far off. You are the God who comes close. Remind me of your nearness when I feel alone or isolated. Thank you for your ever-present help. Today, as I take care of my children, teach me to see the ways you are present in my life.

# THE SIMPLE GOSPEL

*"I thank you, Father, Lord of heaven and earth,*
*that you have hidden these things*
*from the wise and understanding*
*and revealed them to little children."*

MATTHEW 11:25 ESV

Take a deep breath. As you sit here and give what you have to God, you can take heart that the best way to know him is to embrace humility. Worldly wisdom is not a requirement for Godly knowledge; in fact, it can be a hindrance. Pride will only get in your way. Pride says that you have enough, that you are enough, that you can do enough. Humility quietly says that all you need is found in Christ. As a mother you can find true rest knowing that the simple gospel is your highest calling.

Today, seek to become childlike in the way that you view God. Don't let your age or responsibility as a mother keep you from remembering that you too are one of God's little children. Let go of the burdens that you carry as a mom and find joy in the simplicity of the gospel!

God, help me to let go of my pride. Teach me how to see you with simplicity. Renew within me a childlike spirit, that I might depend on you as my good and faithful Father. You have hidden your ways from the wise and have revealed them to little children. Teach me to embrace humility and to see you rightly.

# DELIBERATE REFUGE

*This God—his way is perfect;*
*the word of the LORD proves true;*
*he is a shield for all those who take refuge in him.*

2 SAMUEL 22:31 ESV

To take refuge in God is a deliberate act. He is a shield for those who choose to take refuge in him. You need refuge. When life is smooth and your days feel easy to navigate, you need refuge. When life is difficult and heavy, you need refuge. As the world around you changes, you can rest in the fact that his way is perfect and never changing. When circumstances uproot your life, God's Word is still true. He is and always will be the safest place for you to run when troubles arise.

As a mother, you a responsible for yourself but also for your children. Today, let them see you run to Jesus. Let them see you find refuge in him when everything around you feels unsteady. As they run to you, their safe place, lead them to the safest place—the arms of Jesus.

Thank you, God, that you are dependable. The world is ever changing, but you are a steady refuge; you never change. Your ways are perfect, and your Word proves true. Teach me how to find shelter in you. Teach me how to run to you when trouble arises.

# LEARN FROM GOD

*Guide me in your truth and teach me,*
*for you are God my Savior,*
*and my hope is in you all day long.*

PSALM 25:5 NIV

Teacher is one of the many hats that you wear as a mom. From the moment you wake up, you are actively and passively teaching your children. You teach them to tie shoes, to add and subtract, to wash their hands, to navigate relationships. You use your words and your deliberate guidance to help them successfully walk through their days. Not only that, but you also teach them by example. They watch you. They watch how you interact with the world around you. They watch how you respond to joy, to trials, to stress, to pain. They see you in your rejoicing and they see you in your sorrows, all the while absorbing.

Turn this attitude toward your heavenly Father. Let him teach you actively through his Word and instruction, but also learn from him as you observe who he is. Learn from him today as you refuse to take your eyes off him. Learn from him and let an everlasting hope spring out of that deep well.

Father, thank you that you are a God who interacts with me. Thank you for being a patient and kind teacher. As I walk through my day, give me the grace to learn from you. Help me to become more like you. Help me to keep my eyes on you for consistent guidance.

# THE STORM CALMER

*Soon a fierce storm came up. High waves were breaking into the boat,*
*and it began to fill with water. Jesus was sleeping at the back of the*
*boat with his head on a cushion. The disciples woke him up, shouting,*
*"Teacher, don't you care that we're going to drown?"*
*When Jesus woke up, he rebuked the wind and said to the waves,*
*"Silence! Be still!" Suddenly the wind stopped, and there was a great calm.*
*Then he asked them, "Why are you afraid? Do you still have no faith?"*
MARK 4:37-40 NLT

You know the God who can calm the seas. If he can subdue the waves, then he can calm the storms in you. He can calm the storms within your child. Be encouraged today that as you cry out to him for peace, you can also cry out to him for your child's peace. Where your child is troubled, hurt, or doubting, trust in God. You are all little and learning.

Together, as you walk through the day, let God rebuke the winds. Let him handle the fierce storms. Even when your boat begins to fill with water, it's not too late to experience the great calm that Jesus can bring. This is true for you and for your children. In the midst of a tantrum or a great barrage of emotions, you can experience peaceful waters.

God, thank you for your ability to calm the storms! I praise you for your strength and your power. Let that power be on display in my life. Today, whatever troubles arise, teach me how to depend on you for peace. Remind that it's never too late to ask you for help. You care about the storms in my life and in the lives of my children. Strengthen our faith to let you be the one who handles those storms.

# ENDURING TEMPTATION

*No temptation has overtaken you except what is common to mankind. And God is faithful; he will not let you be tempted beyond what you can bear. But when you are tempted, he will also provide a way out so that you can endure it.*

1 CORINTHIANS 10:13 NIV

Temptation is not a one-size-fits-all situation. It also isn't limited to certain categories of sin. Temptation can creep into your life in big ways and in small ways. As a mom, you might be tempted to respond to your children in anger. You might be tempted toward laziness or frustration. We are promised a reprise from temptation no matter how big or small.

Throughout your day, seek to remember that God is faithful to lighten our burdens and provide a means to endure temptation. His promises are true, and he does not promise help where it will not be given. Be aware of where temptation is in your daily walk and seek to cast that burden onto the Lord. What tempts you today does not define you. Choose instead to be defined by the love of Christ and place your confidence in his ability to help you endure whatever you face.

Thank you, God, that you sent your Son die for me. He is not a stranger to temptation, so I have an advocate who understands my own temptations. You provide help when I need it. As I'm tempted today or this week, remind me through your Holy Spirit that you will provide me a way out so I can endure it.

# WINNERS DON'T QUIT

*Never become tired of doing good.*
2 Thessalonians 3:13 ncv

God knows that we are easily discouraged. He knows how fickle we can be even when we have the best of intentions. His Word reminds us not to grow weary of doing good simply because he knew that we would. Mothering can feel endless. Your to-do list never stops and you might be less than appreciated. God sees you. He sees the good that you do. It is not lost or hidden from him. He is aware of each sacrifice that you make, and he gently reminds you to keep going.

With kindness he urges you not to quit because he knows the great reward that awaits you. In your weariness remember that a day is coming when he will wipe away every tear and death will be no more. Today, no matter how much good you've done, press on, don't quit. He sees you; he knows you. The work you do counts.

Thank you, God, that you know me. My weariness doesn't surprise you. Even at my worst, Christ's blood covers me. When I am exhausted and ready to quit, you see me and uphold me. You sustain me when I can't keep going. Today, encourage me where I am weary and want to quit. Help me to depend on you instead of feeling discouraged by my tiredness.

# CHOOSE YOUR MASTER

*"No one can serve two masters. Either you will hate the one and love the other, or you will be devoted to the one and despise the other."*

MATTHEW 6:24 NIV

You probably tell your kids all the time, "You can't have it both ways." You do your best to explain to them that you often need to choose one thing or the other but not both. This is applicable in your walk with God as well. You cannot serve two masters. As a follower of Christ, you are urged to follow him wholeheartedly.

Today, think about the things that might be edging away at that wholeheartedness. What is getting in the way of full devotion to God? As the Holy Spirit brings those things to mind, be confident that you can carry them to God. He knows that you are prone to wander, and it does not intimidate him. As you seek to serve him well, he will meet with gentleness and will guide you with compassion. If you've felt yourself straying, there's no need to walk back in fear. You can confidently approach the throne of grace and he will be faithful to give you the help you need.

Thank you, God, that know my weaknesses. You are aware of everything pulling at my attention and my heart. Help me to love you wholeheartedly and without distraction. Today, as I seek to serve you only, guide me in surrendering things that have pulled me away from you.

# GREAT COMPASSION

*As those who have been chosen of God, holy and beloved, put on a heart of compassion, kindness, humility, gentleness and patience; bearing with one another, and forgiving each other, whoever has a complaint against anyone; just as the Lord forgave you, so also should you.*

COLOSSIANS 3:12-13 NASB

God's love for you is great. It's endless, deliberate, all-encompassing, and vast. Out of this knowledge that you have been chosen and adopted as his child, you are reminded to treat others the same way. Let this Scripture be a mantle over your home. Let it be a reminder to deal with your children with patience and gentleness, bearing with each other, full of compassion. Meet your children in this way and they will learn to do the same with each other.

As your children look to you as an example of how to put on a heart of compassion, kindness, humility, gentleness, and patience, remember that you can look to Christ. As they follow your lead to bear with one another and forgive, remember that you can look to Christ. He is the epitome of all of these things, and he is eager for you to learn from him just as your children learn from you.

Thank you, God, that you've given me such beautiful instructions on how to live in peace with others. Help me to teach my children out of the security of knowing that I've been adopted as your child. Help me to look to Jesus when I am failing. You have equipped me with the Holy Spirit who advocates for me and bears fruit in my life as I walk with my eyes on you.

# UNTO THE LORD

*Whatever you do, work at it with all your heart, as working for the Lord, not for human masters, since you know that you will receive an inheritance from the Lord as a reward. It is the Lord Christ you are serving.*
COLOSSIANS 3:23-24 NIV

Motherhood can feel like a thankless job. You are consistently pouring yourself out and might not be receiving the appreciation you want. If you are working unto man, then this disappointment can be crushing. It can become a heavy burden that turns your acts of service into bitter obligations. Instead, remember that your work is unto the Lord. Each Band-Aid placed on a scraped knee, each baking dish scrubbed clean, each refereeing of never-ending bickering, each school drop off, each math problem worked through are all done unto the Lord. The big and the small. It all counts, and it is all seen by God. He is consistently aware of you even when you feel unseen.

As you move about your day, find inner satisfaction in the fact that all you do is worth it no matter the recognition you get because God won't forget. The day will come when you reap rewards for your service. Your inheritance is not here on earth but in the age to come.

Thank you, God, that you see me. You are a kind and good God. Help me to remember that I'm working unto you and not unto man. When disappointment or bitterness creeps in, help me to turn to you and have my spirit renewed. Grant me the perseverance to keep serving my family in a way that is honoring to you.

# BLESS THE LORD

*Bless the LORD, O my soul,*
*and all that is within me,*
*bless his holy name!*
*Bless the LORD, O my soul,*
*and forget not all his benefits*

PSALM 103:1-2 ESV

One of the quickest ways to change your course is to practice thanksgiving. It's easy to become so lost in your daily tasks of mothering that when you finally have time to sit and seek the Lord you might feel lost or frazzled. If you are unsure of how to approach God, start with praise. He is never changing. He is always good even if we doubt his goodness. He is always faithful even if we doubt his faithfulness.

Walking in deliberate thanksgiving can move you from a place of frustration, sorrow, or bitterness to a place where humility can remind you of the greatness of God. When we see him rightly, we can see ourselves rightly. Thanksgiving moves your eyes off your own struggles and toward Christ, the great redeemer, whose work on the cross is all encompassing and whose grace is more than sufficient.

Thank you for your goodness, God! Remind me of all you've done. You are great, and you are kind. When I feel unsure of how to seek you, remind me of how wonderful you are. Teach me to praise you and to walk in thanksgiving in the midst of the busyness of mothering.

# AS REAL AS BEDROCK

*You're as real to me as bedrock beneath my feet,*
*like a castle on a cliff, my forever firm fortress,*
*my mountain of hiding, my pathway of escape,*
*my tower of rescue where none can reach me.*
*My secret strength and shield around me,*
*you are salvation's ray of brightness shining on the hillside,*
*always the champion of my cause.*

PSALM 18:2 TPT

Delight in the reality of a good God today. Feel the ground beneath your feet. Feel the breath in your lungs. He is your creator and sustainer. Let him fill your heart with a song. No matter your circumstances, he surrounds you and is your shield. He is as steady as the sun. In this moment, even if just for few seconds, draw closer to him through worship.

The demands of motherhood are a consistent pull on your attention and your energy. You might feel like you don't have very much to give but even the smallest fractions of time count when you turn your eyes and focus on who God is and what he's done. When you feel stretched thin in the middle of your day remember that he constant, he is faithful to rescue you, and he is for you. Praise him that he is a personal God who is as real as anything you can touch.

Thank you, God, that you are close to me! You are real and personal. Help me to remember that you are steady and always available when I need you. Even if just for a moment, help me to turn my heart toward you in praise.

# PEACE BRINGS HEALTH

*A peaceful heart leads to a healthy body;*
*jealousy is like cancer in the bones.*
PROVERBS 14:30 NLT

Do you compare yourself to others around you? We live in an unprecedented time with a deluge of information available to us all the time. We have unlimited access to windows into the lives of other people. We see precisely what they want us to see but that doesn't stop us from making assumptions about what we think their full life looks like. You are responsible for your family. You have been given to them. You can stand in confidence that what you have to offer is what they need. They don't need a mom who has it all together; they need a mom with a gentle heart.

Jealously will quickly steal your ability to be present. Someone will always have what you don't; someone will always have strengths where you have weaknesses. Today, remember that God has chosen you specifically to be the mother of your children. He equips you and you need not covet what anyone else has. Turn to Christ for your confidence today; he will be faithful to strengthen you.

Thank you, God, that you have made me uniquely for the job of mothering my children. When I am tempted to compare my life to others, remind me of all that you have done for me. Help me to have a right perspective and to see clearly. Turn my eyes to you in praise instead of looking to others in jealousy.

# IN THE VALLEY

*How long must I wrestle with my thoughts
and day after day have sorrow in my heart?
How long will my enemy triumph over me?
But I trust in your unfailing love;
my heart rejoices in your salvation.
I will sing the Lord's praise,
for he has been good to me.*

PSALM 13:2, 5-6 NIV

Do you have something in your life that has felt like a consistent battle? Have you felt the heaviness of sorrow settle in like a fog? If you are feeling consistently defeated, know that even then you can trust the Lord. His love is unfailing. Remember that you can praise him for what he has already done. Bolster your faith by remembering his good works.

Motherhood can be equally joyous and painful. Perhaps your journey to becoming a mom wasn't smooth. Maybe you've experienced a loss that has left you broken. Maybe you've found yourself disappointed or unprepared by the immense sacrifices you're making for your children. Whether you are muddling through a valley of motherhood or rejoicing on a mountain top, you can sing the Lord's praise. There is truth to cling to that transcends the details of your life. Bring your heart, whole or broken, to the Lord and remember that his unfailing love is what sustains you.

Thank you, God, that I can trust in your unfailing love. I can praise you when I am broken and when I am full of joy. Your goodness never changes. Help me to rejoice in my salvation even when I am weary and heavy laden. You are the God who will triumph over my enemies.

# ENCOURAGING WORDS

*Don't use foul or abusive language.*
*Let everything you say be good and helpful,*
*so that your words will be an encouragement to those who hear them.*
EPHESIANS 4:29 NLT

As a mom, you know how influential your words are. Your children listen closely and the things you say deeply affect them. If you struggle to control your tone and your language, then this might also be an area that is a source of shame in your life.

Run to God who is merciful and faithful to forgive you when you come to him and confess. Christ's work on the cross is all sufficient for you. Let your words encourage your children; let them be life giving and kind. When you are tempted to speak rashly or out of anger, trust that God is faithful to provide you with a way out of temptation. Let your words be a balm to your children, and when they aren't, be quick to ask for forgiveness.

Thank you, God, that you help me where I am weak. Forgive me for the times that my words have been hurtful toward my children. When I am frustrated, grant me self-control. Give me words to speak that are life giving and uplifting. Thank you for your kindness and gentleness where I am lacking!

# MORE OF HIM

*"He must increase,*
*but I must decrease."*
JOHN 3:30 ESV

As far as jobs go, motherhood tops the list when it comes to ways to decrease. You will constantly be giving of your time, your energy, your physical body, and your emotions. Motherhood is, by definition, a lifelong sacrifice. As you pour yourself out for your children today, remember that Christ has poured himself out for you. When mothering strips you bare, remember that Christ was stripped bare for you. As you decrease, may he increase.

No matter how much you give of yourself, let it remind you that your decreasing is not in vain. It has meaning and purpose. May you reflect Christ as you draw your children in close and give what you can. May Christ be glorified as you move throughout your day, meeting needs and guiding your children.

Thank you, God, that as I pour myself out, you will be glorified! May I honor you with how I serve my family. As I decrease and you increase, may my life be a reflection of Jesus. You are worthy of my sacrifice. Remind me of what Christ has done for me, that I might joyfully decrease.

# AN EVERLASTING INHERITANCE

*We will not hide these truths from our children;*
*we will tell the next generation*
*about the glorious deeds of the Lord,*
*about his power and his mighty wonders.*

PSALM 78:4 NLT

As a mother, you have an instant legacy. No matter your financial situation, you have a storehouse of riches to pass on to your children. Maybe you feel like you don't have a lot to offer your kids. You have the unique privilege of gathering your children, as a hen gathers her chicks, and declaring the goodness of the Lord. There will be moments that feel sweet and tender and moments that feel like hard work. In both situations, seeds are sewn, and fruit will be harvested when the time is right.

Where you are lacking, God is strong and more than sufficient. Lean on his strength. Declare his ability to your children. Talk to them about what he has done in your life and what he has done in theirs. This an everlasting inheritance that you are fully equipped to give your children. Rejoice together!

Thank you, God, that I can pass truth to my children. I can tell them of your goodness and of your glorious deeds. Give me the words to say when I feel lost in this area. Help me to communicate your mighty wonders to them in ways they will understand.

# A SEASON FOR EVERYTHING

*To everything there is a season,*
*A time for every purpose under heaven.*
ECCLESIASTES 3:1 NKJV

Motherhood is full of seasons. You move from one to the other with little control of beginnings and endings. Nothing lasts forever. You conquer something, and it changes. The baby's sleep schedule changes, the toddler's language develops, the child's interests evolve, the teenager or young adult navigates life without you. Maybe you relish the ever-altering seasons of motherhood or maybe they leave you feeling like you can't quite keep up.

In either situation, remember that each season has a purpose. Each one, no matter the length, is orchestrated by God. He is the designer who is good and kind, and he leads you with gentleness. If you're feeling lost in your current season of mothering, bring your worries to him and ask for direction. He will anchor you and remind you of his unfailing love.

Father, whatever season I'm in, remind me of your faithfulness. Help me to depend on you when life is quickly changing. When I can't keep up, keep me steady and remind me of your unfailing love. You have a purpose for each season I walk through. Help me trust in you to lead me.

# FULLY PROTECTED

*Your perfection and faithfulness are my bodyguards,*
*for you are my hope and I trust in you as my only protection.*
PSALM 25:21 TPT

Looking around at the world right now might cause you to be fearful or anxious. It might feel like a tumultuous time especially as a mother. Not only do you need to navigate the world, but you are leading your children through it as well. Today, take a deep breath and let the Holy Spirit remind you that God's faithfulness is your bodyguard. His ways are perfect, and he holds you and your children closely. Your hope can be firmly rooted in Christ and his promise to make all things right.

Trust in the Lord not only for your protection but for your children as well. If you are carrying the burden of fear or anxiety, know that God is able to shoulder those burdens and replace them with peace and hope. When life is uncertain and new challenges arise, let him lead you and protect you. When the world tells you to be afraid, put your hope in Christ.

Thank you, God, that you are my bodyguard. No matter how uncertain the world is, you are a constant source of hope. Help me to turn to you with my fear and anxiety and let you replace them with peace and trust. I trust you to lead me and my children through our days. Thank you for your steady leading!

# MEET WEAKNESS WITH MERCY

*"Why worry about a speck in your friend's eye when you have a log in your own? How can you think of saying to your friend, 'Let me help you get rid of that speck in your eye,' when you can't see past the log in your own eye?"*

MATTHEW 7:3-4 NLT

As a mother you have a front row seat to the sins of your children. You are around them more than anyone else. You see them at their best and you see them at their worst. Today, let God remind you to meet them with the same grace you want. Their sins are neither better nor worse than your own. You are all children, learning to follow Jesus more closely each day. Don't judge so harshly. Their sins are not yours, nor are they a reflection of you. You need not shoulder them.

Let God's kindness lead you to repentance today. Let his kindness lead them to repentance today. The same Holy Spirit within you is also within them. Let this be freeing as you guide them to Christ, relinquishing control to him and trusting him for your forgiveness and for theirs.

Thank you, God, I can come to you for forgiveness. It is not my job to judge my children. Help me instead to come to you in repentance when needed. Help me to see myself rightly, that you might be glorified in my life. Teach me to lead my children to you.

# FEBRUARY

Love takes no pleasure in evil but rejoices
over the truth. Love patiently accepts all
things. It always trusts, always hopes, and
always endures. Love never ends.

1 Corinthians 13:6-8 NCV

# HE GIVES PEACE

*"Peace I leave with you; my peace I give you.*
*I do not give to you as the world gives.*
*Do not let your hearts be troubled and do not be afraid."*
JOHN 14:27 NIV

God does not give as the world gives. He gives true peace that comes from being firmly rooted in his love. He does not arbitrarily give commands. If he tells you not to let your heart be troubled, it's because he can back it up. He wouldn't tell you not to be afraid without the means necessary to calm your fears. True peace is not something that you can manufacture yourself. It's a gift from Jesus, given abundantly to world full of strife and brokenness. Everywhere you look people are longing for true peace. They are desperate for it, searching for it, trying to create it themselves.

Today, you can rest in the knowledge that no amount of striving will create the peace that Jesus can give. You can create peaceful spaces in your home, keep a low stress schedule, and do your best to calmly walk through life, but none of this provides the same peace that comes from being rooted in Christ Jesus. This should feel like a burden has been lifted from you. The work has already been done; all you need to do is receive what has been offered.

Father, thank you that your peace is not like the world's peace. You give freely and abundantly. Help me to receive what you are offering. Teach me how to depend on you when I am anxious. Forgive me for the times I have tried to muster up my own peace. Help me instead to rest in what Christ has done on the cross.

# PRAISE GOD

*That my soul may sing praise to You and not be silent.*
*O LORD my God, I will give thanks to You forever.*
PSALM 30:12 NASB

Thanksgiving is the doorway to the presence of God. In your thankfulness, you are able to turn your attention to what God has done instead of focusing on what is going on around or inside you. Your deliberate praise, no matter how weak, has the power to lift you out of the mire and set your feet firmly on a rock. Thanksgiving can sustain your faith when you're weak and provide a starting point when you feel lost.

As you begin to see the hand of God everywhere, he will strengthen you. As you begin to recognize what he has done, you'll find a greater understanding of his character. As you begin to focus on what you have over what you don't, you'll find yourself prone to contentedness over comparison. Today, let your soul sing praise to God! He has done great things and he is always moving. Choose to give him thanks because he is worthy.

Thank you, God, for your goodness! Teach me to walk in thanksgiving even when I don't feel like it. Let my praise to you transform the way I think. Give me the grace to turn my eyes away from my own troubles and toward who you are. Help me to have eyes to see what you have done.

# YOU ARE REDEEMED

*"Fear not, for I have redeemed you;*
*I have called you by name, you are mine."*
ISAIAH 43:1 ESV

Despite the wanderings and short comings of the Israelites, God chose them. He called them redeemed even when they turned their backs on him. He spoke words of encouragement to them through the prophet Isaiah even after they made the wrong choices over and over again. He continued to guide them, fully knowing they would likely not follow each time.

God is not far off waiting for you to do the right thing. He's not sitting frustrated that you don't spend enough time with him. He's not an annoyed king, confused about why his people can't just get it together already. He sees you and calls you by name. You are his valued child, able to be close to him because of what Christ did on the cross. He sees you through what Jesus has done. There is not a path that you can take that would make you irredeemable. There is not a place that you can wander where you suddenly don't have the ability to turn back to him. Surely if the Israelites can wander the desert for years in stubbornness, you can depend upon Jesus today and be redeemed.

You have called me by my name. you know exactly who I am and what I am walking through. You and you alone redeem me. Teach me how to turn to you, no matter how far away I might feel. Help me to walk in security and not in fear because of what you have done.

# BECOMING LIKE HIM

*The Lord is the Spirit, and where the Spirit of the Lord is, there is freedom. And we all, who with unveiled faces contemplate the Lord's glory, are being transformed into his image with ever-increasing glory, which comes from the Lord, who is the Spirit.*

2 CORINTHIANS 3:17-18 NIV

It's common to become like those you spend the most time with. You've probably seen this at work in your life and in the lives of your children as well. You've likely seen this have a positive or negative impact. Sometimes without even thinking about it, you pick up mannerisms, habits, ways of speaking, and opinions. Likewise, as you focus on the Lord, you will become more like him. The more time you spend in his presence, the more you'll begin to reflect him. As you soak up the Word and turn your attention toward him, his nearness will influence you in ways you might not even notice right away.

Because of Christ's sacrifice on the cross, you've been given full freedom to be close to the Father, contemplating his glory and being transformed into his image. Praise God for the way he teaches and influences you. As you climb into the Father's lap, rejoice that he requires no work of you other than being near to him. Christ has done the work that was needed to bridge the gap between you and God. Now, you are given freedom and life as his child.

Thank you, God, that as I seek to be near you, you are transforming me into your image! Christ's work on the cross means I don't have to work for that transformation. Teach me how to dwell with you and live in freedom. Help me to keep my mind focused on your glory.

# HE EQUIPS YOU

*His divine power has given us everything we need for a Godly life through our knowledge of him who called us by his own glory and goodness.*

2 PETER 1:3 NIV

Motherhood can quickly reveal many areas you might feel ill equipped or unqualified in. Maybe you don't have access to the resources you wish you had, or maybe you feel insecure in your own abilities. The truth is that you have been given everything you need for a Godly life. You are perfectly equipped to love, be at peace, have joy, and walk in patience. The reason you are so perfectly equipped is because you have unlimited access to he who is completely perfect.

You, a child of God and follower of Christ, are given everything you need because of who you know not what you have. When you feel ill equipped, turn to the one who has unlimited resources. When walking in love is hard, turn to the one who loves abundantly with ease. When mustering up patience leaves you gritting your teeth, turn to the one who is never rushed or frazzled. Today, glean each and every thing you need from your generous and completely sufficient Father.

Father, thank you that you have given me everything I need. Because of who you are, I am never in want. Teach me how to depend on you in all of my lacking. I praise you for your perfection and your generosity. Instead of mustering up what I need myself, or hastily hunting for it, teach me how to simply come to you as a beloved child.

# LET HOPE ARISE

*Restore to me the joy of your salvation,*
*And uphold me with a willing spirit.*
PSALM 51:12 ESV

Take a moment and reflect upon the first time your salvation truly impacted you. Whether it's been days, months, or years, you may have strayed from the joy that you felt in those first days as a believer. Remember the freedom and excitement you felt with each new truth that you uncovered, the words in Scripture leaping off of the page and making a home in your heart. Remember the way you felt loved in your brokenness and joy where there used to be sorrow. Remember how you felt lighter when you realized that salvation is a gift and requires nothing of your own merit. Remember the hope you knew when you learned that Jesus is coming back to make all things right.

Today, let God restore you to that same place again. As you delight once again in those truths, you'll find your current troubles easier to bear. As you reflect upon the joy that you once had, you'll see that what God has done before, he can do again. When you first followed Jesus, a miracle occurred. That miracle can happen again. Let hope rise up within you. Where you are dry, he can bring rain. Where you are broken, he can bring healing. Where you are discouraged, he can comfort you. He has done it before; he can do it again.

Thank you, God, for my salvation! Renew my spirit. Help me to remember the joy that I had before and give me the faith to trust you for it again. Restore the tired areas of my faith. Forgive me for being discouraged instead of trusting you for joy and refreshment.

# A VALUED PART

*You are the body of Christ,*
*and each one of you is a part of it.*
1 CORINTHIANS 12:27 NIV

You are necessary. You are an important part of the body of Christ. You are needed. Your role as a mother doesn't disqualify you from your role in the body. If you ever feel isolated as a mother, you can take solace in the fact that you are not alone. You are a distinct and valued part of the body of Christ.

As you are changing diapers, driving kids to school, cooking dinner, or managing your job schedule, you might not feel like you are contributing the body. Know that each of the tasks in front you are an opportunity to serve in love. As you love your children, even in the smallest ways, you are ensuring that the body is thriving and healthy. Your service to your children is a direct service to the body. You are loving and raising up part of the next generation of believers. Take heart that you are never separate from the body even though motherhood can feel isolating.

Thank you, God, that the body of Christ exists. We each have an important role and I am needed even when I don't feel like I am. Thank you for the role that you've given me in this season of my life. When I am discouraged about being part of the body, help me to depend on you for encouragement.

# SWEEPS AWAY OFFENSES

*I have swept away offences like a cloud,*
*your sins like the morning mist.*
*Return to me, for I have redeemed you.*
ISAIAH 44:22 NIV

You are just as human as your children. You have the same ability to make the wrong choices, to use the wrong words, and to cause pain to others. Your children in their childishness have the same propensity toward sin as you do as an adult. As a mom, you do your best to teach them to forgive when they are hurt or offended. You teach conflict resolution and humble kindness. But do you apply these same concepts to yourself? When you make the wrong choice, and opportunity abounds for this, do you remember that God is waiting in kindness as your redeemer? He is the sweeper of offenses.

As you teach your children to keep a short record of wrongs, God holds you gently, ready and fully able to wash away your sins. Let that forgiveness sweep over you today. Revel in the new mercies that you've been given. If yesterday was full of yelling and short tempers, remember that as you confess and repent, today you have been equipped anew.

Thank you, God, that you sweep away my offenses like a cloud. You have redeemed me and my sins are covered by Christ's blood. Help me to teach my children of your redemptive heart and help me to remember that truth as well. Teach me to turn to you with my sins instead of holding onto them tightly. You are big enough to handle my wrongdoings. No matter how many times I fail, you are waiting for me to return to you.

# WIPING TEARS

*"He will wipe every tear from their eyes, and there will be no more death or sorrow or crying or pain. All these things are gone forever."*
REVELATION 21:4 NLT

Hope is a marvelous thing. Can you imagine a day with no pain? With no tears? Motherhood is riddled with tears: of joy, of pain, of perseverance, of fortitude. But one day all of that will be wiped away by your compassionate Father. The perfection that the body of Christ will be welcomed into can serve as a motivator each day that you are waiting for Christ's return. Spend time today gleaning hope from the promise of what's to come. This life is full of pain. If your heart is heavy with burdens, you can be assured that you are seen and known, and God is reminding you to hold on for a little longer.

Have you ever been hiking with your children? You know that the view at the end, be it a sunset on the horizon, a waterfall, or a mountainous vista are well worth the hard work of getting there. You remind your children to hang on, to just keep walking, to think about what is to come. The same is true when it comes to you and your life. God knows that the day is coming that will be well worth the work of this life. Just keep walking with your eyes steady on him.

God, thank you that you have given me a glimpse of what is to come. One day I will be without tears, sorrow, crying, or pain. When that day feels far, remind me that you are with me, leading me steadily. Give me strength when I want to quit and fortitude when I am weary. Your plan is glorious; help me to keep my eyes on Christ as I wait for his return.

# ENCOURAGED DAILY

*Encourage one another daily, as long as it is called "Today,"
so that none of you may be hardened by sin's deceitfulness.*

HEBREWS 3:13 NIV

As a mother, you know how much you need encouragement. You know how much it means when someone acknowledges the work you do and reassures you that you are doing a good job. Even a few simple words can be incredibly life giving. Knowing that you are seen and not alone goes a long way in keeping your heart soft. The same is true when it comes to your faith. You are commanded to encourage others daily. The expense of not doing this is being hardened by sin's deceitfulness. With the diligence of your words, you have the opportunity to actively protect each other from sin.

Motherhood can feel isolating and you might think you simply don't have the time or energy for deep friendships. The command given in Hebrews is not a trite reminder or a suggestion; it's a warning. It is in your very best interest to remind your brothers and sisters of the freedom, love, and mercy found in Christ. This can look like a simple text, a quiet hug, or a lengthy conversation. Time is not the commodity here. All that is needed is sincerity.

Thank you, God, for the reminder to encourage those around me. I know how much I need life-giving words, so help me remember to edify others as well. Give me words to say when I am unsure and help me to sincerely speak truth to those around me.

# WON'T LAST FOREVER

*"Now is your time of grief,*
*but I will see you again and you will rejoice,*
*and no one will take away your joy."*
JOHN 16:22 NIV

Active motherhood is fleeting. You've probably heard that the days are long, but the years are short. Often you are told that you should cherish the moments you have because they won't last long. Joy is fleeting. It's important to remember that grief is as well. Jesus reminds you that your time on earth, without him, is a time of grief. As you wait expectantly for his return, you are ever aware that things are not as they should be. Systems are corrupt; the world is broken and longing for restoration. Creation groans in eager anticipation for things to be returned to the way God designed them to be.

In your waiting, Jesus reminds you that your grief will not last forever. He is coming back. We don't hope he will return; we know he will. At that time, no one will be able to take away your joy. You won't have to mindfully cherish fleeting happiness because it won't be fleeting. As you navigate seasons of joy and pain, you can take heart knowing that there will be a day when you will only experience joy.

God, thank you for the different seasons you have me walk through. Teach me how to view all of them, the joyful and the painful, as temporary. Help me look toward Jesus' return with eager anticipation. May my hope be rooted in what you have promised and not in what the world tells me I should value.

# NEIGHBOR CHILD

*"'Love the Lord your God with all your heart and with all your soul
and with all your mind and with all your strength.'
The second is this: 'Love your neighbor as yourself.'
There is no commandment greater than these."*

MARK 12:30-31 NIV

Though they may not be the first person that comes to mind, your child is your neighbor. It can be easy to forget that they are more than just a part of yourself. Love them as you would love yourself. Just because they are your children doesn't mean that it will always be easy to love them. Today, ask the Lord to renew your love for them. Where you have been impatient, repent and ask for forgiveness. Where you have been angry, repent and ask for forgiveness. Where you have not been present, repent and ask for forgiveness. Love them well as this is the second greatest commandment after loving the Lord with all of your heart.

As a mother you might feel like you don't have time for ministry. In this season, your children are as much a ministry as anything else. Pouring your life out to love them well is just as valuable and needed as any other ministry you could be involved in. Let God empower you to love them as you love yourself.

Father, help me to see my children as my neighbor. Teach me how to love them well. When I fail, give me the grace to repent and ask for forgiveness. You are my teacher and you help me when I need it. Thank you for the opportunity to pour my life out for my kids. As I seek to love them as I might love myself, let it lead them closer to you.

# FAITH OF CHILDREN

*"Let the little children come to me, and do not hinder them,
for the kingdom of God belongs to such as these."*
LUKE 18:16 NIV

Your children can be direct leaders to Christ. One of the joys of parenting is discovering the world all over again. Let your children lead you in that way. There are treasures to be found in watching how they interact with Jesus. Their faith is simple, and their confidence is great.

You can learn about interacting with Jesus from the way he interacted with children. He didn't ask them to come to him so he could teach them, correct them, or cure them. He blessed them. He prayed for them and he showered them with love and affection. This is how he desires to interact with you. He doesn't ask you to seek him so he can make you better or tell you all the ways you're failing. Christ has great affection for you, and his kindness is what leads you to repentance. Today, learn from the sweet and trusting faith that your children have. Let it draw you to Christ so you experience his love for you.

Father, thank you that I can come to you like a child. Help me to learn from the way Jesus interacted with little children. Renew a childlike faith within me. Remind me of who I am to you—a child before a father. Today, may I receive the affection of Christ and glorify your name.

# NO SEPARATION

*I am convinced that nothing can ever separate us from God's love.*
*Neither death nor life, neither angels nor demons, neither our fears for*
*today nor our worries about tomorrow—not even the powers of hell can*
*separate us from God's love. No power in the sky above or in the earth*
*below—indeed, nothing in all creation will ever be able to separate us*
*from the love of God that is revealed in Christ Jesus our Lord.*

ROMANS 8:38-39 NLT

Your tiredness, lack of discipline, endless nights of tending to a
baby, or impatient reaction cannot separate you from the love of
God. Motherhood can be isolating but *nothing* can separate you
from God's love. No matter what you feel is in the way of your
time with God, nothing can come between you and his love. It is
constant and beyond human intervention. It is out of your control
and out of your power. His love is ever reaching, ever sustaining,
and ever present.

Though you might look at your relationship with God as a success
or a failure, he only sees you through eyes of love because of what
Christ did on the cross. On your most weary days, this is still true.
When you have nothing left to cling to, the love that God has for
you is revealed through Jesus and can never be changed.

God, thank you for your great love! When I feel isolated or
alone, remind me that your love is always present. Teach me
how to lean on it and have confidence in it. Remind me that
I am firmly rooted in your love no matter what my days and
nights look like. Even in this busy season of motherhood, you
hold me closely and love me fully.

# GOD'S WORKMANSHIP

*We are his workmanship, created in Christ Jesus for good works,*
*which God prepared beforehand, that we should walk in them.*
EPHESIANS 2:10 ESV

Do you remember staring at your child for the first time? In awe of each freckle or dimple, you traced the lines of their face and breathed them in. You memorized how they smelled, how they fit into your arms, and how they sounded. You looked at your new child with awe and wonder, amazed at each tiny part. A new child is like poetry: beautiful and intricately designed.

This is how God sees you. You are his most delightful creation. You are his workmanship. He crafted you with care, purpose, and love. Each part of you was planned out and executed to perfection. There is no part of you that is accidental or overlooked. You might be prone to look at yourself and see flaws or things you wish were different, but that is not how God sees you. You were created in Christ Jesus that you would walk in the good works that God prepared for you. He wants to see you walk in the freedom that Christ bought for you, fully belonging and fully free.

Father, help me to see myself the way you see me. Teach me how to see you as a kind and loving father who created me as an artist creates a masterpiece. I am your workmanship and I am thankful that you designed me the way you did. In areas where I see flaws, help me to change my perspective. Help me to walk in the freedom that Christ gained for me on the cross.

# FOLLOW CHRIST'S EXAMPLE

*"I have given you an example to follow.
Do as I have done to you."*
JOHN 13:15 NLT

For better or for worse, your children probably mimic you in a lot of ways. There are times when they display the best of you and there are times when they might display qualities that you wish hadn't been passed on. It's so easy for your children to be a reflection of who you are because you are the one they spend the most time with. They know you. They recognize your voice, know your mannerisms, and see how you interact with the world around you.

Likewise, you are to mimic Christ. Your following of him should come from a storehouse of time spent with him. He should be the one you copy because he is the one you spend the most time with—the one you are consistently observing. Like a child, you can learn from looking at his example. How did he speak? Who did he love? What was his character like? Today, as you walk through your day, ask the Lord to show you ways to further follow his example.

Thank you, God, that you've given me an example to follow. When I am unsure of how to act or what to do, I can look to you for clarity. When I stray and follow the world's examples, help me to navigate my way back to you. Teach me how to be more like you.

# HE WILL HEAL YOU

*The people all tried to touch him,*
*because power was coming from him*
*and healing them all.*

LUKE 6:19 NIV

Over and over again we are given examples of how Jesus healed people. Most of his ministry was focused on meeting the tangible needs of those around him. He consistently healed and fed people. He cares deeply about what you need. He wants to see you whole. He is the one who can awaken the dead and make blind eyes see. He is capable of healing your brokenness, whether it is physical, relational, mental, emotional, or circumstantial. He doesn't just apply Band-Aids and a quick salve; he is a true healer, making the deepest parts right again.

Bring your brokenness to him. Let him wipe your tears; give him your pain and ask as a child asks a father. From that place of closeness, you will grow in trust whether or not you receive physical healing. Physical healing doesn't always come when you want it, but his nearness is what your spirit needs.

God, thank you that you have the power to heal me! As I seek you for healing, I want to become closer and closer to you. Renew my faith for healing. Teach me to come to you as a child goes to their father. I trust that you have the ability to heal me fully and completely.

# HARVEST GOODNESS

*"The seed on good soil stands for those with a noble and good heart,
who hear the word, retain it, and by persevering produce a crop."*

LUKE 8:15 NIV

When you hear the word of God, it will either fall on the good soil of a soft heart or wither on the rocky ground of a hardened heart. You can choose between bitterness and softness. Despite your circumstances or shortcomings, you can receive the word of God with a soft heart. If you find yourself feeling like there's a situation in your life that seems insurmountable and you can't imagine your heart being soft, you can find solace in the fact that God is in the business of changing hearts.

It's among God's top priorities to change repentant hearts and make them soft. Then, as you hear the good Word, as it absorbs into your heart, God reminds you to persevere. By persevering, you will produce a good crop. You've already done the hard work of letting God soften your heart; just don't quit! There isn't an instruction here to master anything in a week or to live perfectly, the only direction given is just don't quit. By persevering, a good crop will be produced. Today, if there are areas of your heart that feel hard, confidently ask the Lord to create good soil, so you might retain the Word and persevere.

Thank you, God, that you can change my heart. Where I am holding to bitterness, please make my heart soft. I want my heart to be noble and good so I retain your Word and persevere to produce a crop. Help me to turn to you where I am weak.

# SEEK WISDOM

*Know that wisdom is such to your soul;*
*if you find it, there will be a future,*
*and your hope will not be cut off.*
PROVERBS 24:14 ESV

Wisdom has very little to do with your ability or your intellect. Wisdom is a commodity of the kingdom of heaven. It's not something you've been born with, that you can boast about, or that you can attain by your own merit. Wisdom is found, given, and bestowed upon you. You are promised that if you seek the Lord, he will grant you it. He will teach you how to think the way that he does. Wisdom requires humility because in order to obtain it, you have to recognize your lack and ask for help. In your willingness to admit your need for him, God is faithful to provide wisdom. He will not turn away a contrite spirit. It is in his very nature to guide you and equip you. Not only will he grant you wisdom when you ask for it, he promises that your hope will not be cut off.

As you live according to the wisdom of God, you will be filled with unending hope for what is to come. As you further your understanding of how Godly wisdom operates, you see glimpses of what life will be like when Jesus returns and all is as it should be. This is why your hope will not run dry: with each glimpse of how God designed things to be, you can trust that one day, they will be that way again.

Thank you, God, that you grant wisdom to those who seek it. Help me to lean on you instead of using my own intellect or abilities. Teach me how to seek you when I need help. Today, as I seek to live with Godly wisdom, renew my hope. Help me to keep my eyes steady on what you have planned.

# ABIDE FIRST

*The Holy Spirit produces this kind of fruit in our lives: love, joy, peace, patience, kindness, goodness, faithfulness, gentleness, and self-control.*
GALATIANS 5:22-23 NLT

The fruit of the Spirit is not a check list. You are not required to achieve patience, kindness, goodness, faithfulness, gentleness, self-control, peace, love, or joy. The list provided in Galatians is not meant to create shame. Instead, it's to explain what your life will look like when you live by the Spirit. You've been given a one-item to-do list. Abide in the Spirit. You can delight in the freedom that life in the Spirit brings.

As a mother, when do you have a list that only has one item on it? On any given day you tend to laundry, dinner, your job, mopping the floors, teaching your children, or going to the gym. Here, in the quiet place with the Lord, rest in the fact that he requires very little of you. You are asked to walk by the Spirit, abiding in the love of Christ. The fruit will follow. Abide first, then bear fruit. If you try to do it in reverse, you'll find yourself striving and working for your faith instead of receiving it as a gift from God.

Father, thank you that you've given me a means to measure if I'm walking in the Spirit. When I abide, the Holy Spirit produces the fruit. Teach me to shorten my to-do list when it comes to my time with you. Despite long lists in other areas of my life, when it comes to you I can rest in the work Christ has done.

# UNDESERVED REDEMPTION

*To the praise of the glory of His grace, which He freely bestowed on
us in the Beloved. In Him we have redemption through His blood,
the forgiveness of our trespasses, according to the riches of His grace
which He lavished on us.*

EPHESIANS 1:6-8 NASB

God is consistent and always good. His truth never changes and
what he has done to redeem you cannot be erased. No matter
how long you've been following Jesus—whether years, months,
or days—you can always revel in the foundations of your faith. No
matter what happens in your life, this will always be true; you have
been redeemed by the blood of Christ because of the incredible
grace that God has lavished upon you.

There isn't a day too dark or a task too mundane that can
overshadow the glory of the basics of the gospel. Whether you
feel lost in unexpected difficulty or lost in the daily tasks that
motherhood necessitates, the gospel is for you. No matter the
depth of your biblical knowledge, the redemption and forgiveness
you've received should stir your heart. Let the Holy Spirit soften
your heart today to sit in thanksgiving for what has been done for
you. May you walk throughout your day humbled by the richness
that has been bestowed on you.

Thank you, God, for what you have done. The gospel is such a
good and perfect plan. May I continuously marvel at what Jesus
did for me. May I never lose sight of his sacrifice and of the
riches of your grace. Help me to walk in humility as I look to
you for guidance. No matter what I walk through, help me to
always return to the foundations of my faith.

# DON'T HIDE

*If we claim we have no sin, we are only fooling ourselves and not living in the truth. But if we confess our sins to him, he is faithful and just to forgive us our sins and to cleanse us from all wickedness. If we claim we have not sinned, we are calling God a liar and showing that his word has no place in our hearts.*

1 John 1:8-10 NLT

There is no use in hiding. It is fruitless to try and deceive God about who you are and what you've done. He knows you full well; your actions don't surprise him, nor can they be hidden from him. Do your children ever try to hide from you? Have you had the toddler claim they didn't eat the piece of chocolate only to look at you innocently with melted evidence all over their face? Perhaps this is how God sees us at times, affectionately and ever aware. He knows you inside and out, all of your triumphs and all of your sins.

To try to live like you are without sin only results in you fooling yourself and treating God's knowledge as though it is inaccurate. Instead, submit yourself to his omniscience and humbly confess to him what he already knows. Go to him in your sin and let him forgive you and cleanse you of wickedness. It is his desire that we would come to him willingly, like a child approaching a loving father. Today, be transparent with your Father. Communicate with him openly and find the freedom that comes from a right and humble understanding of yourself and your actions.

Thank you, God, that you see me fully. I cannot hide from you. Teach me to see myself rightly and to approach you with confidence that you will grant me forgiveness. You are faithful to forgive me and cleanse me of wickedness. Teach me to turn to you instead of being stubborn in my sin. Soften my heart today!

# INTERCEDING FOR YOU

*He is able, once and forever,*
*to save those who come to God through him.*
*He lives forever to intercede with God on their behalf.*
HEBREWS 7:25 NLT

Jesus is on your side. He is your constant advocate. Because of what Christ did on the cross, you can be near to God. Jesus lives to intercede for you. Let that soak in for a moment. Jesus Christ, the Son of God, in all his glory, perfection, kindness, and love, prays for *you*. He speaks to God about you, for you, and on your behalf. In your darkest moments you have an incredible support. He upholds you before the Creator of the universe. He sacrificed his very life on the cross and continues to lay his life down for you as he intercedes with God on your behalf. This is not a trite encouragement that you aren't ever alone. The reality of these interactions is life changing.

In the midst of mothering, when you are overwhelmed, exhausted, or discouraged, Jesus is on your side. You can approach him in whatever state you find yourself and know that he is speaking to the Father for you. Let the reality of what Christ has done and *is doing* impact you as you walk through your day.

I praise you, God, for what you have done through Jesus! I have an advocate and a support throughout all of my days. As I go about my day, help me to remember that Jesus is on my side. May it truly impact how I feel and act.

# TRUST THE LORD

*Trust in the LORD with all your heart;*
*do not depend on your own understanding.*
*Seek his will in all you do,*
*and he will show you which path to take.*
PROVERBS 3:5-6 NLT

It might feel like everyone around you depends on you. You manage schedules, nurture, feed, clothe, teach, and discipline your children more than anyone else. Don't let this create a sense of independence. Dependence upon the Lord is a practiced discipline. It takes diligence to consistently say, "I trust you Lord; lead me." The work of building this habit will never be in vain. God promises that as you seek him, he will show you what to do. Your understanding is limited but his is infinite. He knows what is best for you and he knows how each moment of your life interacts with the others. He, in his great power, knowledge, and goodness is the most reliable source you'll ever find. He is worth depending on.

Today, let the command to trust in him bring freedom and a sigh of relief. You don't need to have it all figured out. You don't need to carry the weight of independence. With open hands, release your burdens to God. Seek him and he will lead you.

Father, thank you for the true freedom that comes from depending on you. Teach me how to lean not on my own understanding. When I am tempted to blaze my own path, remind me to surrender to you and seek your face instead. You are a strong foundation who is infinitely wise, good, and loving. I can trust you because of who you are. Teach me to develop the habit of consistently turning to you.

# HE EXULTS OVER YOU

*"The Lord your God is in your midst,*
*A victorious warrior.*
*He will exult over you with joy,*
*He will be quiet in His love,*
*He will rejoice over you with shouts of joy."*

ZEPHANIAH 3:17 NASB

You've already done the hard work of setting aside your to-do list to sit and seek the Lord. You've purposed in your heart that time with him is not only important but to be prioritized. Maybe you have ample time to yourself right now, or maybe you have just a few minutes before the toddler finds you or the baby wakes up from their nap. Even if your time is brief, read this Scripture again. Let it wash over you.

God is with you and he delights in you. He exults over you with joy. He is capable of quieting you and calming your storms. Let his love for you define your identity today. Let it satiate you no matter how tired, worn out, or overwhelmed you might be. There is not a required timeline for you to rest in his love. It's not withheld from you until you devote five minutes, ten minutes, or an hour to seeking God. He is in your midst and you have full access to his goodness. As he rejoices over you today, let how he sees you encourage you to love those around you with the same fullness.

Thank you, Father, that you are a God who rejoices over his children. You are such a kind and good father. As you rejoice over me, let my perspective of myself be changed. Help me to see myself as you see me and let that impact how I love those around me. No matter how brief my time is, you are in my midst and you exult over me.

# REALISTIC EXPECTATIONS

*The LORD is like a father to his children,*
*tender and compassionate to those who fear him.*
*For he knows how weak we are;*
*he remembers we are only dust.*
PSALM 103:13-14 NLT

God does not have unrealistic expectations of you. Perhaps when you became a mother you saw it as being different than it is. Maybe you thought you'd be more patient, more excited, more sufficient in meeting your child's needs. While you might find yourself disappointed in your shortcomings, God is not. He is well aware of all the ways you are lacking. He does not dangle our failures over us. He is a good father, abounding in compassion and tenderness.

In the midst of your weaknesses and failures, he has redeemed you. Let your lacking make space for his grace to be displayed. Let him speak to you gently about what he thinks of you. He is tender and he is compassionate just as you are toward your children. You don't expect your toddler to cook dinner and you don't expect your teenager to manage a company. You have realistic expectations of your children because you know what they can handle, you know who they are, and you know what they are capable of. If you can see your children rightly, then how much more clearly can God see you?

Thank you, God, that you know all of me. You see all of my weaknesses and failures and you are tender and compassionate toward me. Teach me how to adjust my expectations and to lean on you where I am weak. Thank you for being such a tender father. Today, when I am overwhelmed with what I cannot do, remind me of your greatness and all that you can do.

# FULLY SEEN AND UNDERSTOOD

*You keep track of all my sorrows.*
*You have collected all my tears in your bottle.*
*You have recorded each one in your book.*

PSALM 56:8 NLT

You are seen and understood. Not a single heartbreak is unseen. More so, you are validated. God is not a father who brushes off our pain. He doesn't tell you to get over it or to move on more quickly. He treasures your tears: of sadness, of anger, of happiness, of frustration. He collects all of them and keeps track of your sorrows. He is attentive and present.

Do you ever struggle to give your full attention to your children? In the midst of everything else you might having going on in life, it can be difficult to validate their big emotions and meet them with kindness each time they need it. While your intentions are to love, there are times your humanity probably gets in the way. This is not a struggle that God has. He, in his great power and goodness, always meets your sorrows with compassion. He is infinitely capable of validating you and keeping track of your hurts. Let his kindness stir you to draw closer to him. Let his kindness stir you to teach your children about who he is. Let his kindness and attentiveness be elevated by your weakness.

Thank you, God, that you see me and you know me. You are attentive to my hurts and you comfort me in them. Help me to love my children in the same way you love me. Where I am weak and prone to fail, teach my children about your greatness. You see them and you meet them with kindness.

# SEE YOURSELF RIGHTLY

*"Healthy people don't need a doctor—sick people do." Then he added,
"Now go and learn the meaning of this Scripture: 'I want you to show
mercy, not offer sacrifices.' For I have come to call not those who think
they are righteous, but those who know they are sinners."*

MATTHEW 9:12-13 NLT

Humility is necessary to walk in correct relationship with Jesus.
Having an accurate perspective of yourself allows you to have an
accurate perspective of who he is. If you don't understand your
own lowliness, you won't see the magnitude of his goodness.
Especially if you have been walking with the Lord for a number of
years, it's important to remember your daily need for redemption.
Don't consider yourself loftier than you should, taking the place of
honor in your own life. Despite your accomplishments, skills, or the
longevity of your faith, you are consistently in need of a Savior.

Today, ask the Holy Spirit to reveal areas of your life where instead
of depending upon the grace of God, you have taken unnecessary
pride in yourself. As he reveals those areas to you, humbly confess
them and be confident in God's desire to show you mercy. As
you correct your perspective of yourself, you will be able to
comprehend his greatness more accurately. You will also begin to
see those around you with greater compassion as you direct your
eyes toward what Christ has done and not what you can do.

Father, help me to see my constant need for you. Forgive
me for the times I have seen myself as righteous by my own
accord. I know that I am a sinner and that I am in desperate
need of the redemption of Christ. Help me to see where I have
depended on myself and where I can depend more on you.
Thank you for the gift of your mercy.

# MARCH

Let us run with endurance the race
that is set before us, looking to Jesus,
the founder and perfecter of our faith,
who for the joy that was set before him
endured the cross.

HEBREWS 12:1-2 ESV

# ENCOURAGE A FRIEND

*Let us consider one another in order to stir up love and good works, not forsaking the assembling of ourselves together, as is the manner of some, but exhorting one another, and so much the more as you see the Day approaching.*
HEBREWS 10:24-25 NKJV

You are not an island and you were not made to function as one. It can be easy to become so absorbed in your life as a mom that you don't invest in friendships and community the way you used to. Perhaps you don't have the time or it feels like it takes too much energy.

Remember today that God has made you to need others. While you might not have hours to give, you can give freely of what you have. An encouraging text, a quick note—these things take little effort but provide great fuel for maintaining friendships. If you are feeling lonely, be the friend who reaches out. Be the one who exhorts as you wait eagerly for Christ's return.

Thank you, God, for the body of Christ! No matter where I am in my relationships right now, give me the grace to reach out and encourage someone else. Teach me how to stir up love and good works. When I am feeling alone, let me consider someone else and meet them where they are. Bring to mind someone I can encourage today.

# CAST YOUR CARES

*Humble yourselves under the mighty power of God,*
*and at the right time he will lift you up in honor.*
*Give all your worries and cares to God, for he cares about you.*

1 PETER 5:6-7 NLT

The king you serve is not a tyrant. He is not far off or cold. He is warm, personal, close, and fatherly. When he asks you for humility to recognize his mighty power, it goes hand-in-hand with his kindness. He doesn't ask for obedience without reward. He promises that he will lift you up in honor. He reminds you of his power and immediately tells you to give him all your worries. In his great power and great love, he can handle your cares.

Today, cast them upon him. Without refrain, throw your troubles on him. You don't need to package them up neatly or present them calmly. He is not intimidated by your anxieties, fears, or emotions. Come to him like your children come to you: unafraid, messy, and trusting.

Thank you, God, that you are mighty! You are kind. As I seek to humble myself, remind me of your goodness. As I seek to serve you, remind me that you promise to lift me up. As I seek to cast my cares upon you, remind me that nothing is too big or messy for you to manage. You are fully able to care for me.

# BREATHE EASY

*"Come to me, all who labor and are heavy laden, and I will give you rest. Take my yoke upon you, and learn from me, for I am gentle and lowly in heart, and you will find rest for your souls. For my yoke is easy, and my burden is light."*

MATTHEW 11:28-30 ESV

You've been given an invitation to breathe easy. You've been invited to confidently approach and receive exactly what you need. God, who is gentle and strong, is asking you to learn from him. Walk in his ways today and you'll find that it brings a feeling of lightness. Don't carry heavy burdens by yourself. Run to him the same way you hope your children will come to you when they are tired, troubled, or hurting.

Whatever is heavy on your heart today, bring it to God. Take a few minutes and speak with him about it. He doesn't give you a list of requirements in order to rest in him. Right now no matter what's happening around you, no matter how much time you have, no matter how heavy you feel, you can find rest in Christ.

Thank you, God, that you provide me with a place of true rest. Thank you for carrying my burdens and that following you is light and life giving. Teach me to come to you first when I am tired. Help me to turn to you when I'd rather turn to worldly things for rest.

# BUILD UP PERSEVERANCE

*You know that the testing of your faith produces perseverance.*
JAMES 1:3 NIV

We aren't promised that life will be easy. As a mother, you know this full well. You face trials each day. God hasn't said that we will be without struggles, but he does promise that trials and the testing of your faith will produce perseverance. The hard things you go through are not purposeless. They are making you stronger. Like a runner trains for a marathon, you are building the muscles of perseverance as you face difficult circumstances. With each valley you walk through, you can gain confidence.

Today, instead of focusing on what is hard, keep your eyes on Christ as he leads you. You are stronger than you realize. Look back and see how far you have come. What feels impossible today is strengthening you for tomorrow.

Thank you, God, that the trials we face can have meaning. You can use them to produce perseverance. You are developing within me a faith that will last. You know what is best for me and I can be confident in your leading even when I find myself in valleys. I praise you for your strength!

# WALK IN THANKSGIVING

*Rejoice always, pray continually,*
*give thanks in all circumstances;*
*for this is God's will for you in Christ Jesus.*
1 THESSALONIANS 5:16-18 NIV

As motherhood consumes your time, energy, and resources, you might suddenly find yourself in a place with God that you haven't navigated before. Your relationship with him will look different than it used to when you weren't focused on the constant care of your children. In this time when you're adjusting to new realities of life, it might feel as though you don't know what God's will for you is anymore. The mundane can take over, and endless laundry, dishes, and homework help might make you feel purposeless.

Thankfully, God gives direction. His will for you in Christ Jesus is that you would rejoice always, pray continually, and give thanks in all circumstances. When you're not sure where to go, start there. Proclaim his goodness, pray for those around you, and walk in thanksgiving.

Thank you, God, that you give clear direction. Teach me how to walk in thanksgiving and to pray continually, knowing that these will always bear fruit because you promise they will. I praise you for your goodness and for all that you have done. Though I feel directionless sometimes, remind me that with my eyes on you, you will lead me where I need to be.

# HE LEAVES THE 99

*"If a man has a hundred sheep and one of them gets lost, what will he do? Won't he leave the ninety-nine others in the wilderness and go to search for the one that is lost until he finds it?"*

LUKE 15:4 NLT

You individually are seen by the good shepherd. He sees all of you, and still calls you his own. His eyes are on his flock as a whole and on you specifically. He is acutely aware of you and whether or not you are accounted for. Not only that, but when you are lost, he promises that he will search for you *and* find you. You are worth searching for. You are worth God's time and resources. There isn't a single sheep whom he would forsake because he has enough or cannot be bothered.

As you go about your day, remember that God's faithfulness to you can be a great encouragement. Because of Christ's sacrificial work on the cross, you are hemmed into a flock that is sustained and well cared for. Remember that he is the one who is ever aware of you. A shepherd does not forsake his sheep because of how the sheep feels. Lean into his lovingkindness and let him change your heart. Even in your doubts or struggles, you are safe and you are loved.

Thank you, God, that you are a good shepherd. You care for me and when I am lost, you will always find me. When I am discouraged, remind me that I am well loved and safe. Teach me how to depend on you to lead me as a shepherd leads a flock.

# SET THE TONE

*Brothers and sisters, think about the things that are good and worthy of praise. Think about the things that are true and honorable and right and pure and beautiful and respected.*

PHILIPPIANS 4:8 NCV

As a mother, you have the unique role of setting the tone in your home. This often starts with your thought patterns. Where your thoughts are focused is where your heart will be and this will dictate the fruit you see in your life and in your home. Are you focusing on what is stressful, out of your control, overwhelming, and negative? Have you noticed that on those days, you feel anxious, short tempered, tired, or snappy?

Today, seek to focus on what is good, beautiful, and respected. You are responsible for where you direct your attention. If you are dwelling on the negative, such will be the fruit in your life. You are responsible for the thought patterns that you feed. If certain news outlets cause stress, stop reading them. If social media causes you to focus on what you don't have, take a break. Today, ask the Lord to equip you to develop a healthy thought life.

Thank you, God, for reminding me how influential my thoughts can be. Teach me how to dwell on what is good, right, and lovely. When I find myself straying, may the Holy Spirit speak to me and help me to change course. Give me the strength to cut off habits that negatively affect my thought life.

# UNCEASING MERCY

*The faithful love of the LORD never ends!*
*His mercies never cease.*
*Great is his faithfulness;*
*his mercies begin afresh each morning.*
LAMENTATIONS 3:22-23 NLT

God knew that you would constantly need a fresh start. His perfect design of seasons, beginnings and endings, sunrises and sunsets, speaks to his affinity for rest, restoration, and renewal. He knew that you would need to close the door on difficult days and wake up to start fresh. No matter what yesterday held, today is different from the moment you opened your eyes.

If yesterday was marked by stress over schedules, conflict with your children, pain over strained relationships, or difficult family dynamics, know that today you have the opportunity to delight in God's faithfulness and declare fresh mercy over your life and over your children. God is the master of do-overs. He knows we are prone to fail and his mercies never cease. There is no need to carry yesterday's burdens into today.

Thank you, God, that your mercies are fresh every morning. Help me to be a mom who depends on your unfailing faithfulness. Help me to treat my children the same way you treat me: with kindness and grace whenever they need a fresh start. Teach me how to come to you for renewal when I'm stuck in yesterday's hurts and struggles.

# YOU BELONG

*Instead, we will speak the truth in love, growing in every way more and more like Christ, who is the head of his body, the church. He makes the whole body fit together perfectly. As each part does its own special work, it helps the other parts grow, so that the whole body is healthy and growing and full of love.*

EPHESIANS 4:15-16 NLT

You are a unique part of the body of Christ. You are needed and necessary for the body to grow and be full of love. When you feel lost in motherhood, know that what you do is incredible and needed. The cereal you pour, the bedtime songs you sing, the job you do each day has intrinsic value. Whether you stay home full time, work full time, or do a bit of both, you are needed for the body to fit together perfectly. God promises that as you speak and operate in the love of Christ, you are ensuring that the entire body is healthy.

You have a unique role to play and it cannot be diminished by whether or not you see it as successful. Your love, given to you by Christ and poured out for your children, is an integral part of the body. As you walk with the Spirit and speak the truth in love, you are growing more like Christ. There is no more important work than this.

Thank you, God, that you encourage us to speak the truth in love. Thank you for holding the body together and for giving me an important role to play. Help me to seek to be more like Jesus each day. Show me areas of my life where I can grow further in love. I am an important part of the body. Remind me of the importance of others as well.

# FULLY KNOWN

*You discern my going out and my lying down;*
*you are familiar with all my ways.*
*Before a word is on my tongue,*
*you, LORD, know it completely.*
*You hem me in behind and before,*
*and you lay your hand upon me.*

PSALM 139:3-5 NIV

You are fully known. Do you ever feel misrepresented, unknown, or misunderstood? Those feelings can quickly cause loneliness and isolation. You are not isolated from God. He is highly personal and acutely aware of you. He sees the tears you hide from your children; he sees your shortcomings and your fears. He keeps track of you. The needs of your children are unending, and you might feel the heaviness of having to be on all the time. There is one who cares for you in this same way. He hems you in, he guides you, he doesn't miss a thing.

Today, lean into an awareness that God knows everything about you and won't ever run from you. There is no part of you that is hidden from him, yet his love is unfailing and unchanging.

Father, thank you that you are personal. You are close, not far. Your nearness is a comfort to me! Through your Holy Spirit, let your nearness chase away loneliness. When I don't feel cared for, remind me that you are the one who shepherds me lovingly. Today, help me to feel secure in your unchanging love.

# LOOK TO CREATION

*Go to the ant, O sluggard;*
*consider her ways, and be wise.*
*Without having any chief, officer, or ruler,*
*she prepares her bread in summer*
*and gathers her food in harvest.*

PROVERBS 6:6-8 ESV

If you take the time to slow down and observe, you can see that God has provided countless opportunities for you to learn from his creation. The ant prepares for the future and works diligently. The sunset speaks of creativity and glory. The tree grows deep roots and thrives. The sparrow is fed and the lilies are clothed. God's creation is intricate and full of purpose.

As a mother, you have the blessing of learning all these things through the eyes of your child. Their amazement at a bee collecting nectar or a wave crashing onto the shore is delightful. Slow down and take time today to see the world like they do. Ask God to reveal himself and his character to you through all he has made. It is all good. Your children can see that clearly and are amazed. Let your eyes widen and your heart soften for even just a moment.

Thank you, God, that everything you've made brings you glory. Your love for me can be seen in how you've designed the world I live in, full of life and beauty. Help me to see the world the way my children do. Refresh my spirit as I praise you for the good things you have made.

# BLESSED AND KEPT

*"The Lord bless you, and keep you;*
*The Lord make his face shine on you,*
*and be gracious to you;*
*The Lord lift up His countenance on you,*
*and give you peace."*

NUMBERS 6:24-26 NASB

As you sit here, seeking God even if just for a moment, let this prayer be spoken over your home. Let the words wash over you and your children. May the Lord bless you; may he provide you with exactly what you need to get through the day. May the Lord keep you; may he hold you close and keep you from straying from the narrow path. May the Lord make his face shine on you; may you experience the glory of who he is and see the kindness with which he sees you. May he be gracious to you; may you experience the undeserving grace that is a free gift to you because of what Christ accomplished on the cross. May the Lord lift up his countenance upon you; may you know that you are seen by God and that he doesn't take his eyes off of you. May he give you peace; may your heart be at rest and your mind be at ease as you trust him fully and walk through your day leaning on his strength.

Let this blessing from Numbers wash over you and stir up within you affection for your Father.

Thank you, God, that you see me. You've given me your Word to meditate on. As I read it, may it point me to you. Help me to walk in truth and to be impacted throughout my day by the truth that you place on my heart. Stir up within me an affection for you as I learn more about your character and how you see me.

# PERFECT UNITY

*"I have given them the glory you gave me, so they may be one as we
are one. I am in them and you are in me. May they experience such
perfect unity that the world will know that you sent me and that you
love them as much as you love me."*

JOHN 17:22-23 NLT

Unity within the body of Christ is the channel that displays who
Christ is to the rest of the world. The Word says that by unity they
will know that God sent his Son and that he loves the world as
much as he loves his Son. Striving for unity is a noble cause but it
isn't without its challenges. As a mother, you've seen the value of
picking your battles with your kids. The same is true within the body
of Christ. With the discernment of the Holy Spirit, you can walk in
wisdom, knowing what is worth a discussion and what is not.

As you keep your eyes on the cross and walk in humility, you'll find
that bearing each other's burdens is more important than insisting
on your own way. As you walk in peace with each other, you can
have confidence that you are actively displaying the love of Christ.
You might feel like you don't have the time for ministry. Take heart
in knowing that loving those around you well displays the love
of Christ just as effectively and fully as any ministry you could be
involved in.

Thank you, God, that you've given me clear instructions on how
to show the world that you love them. Today, help me to walk
in humility, bearing the burdens of others. Help me to discern
what to focus on and what to keep to myself when it comes to
communicating with my brothers and sisters. Teach me to walk
in wisdom.

# PRESENCE OVER PRODUCTIVITY

*"My dear Martha, you are worried and upset over all these details!
There is only one thing worth being concerned about. Mary has
discovered it, and it will not be taken away from her."*

LUKE 10:41-42 NLT

When your to-do list is never-ending and you feel stretched thin,
it seems counterintuitive to sit still. Yet this is exactly what Jesus
recommends. His ways are not like the world's ways. He is the ruler
of the upside-down kingdom where the first is last and striving
is unproductive. The world will tell you to do more, be more,
know more. Jesus calls you to a life that is defined by the simple
obedience of sitting at his feet. He knows that is the place where
true connection is found. This can be modeled perfectly in the life
of a mother.

How often have you been so busy working for your children that
you've missed the connection of an extra-long hug, a snuggle on
the couch, or a slow and peaceful bedtime routine. Your presence
is more important than your productivity both with Christ and
with your children. Today, slow down and soak up the love of Jesus
which is given to you freely and abundantly.

Thank you, God, that in your presence I can find true rest. Help
me to slow down and seek that which is truly life giving. Help
me to put aside my to-do list and prioritize presence over
productivity. You are concerned with the state of my heart and
with my rest. I praise you that you are a God who is personal
and present. May my life be defined by a longing to be with
you more than a longing to be productive.

# CHOOSE MEEKNESS

*"Blessed are the meek,*
*for they shall inherit the earth."*
MATTHEW 5:5 ESV

At the beginning of Jesus' ministry, he offered up one his most iconic and quoted sermons. The Sermon on the Mount is full of reminders about who is truly rich. Where the world might tell you to spend your time hoarding power, influence, and material gain, Jesus elevates meekness, purity of heart, and those who hunger and mourn. He reminds you that while meekness might feel like surrender, really it's an extreme confidence in who God is and what is to come.

You needn't insist upon your way, your opinion, or your own rights because your confidence does not lie in yourself or what you can do. You can afford to give up control because you know who is truly in control. Meekness says to release your grasp where the world will tell you to hold on tighter. Meekness says to let God's power be displayed in your weakness where the world will tell you to elevate yourself. Today, look to Christ's example of meekness and let it transform your perspective.

Thank you, Jesus, for your example. You have unlimited power and ability and yet you chose to be meek. You submitted yourself to the will of the Father knowing that he would care for you. Help me to walk in meekness. Teach me how to elevate your name instead of insisting upon my own way.

# GLORY TO COME

*Our present troubles are small and won't last very long. Yet they produce for us a glory that vastly outweighs them and will last forever! So we don't look at the troubles we can see now; rather, we fix our gaze on things that cannot be seen.*

2 CORINTHIANS 4:17-18 NLT

"Your present troubles are small and won't last long"? This might feel like a trite observation. Your present troubles may in fact feel quite large and long-lasting. Your present trials might be traumatic and painful. You may be walking through darkness that feels as though it is consuming you. Whether your present troubles are big or small, God knows. He is acutely aware of your struggles. Yet, you are still told that they are small and won't last long compared to the produced glory that is to come. Imagine then, the great and incredible glory that awaits you as a follower of Christ.

If God knows the pain of this life and can call it small, then how infinite and perfect is the glory to come! Let the great hope of what is to come spur you on. Let it produce fortitude within you. You are even given clear instructions on how to accomplish this: don't focus on what is happening right now; fix your eyes on what is to come. Even though you cannot see him now, fix your eyes on the return of Christ. There will be a day that he makes all things right. May the anticipation of that day help you to look beyond your current troubles.

Thank you, Jesus, that you are coming back again! The glory to come outweighs my current troubles. Help me to fix my eyes on you and to find hope when I feel overcome by my troubles. Help me to see my trials as a means of producing glory in my life.

# HIS PLANS ARE GOOD

*"For I know the plans I have for you," declares the LORD,*
*"plans to prosper you and not to harm you,*
*plans to give you hope and a future."*
JEREMIAH 29:11 NIV

Motherhood is full of unknowns. Is my child healthy? Is my child thriving? What will they be like when they're older? Am I doing enough? Despite your great love for your children, you cannot possibly plan for everything, and you personally cannot guarantee specific outcomes. Where you are limited in your humanity, God is unlimited. He knows exactly what the future will hold for you and for your children. Where you cannot possibly see clearly, he sees all of your tomorrows perfectly. He promises you that there is hope and that his plans are fully and wonderfully good.

When you are feeling overwhelmed about what is to come, about what you cannot control, lean into God's promises. He is the author, orchestrator, and perfecter of your faith. He is fully dependable in the midst of your limitations.

Thank you, God, that you know exactly what lays before me. I can depend on you fully when I am anxious about the future. I praise you for you are great and your goodness never ends. When I begin to worry about my future or my children's futures, lead me to cast my cares upon you.

# HE IS WITH YOU

*"You will call on me and come and pray to me,*
*and I will listen to you.*
*You will seek me and find me*
*when you seek me with all your heart."*
JEREMIAH 29:12-13 NIV

Motherhood may often leave you in want. You can't always give your children everything they want or even need. In your own power, you cannot always be available. This is not the way the kingdom of heaven works. God doesn't operate within human limits and his availability is not circumstantial. Through Jesus Christ, you have direct and unlimited access to the Father. You will not be left wanting. God promises that when you ask for him, you'll find him. He is not a God who taunts you with his presence. He is not hiding, and he doesn't have a list of requirements for you to complete before you can go to him. Through the sacrifice of Christ, God has made himself readily available to us. He has bridged the gap fully and made a way for you to receive what you need.

Today, delight in your ease of access to God. It's as simple as looking and asking. Ask for what you and your children need. It is irrelevant how big or small those needs are. He delights in your communion with him and he is a good father who loves to give his children good gifts.

Thank you, God, that you are available! You are not hard to find. Today, when I'm overwhelmed with my own inadequacies, remind me of your goodness. Give me the grace to come to you and to seek you with confidence, knowing that I'll always find you when I ask.

# WORK IN PROGRESS

*I am certain that God, who began the good work within you,*
*will continue his work until it is finally finished*
*on the day when Christ Jesus returns.*

PHILIPPIANS 1:6 NLT

It's clear on a daily basis that your children are not finished. They are constantly learning, making mistakes, and reminding you of their childishness. It's more difficult to remember that you are in the same boat. As you nurture them and teach them, humbly remember that you are not finished either. God began a good work in you and that work is continuous until Christ returns. There won't ever be a day prior to his return that you are done.

Let this take a burden off your shoulders as you realize that you still have a long way to go. Instead of walking in shame over that issue that you struggle with or that problem you just can't overcome, remember that, like your children, you are learning. Don't forget about God's grace by setting unrealistic expectations for yourself. Instead, walk in humility, letting the Holy Spirit lead you one step at a time, one day at a time, until that glorious day when Jesus comes back and the work is finished.

Thank you, God, that I am not finished. Today, help me to remember that I am a work in progress and I can depend on you as a child depends on a mother. You will finish the good work you began in me. Help me to lean on your grace as I eagerly wait for the day when Christ returns.

# FIND COMFORT IN GOD

*May your unfailing love be my comfort,*
*according to your promise to your servant.*
PSALM 119:76 NIV

Your child falls on the sidewalk and cries, "Mommy!" then runs straight into your waiting arms. For them, the instinct to turn to you when they are hurting is as natural as breathing. Where else would they possibly go? You are their first and best option. They know that you have what they need and that you will provide comfort in the midst of their pain. You will wipe the tears, find the right colored Band-Aid, say the right words, and hold them tight before sending them off to face the world again.

While your challenges are more complicated than a scratch or a bruise, you can learn from your children's instincts. What do you turn to for comfort? Where do your reflexes take you? Do you run to your friends, to food, to busyness? Do you distract yourself or bury your emotions when something causes you pain? May the unfailing love of God be your comfort. It is more than sufficient. When you lean on him, he'll hold you just like you hold your children. He promises to comfort you, and his comfort is much more sufficient than the balm of distraction or substitution. He knows exactly what you need and how to help you face the world again.

Thank you, God, that you provide true comfort. Teach me to lean on you when I'm in pain instead of seeking out other ways to feel better. You bring healing when I ask you. I praise you for your kindness and goodness. Give me the grace to depend on your unfailing love.

# HE IS KIND

*Or do you think lightly of the riches of His kindness and tolerance and patience, not knowing that the kindness of God leads you to repentance?*

ROMANS 2:4 NASB

God is not a tyrant. He is not an angry king. He is not an impatient father. He is infinitely kind. Your perception of God's character impacts the way you respond to him. If you feel that he is nagging you, condemning you, punishing you, or angry with you, you aren't likely to long to spend time in his presence. Take time to think about what leads you to repentance. Is it the kind and consistent conviction of the Holy Spirit or is it guilt, shame, and fear of getting in trouble? The latter will not push you toward a loving God; it will motivate you to hide from him in your shame.

God's kindness is what leads you to repentance. He doesn't reprimand harshly; he gently guides and he speaks clearly. When the Holy Spirit brings conviction, he will also empower you to surrender your sin and accept mercy in your time of need. Today, as you spend time with God, ask him to soften your heart that you might have a true perspective of his character and how he leads you to repentance.

Thank you, Father, that you are kind. I am so grateful that you do not use shame and guilt to pressure me into change. You gently lead and you give abundant mercy. You meet me in my sin and hold my hand as you guide me out of it. Where I have believed that you are harsh or unloving in your correction, teach me to see you rightly.

# UTILIZE THE WORD

*"I'm not asking you to take them out of the world, but to keep them safe from the evil one. They do not belong to this world any more than I do. Make them holy by your truth; teach them your word, which is truth. Just as you sent me into the world, I am sending them into the world."*

JOHN 17:15-18 NLT

God knew that you would feel out of place in the world. He knew that as a follower of Christ, you don't belong here any more than Jesus did. This is why he has equipped you with the Word. You aren't supposed to fit in nor are you supposed to isolate yourself. You aren't supposed to live a life without trial. You are, however, supposed to strengthen yourself with the sword of the Spirit.

The refuge you can find in biblical truths is what keeps you safe from the evil one. If you don't have any other goals, let bolstering your faith with the Word be your goal. Place Scripture around your home where you will see it often. Memorize simple truths alongside your children. Fill your mind and heart with the edifying truth that God has given you for your benefit. Speak Scripture out loud and let it be the language of your home.

Thank you, God, for the gift of the Word. Help me fill my heart and mind with truth. Thank you for equipping me to live in this time even though I know that my true home is with you. Help me navigate my days with Scripture. Bring to mind your truth when I need it most.

# TRUE FRIENDSHIP

*Confess your sins to each other and pray for each other*
*so that you may be healed. The earnest prayer of a righteous person*
*has great power and produces wonderful results.*

JAMES 5:16 NLT

Your brokenness will follow you. Your sins will follow you. The grudges you carry, the hurt you don't want to acknowledge, the conflict you'd like to bury will not only exist when you hide it in darkness, it will thrive and grow roots of bitterness and unforgiveness. God has designed you to live in the light. Confess your sins to one another and pray for each other that you might be healed. This instruction doesn't have limitations. Confess your sins when you speak in anger toward your children. Confess your sins when you covet. Confess your sins when you are unkind to your neighbor.

This can have a monumental impact on your relationships, including those with your children. God doesn't give instruction for no reason. He knows that confession, prayer, and healing are what we need. Be quick to confess and seek healing. Learn to have quick reflexes when it comes to admitting you were wrong so you may walk in righteousness, or right standing, before God and man.

Thank you, God, that you designed me to walk in the light. In the light, I can thrive and walk in righteousness. You say that the prayers of a righteous person have great power! Teach me how to be quick to confess my sins that I, and those I hurt, might be healed.

# LAY DOWN YOUR LIFE

*"There is no greater love than to lay down one's life for one's friends."*
JOHN 15:13 NLT

There is richness in modeling your life after how Jesus lived. It feels contradictory to lose your life in an effort to gain it, but that's exactly what laying your life down looks like. As you serve your children, know that you are displaying the great love of Christ. He sacrificed unto death—a much more drastic outcome than many of us will ever experience in our efforts to love others.

Let the selflessness of Christ toward you stir up love within you for your children. Though motherhood is tasking, tiring, and difficult, it also comes with the rich reward of loving well. There is no greater love than the selfless prioritization of others' needs above your own. This doesn't mean that you will do it perfectly. If serving others has you feeling worn out, let God renew your strength. Go to him for rest and trust in his faithfulness to sustain you.

Thank you, God, for the opportunity to lay my life down each day. May my love for others come from an overflow of the love you've shown me. Help me not to grow weary but to depend on your strength. As I walk through my day, teach me how to love like you love.

# THE BLESSING OF SPACE

*When hard pressed, I cried to the LORD;*
*he brought me into a spacious place.*
PSALM 118:5 NIV

Motherhood can feel crowded. Little hands are constantly grabbing, doors are flung open, and silence is a desperate commodity. You might find yourself daydreaming of a place where you can just be yourself, a place where you simply have space. God promises that when you are hard pressed, you can cry to him and he will bring you into a spacious place. He is capable of giving you peace in the midst of chaos. He knows that your senses are overloaded and he promises you peace. He knows every detail of your day and he still says he can bring you to a spacious place. This is because he knows that true peace has nothing to do with your physical surroundings and everything to do with a confident hope placed in who he is, what he's done, and what he will do.

Today, if you're feeling crowded take a moment to seek the Lord. With God's sufficient grace, look past what is crowding you and set your gaze on what is to come: a glorious day when God makes all things new and Jesus comes back to set up his true kingdom. Until that day, God will sustain you as you cry out to him.

Thank you, God, that you see me when I am hard pressed. You know I need spacious places and peace for my soul. As I cry out to you when I am overloaded emotionally or physically, I know you will meet me and rescue me. Help me to look past what crowds me and set my gaze on you.

# LEAN INTO DISCIPLINE

*"The Lord disciplines those he loves,*
*and he punishes each one he accepts as his child."*
HEBREWS 12:6 NLT

Just as you often know what is best for your child, God knows what is best for you. He doesn't only see in this moment, he sees all of your moments collectively. In his omniscience he knows how each day impacts the next. When you experience the discipline of the Lord, you can find assurance in his unlimited understanding of your life and in his unfailing love. Not only does he know every detail and what needs pruning, he also accepts and adores you.

This foundation of wisdom and love is the most perfect base for discipline. As a mother, you are well aware of this. There is a vast difference between godly discipline and punishment. One produces growth, togetherness, and peace while the other alienates and creates shame. When God disciplines you, you need not shy away from it. Lean into his discipline, knowing confidently that he is a good and gracious father.

Thank you, God, that you are kind in your discipline. I praise you for your great mercy! You prune and shape me, knowing what is best for me and my future. Help me to trust you and to lean on you without shame. Instead of alienating me when an area of my life needs changing, you bring me close.

# GOD'S REQUIREMENTS

*He has told you, O man, what is good;*
*And what does the LORD require of you*
*But to do justice, to love kindness,*
*And to walk humbly with your God?*

MICAH 6:8 NASB

Perhaps motherhood has caused your days to blur together and you've been left feeling like you don't have the same direction or drive you used to. Instead of dwelling on the feeling of being stuck, consider if you're walking in the way God designed. You will be most fulfilled when you are filling the purpose you were designed for. This purpose is a lot less complicated than a calling or a career. It is more about the way you spend your days than the great things you do or don't do for God.

You might have goals or dreams that you set aside, willingly or not, when you became a mother. Though your purpose is different, you are not disqualified by motherhood. God's instructions do not change based on whether or not you have a calling. His instructions remain the same for each of his children: do justice, love kindness, and walk humbly with your God. He is fully capable of leading you successfully in all of those no matter how tired, overwhelmed, or disoriented you feel. Let God's requirements of you be the sieve for your days. Filter your expectations through his Word and let it wash over you, releasing you to confidently adjust how you define success.

Thank you, God, that your requirements are the same for each of your children. You know the season I'm in and what I'm capable of. Help me to define success based on what you've asked of me. Teach me how to do justice, love kindness, and walk humbly with you.

# RELY ON GOD

*Do not throw away your confidence; it will be richly rewarded.*
*You need to persevere so that when you have done the will of God,*
*you will receive what he has promised.*

HEBREWS 10:35-36 NIV

It can be tempting to rely on yourself. As a mother, you are constantly being relied upon. Instead of letting that translate into independence and confidence in yourself, remember to rely on Christ. Let the work that you do each day for others motivate you to put your confidence in what Jesus has done. Hebrews reveals God's promise that when you persevere in your reliance upon him, you will be rewarded. Put your trust in God's provision and he will not leave you disappointed.

This is not a one-sided transaction. God is faithful to give you what he has promised: a completely perfect eternity spent with Christ as he rules and reigns. God knew that you would be tempted to rely on yourself. He knew that the way would be narrow. He isn't surprised by your tendency to forget about his provision and what he has done. He speaks to you through his Word like a good father, gently reminding and equipping his daughter. Let the Lord speak to you about where you have wavered in your confidence in him, then let him gently guide you back to the narrow path.

Thank you, Father, that you are a reliable place to put my confidence. You are worthy of my trust. You will be faithful to give me what you've promised. Help me to depend on you in everything that I do. Teach me how to trust you in a deeper way today than I did yesterday.

# ABIDE IN THE VINE

*"I am the true vine, and My Father is the vinedresser. Every branch in Me that does not bear fruit, He takes away; and every branch that bears fruit, He prunes it so that it may bear more fruit.... I am the vine, you are the branches; he who abides in Me and I in him, he bears much fruit, for apart from Me you can do nothing."*

JOHN 15:1-2, 5 NASB

A branch does not struggle to bear fruit. A branch does not fret over whether or not it will bear fruit. A branch does not worry over whether there is enough fruit or if that fruit is good enough. A branch simply thrives when the right conditions are in place. When the soil is good, and the sun is vibrant, and the rains are steady, the fruit will come at the right time. You can place full confidence in your Father, the vinedresser. Your one job is to abide in the true vine, Jesus Christ. Apart from the vine, you cannot bear fruit.

Are you lacking patience, joy, gentleness, goodness, self-control, faithfulness, peace, love, or kindness? These are the fruit of the Spirit that come from abiding in Christ. Instead of feeling shame that you don't have an abundance of these in your life, turn to the true source. Do the only necessary work for cultivating fruit, staying connected to the vine, and trusting the skills of the vinedresser.

Thank you, God, that you've designed me to bear fruit. Teach me to abide in Christ and depend on you for the working out of my salvation. You are good and trustworthy and skilled. Help me to see your pruning as a loving act of mercy that I might bear more fruit. Teach me to turn to you when I am lacking.

# HE IS ATTENTIVE

*Who covers the heavens with clouds,*
*who prepares rain for the earth,*
*who makes grass to grow on the mountains.*
PSALM 147:8 NKJV

In the same way that God holds the earth together, he holds your life together. In the same way he gives cloud cover, rainfall, and new growth, he is attentive to the details of your life. Maybe you feel like your current season is more than you can handle or maybe you're so busy that you've overlooked his hand in your life.

Today, as you slow down and seek truth, look at the ways he has orchestrated your life. If you take the time to look, you'll see the million little gifts that he gives you each day. Each thing, big and small, can speak to you about how God cares for you. He makes the sun shine, he makes the breeze soft, and he creates new life all across the earth. Look up from whatever is demanding your attention and set your focus on he who is majestic, gracious, and merciful, yet demands nothing.

God, you are the one who holds everything together. You are the one who creates new life and sustains the earth. Teach me to see you as the one who is in control. Open my eyes to see the ways you have provided for me. Teach me to see the ways you have displayed your love for me.

# SEEK GOD'S PERSPECTIVE

*Don't copy the behavior and customs of this world, but let God
transform you into a new person by changing the way you think.
Then you will learn to know God's will for you, which is good and
pleasing and perfect.*

ROMANS 12:2 NLT

When reading this Scripture in Romans it can be easy to think of it
in terms of sin actions. Do not steal. Do not be unfaithful to your
spouse. Do not speak in a foul way. Today, challenge yourself to
think of how you've been copying the behavior and customs of
the world in your heart and in your thought life. Are you taking
on anxiety, fear, anger, or haughtiness? When it comes to culture,
societal values, or politics, are you willfully and pridefully insisting
on your own way or are you asking God for his perspective?

While the world remains in constant conflict, remember to let God
transform not just your actions, but the way you think. Remember
that Scripture has been given to you as an asset and that you
can confidently approach the throne of grace and receive mercy
whenever you need it. Instead of turning to social media or news
outlets to learn about how to navigate the world, turn to God. Let
him speak to you and change the way you think with his kindness
and compassion. As you respond to him with a soft heart, you will
learn more about his will and purpose for you.

Thank you, God, for the reminder not to copy the ways of the
world. Help me apply this to my heart and my thoughts as
well as to my actions. Help me to humbly come to you for
guidance instead of turning to the world's opinion. Teach me
how to search the Scriptures and depend on you for what my
perspective should be.

# APRIL

I have been crucified with Christ. It is no
longer I who live, but Christ who lives in
me. And the life I now live in the flesh I
live by faith in the Son of God, who loved
me and gave himself for me.

GALATIANS 2:20 ESV

# HIGHEST OPINION

*As the Scriptures say, "If you want to boast, boast only about the Lord."*
*When people commend themselves, it doesn't count for much.*
*The important thing is for the Lord to commend them.*

2 CORINTHIANS 10:18 NLT

When God is your compass and your source of confidence, you'll find yourself walking with a quiet stability that cannot be uprooted. A confidence placed firmly in the Lord is what counts. Despite your skills, successes, or resources, the only thing you can truly boast in is the Lord. If you are tempted to walk in pride, turn to the Lord in humility, knowing that he is your creator and sustainer. Likewise, if you are tempted to walk in condemnation or shame, turn to the Lord in humility, knowing that he is the good and perfect judge who sees you through Christ's work on the cross.

Boasting does not only happen in the form of gloating. Your negative opinion of yourself or others is just as boastful, giving power to your own perceptions over the perceptions of God. In all circumstances, seek out God's opinion before your own. Today, look to God for approval as you mother and move throughout your day.

Thank you, God, that I can boast in you. My confidence can by firmly placed in what you have done and in who you are. Through your Holy Spirit, lead me to turn to you where I am prone to look at myself. Forgive me for elevating my opinion of myself over your opinion. Teach me to walk in humility and to proclaim your name above all else.

# HUMBLY OFFERED

*Offer hospitality to one another without grumbling. Each of you should use whatever gift you have received to serve others, as faithful stewards of God's grace in its various forms. If anyone speaks, they should do so as one who speaks the very words of God.*

1 PETER 4:9-11 NIV

Hospitality does not have definite requirements. It's the friendly and generous reception of others. There is not a hidden rule that says your house must be perfectly clean, your kids must be well behaved, and your food must be deliciously executed. God says to use whatever gift you have. Just give what you have. If you have hotdogs and crumbs on your counters, give that. If you have an open door and warm words, give that. If you have a few extra dollars or a car to give someone a ride, give that. Whatever you have is more than enough when given faithfully with kindness.

While you might compare yourself with others or feel intimidated by their resources, know that you are enough in Christ. When it comes down to it, people just want to be seen and known. The same is true with your children; more often than not they crave your attention and your presence over anything else you think they might need. For your children and others you might encounter, what you have is enough. Speak the words of God with the love of Christ and humbly offer whatever you've been given to those around you.

Thank you, God, that you have equipped me to be hospitable. Help me to be bold in offering what I have. Teach me not to overthink generosity and to instead depend on you to fill in gaps where I don't have resources. May others see the love of Christ in my home and in my interactions. Forgive me for the times that I have held back hospitality and renew in me a generous spirit.

# WAIT IN THE QUIET

*The LORD is good to those who depend on him,*
*to those who search for him.*
*So it is good to wait quietly*
*for salvation from the LORD.*
LAMENTATIONS 3:25-26 NLT

God's promises are true and good. His Word never returns void. He doesn't say things that he doesn't mean. If his Word says that it is good to wait quietly for salvation, then you can depend upon that fully. When you come to him and your mind is distracted, your heart is heavy, and life is bustling all around you, it's okay to just sit. In fact, he invites you to sit quietly, no expectations. You don't have to pray the right thing, read the right thing, or walk away with the right tidbit of wisdom. You are invited to sit at his feet and just wait. What other transaction works like this? You give nothing and you receive in abundance. Posture yourself in expectance and he will be faithful to meet you.

Today, set aside your notions of what should define your relationship with God. Lay aside your failures and frustrations and remember the simplicity of waiting quietly. Be refreshed by knowing that he is worthy of your dependence.

Thank you, God, that I can wait quietly for you. In the quiet you meet me and give me what I need. Teach me to sit with you in the silence even when my world feels frantic. You alone can calm my fears and frustrations. Help me to depend on you.

# TRUE PROMISES

*I pray that God, the source of hope, will fill you completely with joy and peace because you trust in him. Then you will overflow with confident hope through the power of the Holy Spirit.*

ROMANS 15:13 NLT

Scripture is full of beautiful blessings and promises. As you let these words sink in, going from your head to your heart, remember that the Word of God is living and active. What is written is so much more than just words on a page. Let the Word change you, encourage you, and sustain you. Let it be the well you run to when you are weary. Let it be the wisdom you seek when you are unsure. Let it be your refuge in times of trial. As you trust in God and in his Word, you will be filled with peace. As you rely on who he is, you will be filled with joy. The Holy Spirit has the power to make you overflow with confident hope.

Peace, joy, hope—doesn't that sound like a recipe for a full and beautiful life? This is what God offers you as you follow him and trust in what he says. As you come across promises in Scripture, pray them over yourself, your home, and your children. Pray them with confidence because you know that God doesn't say anything he doesn't mean or have the resources to back up. Today, as you seek him, let the Holy Spirit bring to mind areas where you need the balm of the Word in your life.

God, thank you for the promises and blessings that you've given me through your Word. Help me to depend on you as my source of hope. When I am overwhelmed, help me to turn to the Bible for guidance. Teach me how to navigate it and to see Jesus in everything within it. As I trust in you, you will fill me with confident hope.

# BEYOND HUMAN LIMITS

*When they looked up, they saw that the stone, which was very large, had been rolled away. "You are looking for Jesus the Nazarene, who was crucified. He has risen! He is not here. See the place where they laid him."*

MARK 16:4, 6 NIV

God raised a man from the dead. If he has the power to do that, what else can he accomplish? He is the God who opens closed doors, who rolls away stones, who created the universe and holds it together. There is quite literally nothing too big for him to accomplish. He doesn't see obstacles the way you do. He doesn't operate within human limits; in fact, he operates unimaginably beyond what humanity can fathom. He makes a way where there isn't one. He cannot be held back, discouraged, or outperformed. Let his greatness impact the way you approach him. He can and will work miracles in your life if you ask. He can change hearts and heal brokenness.

Your Father longs for you to ask him to move. Moreover, as you ask big things of him, you'll find yourself more at home in his presence. Maybe you're waiting on some big help from God right now. He hears you and he is capable of doing incredible things. Keep your eyes on who he is, stay rooted in what he's already done through Jesus, and place your hope in what he's promised to do through Christ's return.

Thank you, God, that you are powerful enough to raise Jesus from the dead. Help me to see that power in my own life. Help me confidently approach you, knowing that you are the one who can make a way where there doesn't seem to be one. Teach me to depend on you and to become closer to you as I ask you to move in my life.

# LOVING THEM

*"Anyone who becomes as humble as this little child is the greatest in the Kingdom of Heaven. And anyone who welcomes a little child like this on my behalf is welcoming me."*

MATTHEW 18:4-5 NLT

As a mother you are caring for your children on a daily basis. You have the opportunity to teach them and help them navigate life. You also have the beautiful opportunity to get down on their level and humble yourself. As you welcome them, with your time, energy, and resources, you are welcoming Christ. As you lay next to them at bedtime, coaxing them to sleep, it's as if you are comforting Christ. As you nourish them and ensure that they are healthy, you are doing it unto Jesus as well. As you pour your life out, giving the best of yourself to your children, you are also pouring yourself out for Christ.

Today, in your exhaustion or weariness, remember that loving your children is loving Jesus. As you wrap your arms around them with kindness and provide a safe place for them to land, remember that what you are doing counts and that it has eternal value.

Thank you, Father, that you've given me the honor of being a mother. Help me to see each opportunity to love my children as an opportunity to love you. When I am tired and I want to quit, help me to see my children the way you see them. Forgive me for the times I have seen them as a burden. Refresh my spirit and renew my ability to love like you love.

# THE ADVOCATE

*The Spirit helps us in our weakness. For we do not know what to pray
for as we ought, but the Spirit himself intercedes for us with groanings
too deep for words.*

ROMANS 8:26 ESV

Have you ever been sitting down and your child wanders over
and curls up in your lap? You ask what they want or what they
need, and they respond with a quiet, "I don't know," but they
stay snuggled up next to you, heavy on your lap, leaning on you,
soaking in your presence. They can't articulate their needs, but you
know exactly what they're after. You know that they crave closeness
and security, nearness and affection.

Let this way of interacting be mirrored in your relationship with
Christ. You don't need to have anything figured out before you go
to him. You just need to know that his nearness is good for you.
Valuing the security of his presence over asking for just the right
things shows that you trust him to handle whatever is at hand. As
you go to him, finding refuge and peace, you can also know that
the Holy Spirit prays on your behalf. He intercedes for you when
you don't have the right words. Today, let yourself be childlike as
you rest in his presence and let your needs be met as the Holy Spirit
advocates for you.

Thank you, God, that I don't need to have everything figured
out. I don't have to come to you with an organized list in order
for you to know what I need. Teach me to value your presence
over lists or discussion. Help me to find rest in your nearness
and to trust everything else to you.

# RELY ON THE WORD

*The word of God is living and active.*
*Sharper than any double-edged sword;*
*it penetrates even to dividing soul and spirit.*

HEBREWS 4:12 NIV

You haven't just been given a manual for living. You haven't just been given a book to read. You haven't just been given a resource for a rainy day. The Word of God is living and active. It cannot return void. God is always true to his promises and you have the incredible ability to speak his promises over your life. The more familiar you become with his Word, the more equipped you will be to walk through your days.

Are you feeling inadequate, overwhelmed, or ill-equipped for the season you are in? Turn to the Word. As though you were headed to an armory, equip yourself for the challenges that life will throw at you. Saturate your mind in truth that you might quickly differentiate between what is Godly and what is not. Protect yourself with Scripture so when you are told lies about who you are, you are so deeply rooted that you cannot be swayed.

God, thank you for the gift of your Word. Teach me how to wield it effectively. May it be my refuge and my resource in every season. Give me the grace to soak up truth even when I feel too tired to get through the day.

# YOUR SOLACE

*You are my refuge and my shield;*
*your word is my source of hope.*
PSALM 119:114 NLT

Throughout motherhood, some of your days might feel like a battle. You fight against bad attitudes, bickering, constant noise, and unmet expectations. It can feel tumultuous to manage the life and health of the little people around you. In the moments that feel chaotic, remember that God is your refuge and your shield. You can depend on him when your daily life feels messy or frazzled. He is capable of giving you peace and hope.

As your children watch you in your humanity and weakness turn to Christ for solace, they will learn that he is the true source of peace. You can offer more to your children in your weakness and humility than you do in your strengths. As you struggle and then depend upon God, they also learn how to do that. As you turn to the Word as your main source of hope, they will see that Scripture is a gift and how to utilize it. Let God be your refuge in the midst of chaos and let your children see it.

Thank you, God, that you do not leave me helpless in chaos. You are my refuge! I can turn to you in my stress and you will protect me and bring me peace. Help me to teach my children that you are worthy of my dependence. Help me to develop quick instincts to turn to the Word for hope. As I seek truth, let my children see that you are faithful.

# PRAISE ALWAYS

*May your name be blessed and built up!*
*For you have answered my passionate cry for mercy.*
*You are my strength and my shield from every danger.*
*When I fully trust in you, help is on the way.*
*I jump for joy and burst forth with ecstatic, passionate praise!*
*I will sing songs of what you mean to me!*

PSALM 28:6-7 TPT

There is never a shortage of reasons for you to praise God. His mercy alone is enough. His goodness alone is enough. His power alone is enough. His protection alone is enough. You could get lost in any aspect of his character, thanking him for how it has impacted your life. Yet, you are given access to all of it.

He doesn't hold back. He doesn't withhold any good thing. He doesn't keep his wonderful attributes to himself because of the great disparity between you. He does not keep his selflessness just because you are selfish. He doesn't keep his patience just because you are impatient. He lavishes good things on his children. He loves abundantly and fully. Bless his name and praise him for who he is. He answers your cries, he shields you, and you can trust him.

Father, I could never run out of reasons to praise you. Teach me to praise you like the psalmist. Your name is great, and your lovingkindness never ends. Today, keep my eyes steady on who you are. Fill my heart with thanksgiving that I might find true joy in worshipping you.

# PERFECT AND UNCHANGING

*Give thanks to the LORD, for he is good,*
*for his steadfast love endures forever.*
*Give thanks to the God of gods,*
*for his steadfast love endures forever.*
PSALM 136:1-2 ESV

The love of God is steadfast. It is never changing and always dependable. His love doesn't fade in storms or waver when you have doubts. Whether or not you look to him, his affection for you cannot be altered. He is the same despite circumstances and the feelings or opinions of man. His love for you is sustaining and life changing. In his steadfast love, you can find true joy, peace, and rest.

As you walk through your days as a mother, sometimes struggling to keep up with the chaos that children can create, he is perfect and unchanging. No matter how your body changes or your hormones rage, he is steady and patient. No matter your changing circumstances or trials, he is secure. Today, let his steadfast love be your refuge. In thanksgiving you will find contentedness and peace.

God, thank you for your unending love. It never changes no matter what change I experience. Help me to fathom that your love endures forever. I can't wrap my mind around it but teach me how to take refuge in it. I praise you for who you are: kind, loving, and good.

# STAND FIRM

*My dear brothers and sisters, stand firm. Let nothing move you.*
*Always give yourselves fully to the work of the Lord,*
*because you know that your labor in the Lord is not in vain.*

1 CORINTHIANS 15:58 NIV

On days that you feel like quitting, stand firm. As you experience pain and difficulty, stand firm. As you navigate unfamiliar terrain, stand firm. *Let nothing move you.* This is the instruction given to you by Paul who had experienced the faithfulness of God in a tangible and life changing way. He knew first-hand how difficult life could be, yet he encouraged the church to stand firm. If he could do it, you can do it. God knows full well the trials you face. He knows the depths of your sorrow and height of your joy. You can put your faith in him because you know that it is not in vain.

What Jesus death and resurrection began will be completed when he comes back. So, while you wait, Paul reminds you to stand firm and to give yourself fully to the work of the Lord. Love extravagantly, serve humbly, trust God wildly, give generously. As you go about your day, no matter how mundane it might feel, know that in your desire to seek the Lord and serve your family, you are doing his work and he will sustain you.

Thank you, God, for the encouragement to stand firm. When I feel weak, strengthen me. Help me to trust in what you say. When I feel like quitting, remind me that my work is not in vain. Help me to depend on Jesus' work on the cross, keeping my eyes firmly on his return.

# ASK GOD

*We ask God to give you complete knowledge of his will and to give you spiritual wisdom and understanding. Then the way you live will always honor and please the Lord, and your lives will produce every kind of good fruit. All the while, you will grow as you learn to know God better and better.*

COLOSSIANS 1:9–10 NLT

When your mind is set firmly upon the larger picture, it can be easier to bare the small hurdles of day-to-day life. As a mom, you are intimately familiar with these hurdles. Daily, your patience is tested, and your emotional capacity might run dry as you navigate all the requirements of motherhood. Making dinner, keeping your home orderly, and managing the activities of others can feel mundane and repetitive. If you find yourself weary by all of this, consider what your motivation is.

In Colossians, you are reminded that if you ask God, he will give you knowledge of his will along with spiritual wisdom and understanding. This can help you keep your eyes less on what you do now and more on what is to come. As you seek him in the middle of what feels mundane, your life will honor him.

Thank you, God, that though my daily life can feel mundane, I can still honor you. Help me to keep my eyes on your will that I might not be made weary by the repetition of motherhood. Teach me how to honor you as I get to know you better.

# WHAT YOU FEED

*Do not love the world or anything in the world. If anyone loves the world, love for the Father is not in them. For everything in the world— the lust of the flesh, the lust of the eyes, and the pride of life— comes not from the Father but from the world. The world and its desires pass away, but whoever does the will of God lives forever.*

1 John 2:15-17 niv

What you feed will grow. What you sew, you will reap. This principle is visible in all areas of life. If you find that you love the ways of the world more than the will of God, it is likely because you are feeding those areas. Where do you spend your time and what do you fill your mind with? If you continuously align yourself with the world, that's where you will feel the most at home and where your desires will lie. In contrast, if you feed your relationship with God with the Word and his presence, that's where you'll find your desires lie.

Let the Holy Spirit gently point out areas of your life that are feeding a love for the world. As he speaks to you in kindness, he will also equip you to redirect your attention. The will of God is worth your attention more than anything the world can muster up. Direct your focus toward what is eternal and lasting.

God, you have not left me alone in the world, ill-equipped to navigate it. Thank you for the Holy Spirit who guides me and points me to you with kindness. Help me to see clearly the areas of my life that are feeding a love for the world. Show me how I can surrender those areas and refocus. I want to align my life with what you are doing.

# GROW IN SALVATION

*Like newborn babies, you must crave pure spiritual milk so that you will grow into a full experience of salvation. Cry out for this nourishment, now that you have had a taste of the Lord's kindness.*

1 PETER 2:2-3 NLT

You know what your children need for nourishment. You are aware of their capabilities and what they require at each stage. God, your Father, knows how to nourish you as well. Notice that milk, the most basic nutrition, is needed to *grow* into a full experience of salvation. You aren't told that you need to *have* a full experience of salvation, but that you will grow into it.

Just as you nourish your children and prepare them for adulthood, so God nourishes you through each stage of your growth. He doesn't expect you to have everything figured out. He doesn't expect you to digest what is beyond you. He knows exactly where you are and how to sustain you in that time. Continue to depend on his kindness and leading as you mature in your faith. Today, be encouraged by the peace that comes from knowing that God does not rush you, nor does he feel disappointed in your growth.

Thank you, God, for encouraging me to grow! You know what I need and you sustain me through each season. Teach me how to crave spiritual milk as I seek to grow more mature in my faith. Show me today how to follow closer to you and lean more fully on you.

# QUIET YOUR HEART

*"Be still, and know that I am God.
I will be exalted among the nations,
I will be exalted in the earth!"*

PSALM 46:10 ESV

Quiet your heart. Quiet your thoughts. Though there might be noise all around you, let your spirit be still and dwell upon who God is. When you choose to be still, you take your focus off yourself and make space for the Lord. In denying your own tendency for busyness or anxiety, you leave room for God to speak to you. He knows that you might be distracted or overwhelmed. He knows that you might have other things on your mind. He also knows that as you turn from those things, he will have the opportunity to meet you where you are and provide true rest.

As you exalt him, you become less and he becomes greater. As you praise who he is and focus on his character, he will strengthen you from the inside out. Today, instead of dwelling on what you cannot change, provide margin for God to move in your life. Commit your distractions to him and ask him for guidance.

Lord, you are great! Help me sit quietly and focus not on myself but on who you are. As I praise you, teach me how to rest. As I turn to you, teach me to dwell more on your goodness and less on my stress. You are trustworthy. As I quiet myself to make space for you, you will care for my every need.

# PATIENT AND KIND

*Love is patient,*
*love is kind.*
1 CORINTHIANS 13:4 NASB

Love is patient, and love is kind. As the fullest possible embodiment of love, God is patient and kind. Not only does he personify those traits, but he cannot behave in any other way. He is always good. Breathe deep and rest in his patience. Where you are inclined to rush or feel anxious, he is steady and consistent. Where you are inclined to look ahead in fear, he is calm and unafraid of what is to come.

Don't project your human weakness on God. If your days are frantic, chaotic, stressful, and overwhelming, run to him. Let his patience and kindness be your refuge. Whether you have two minutes or two hours of quiet, let your heart be still and rest in who he is. With each breath you take, know that he is the one who sustains you. Slow down your thoughts and remember that you were designed for fellowship with him. Near to him is where you will find true rest and love.

Thank you, God, for your patience and kindness. In your presence, I can find true rest and experience true love. Teach me how to see you clearly. Teach me how to look to who you are when I am overwhelmed.

# HE HEARS YOU

*The eyes of the LORD are on the righteous,*
*and his ears are attentive to their cry.*

PSALM 34:15 NIV

As a mother, you know what it's like to be attentive to your child. You are aware of them, whether they are physically near you or not. You are also limited in your ability to be available for them at all times. God, as your Father, is attentive to you, yet he is not limited. You are seen and you are heard. Let the depth of that truth permeate your soul. Let it sink deep down and soften your heart. Let it bring life to dry bones and new breath where you are tired.

He who created the universe sees and hears you. In your lowliness, in your pain, in your faults, God is attentive to you. As his child, you are at the top of his priority list. He is never too occupied or too distracted to attend to you. He knows exactly where you, exactly what you need, and exactly how you feel. Let the way that he provides for you stir your heart in affection for him. Let his attentiveness as your Father draw you closer to him in thanksgiving.

Thank you, God, that you see me and that you hear me. You know exactly where I am and what I need. May your attentiveness to me draw me closer to you. Teach me how to depend on you and see you rightly. As I recognize the way you see me, help me turn to you and seek you when I need assistance.

# INCLINED TO YOU

*This is the confidence we have in approaching God:*
*that if we ask anything according to his will, he hears us.*
*And if we know that he hears us—whatever we ask—*
*we know that we have what we asked of him.*

1 JOHN 5:14-15 NIV

What do you need today? Maybe it's rest, provision, a change of heart, or help in a specific situation. Does what you need cloud your thoughts, keep you from focusing, or drain you of your energy? Turn to the Lord and, in an act of trust, commit your needs to him. Then leave them there. Bring your requests before your King and then behave in such a way that displays your belief in his ability to handle them. Your confidence can be rightly placed in what he says is true: if you ask, he will hear you. He is not far off, dealing with more pressing matters. His ear is inclined toward you and he openly invites you to bring your needs to him.

Today, bring your pressing matters to God no matter if it's a list that is three items or three pages. Asking him for what you need is not only precious communion with your Father but it also shows that you trust in his character. As you cross those items off your list in prayer, let them also be cleared from your thoughts. This isn't to say you can or should easily forget about them, but don't give them the authority to control your thought life or your day. You've placed them into very capable hands.

Thank you, God, that you are a good father and that you hear me. Thank you for the ability to come to you with what I need. Help me to understand more about how you care for me. Help me to trust you with what I need and walk in peace rather than anxiety.

# SO YOU CAN LOVE

*We love because he first loved us.*
1 JOHN 4:19 NIV

Let your love for others flow out of the incredible love you've received from Christ. If you try to muster up that love, you will run dry because the source is limited. The love of God is like a deep well, consistently providing from unlimited resources. If you find yourself weary in loving, ask yourself where you are drawing from. Each day, you have the opportunity to root yourself in God's love. From that place, you can give to others, knowing that he will be faithful to sustain you. You are greatly loved even when you are at your worst. Even just a glimpse of that can stir compassion in you to love others when they are also at their worst.

His unending love is not only available to you when you do the right thing. So it should be when it comes to your relationships with others. They too, are extravagantly loved by God, made in his image, and fully worthy of your love no matter how they behave or how you see them. Today, seek to draw from the deep well of God's love and pass it on to those around you in the same manner that you have been loved.

Thank you, God, for your unending love! Thank you for the way that you have loved me, fully and extravagantly. Help me to draw from that love and to love others in the same way. Show me areas where I have held back and teach me how to display your love. I don't need to love others out of my own ability.

# WELL ATTENDED TO

*[Love] does not demand its own way.*
1 CORINTHIANS 13:5 NLT

The world is constantly telling you to focus on yourself. Everything is marketed toward making you more comfortable, more successful, more satisfied. Everyone seems to want their voice heard and sometimes the noise feels like too much. If you find yourself overwhelmed with the messages you are receiving, choose instead to focus on others. Elevate someone else's voice. Make someone else more comfortable or more successful. You don't have to fight stubbornly for your own good or your own way because you know thoroughly that you are taken care of by the Creator of the universe. His eyes are on you, so you can stop looking at yourself. He is capable of caring for you. You are free to put others before yourself because there is no doubt that your Father is fully capable of meeting your needs as well as theirs.

Maybe there are areas where you've felt stubbornness develop into bitterness. Talk to your Father about it, confess and repent, and enjoy his new mercy. Trust that you are well attended to and turn your attention to those around you.

Thank you, God, for so many examples of how to love well. Help me to be the kind of woman who is focused on the needs of others. I trust you with my wellbeing, so help me to put others before myself. Forgive me for the times I've demanded my own way. Soften my heart and help me to walk in humility.

# A FIRM FOUNDATION

*"The rain came down, the streams rose,
and the winds blew and beat against that house;
yet it did not fall, because it had its foundation on the rock."*

MATTHEW 7:25 NIV

Build your house upon the rock. You've likely heard that before but take a moment to read that Scripture again and pay attention to what comes to mind when you hear that phrase. If when you think about building your house upon the rock you come up with a list of things that you *should* do, it's time to re-evaluate the kind of life Jesus demonstrated for you. His direct commands were things like, rest, repent, believe, ask. The house was strong because it was built upon a firm and truthful understanding of the gospel, not because the structure of the house was perfect. The gospel is what makes the house strong, not the ability or craftsmanship of the house itself.

The house that stood and the house that crumbled were only different because of where they were built, not how they were built. Today, let your confidence lie in what Christ has done, not what you can do because what you can do won't last. Rest in the freedom that comes from knowing that it's out of your hands. As storms come, and they will, you don't need to question the integrity of your house when it is firmly placed upon the rock.

Thank you, God, for the strong and sufficient work of Christ on the cross. When my life is built on him, I will stand firm. I am thankful that my skill is not what defines my strength. Help me to rely on you and not on myself. Today, show me areas where my foundation is weak and help me to turn to you.

# WAIT AND BE RENEWED

*They who wait for the LORD shall renew their strength;*
*they shall mount up with wings like eagles;*
*they shall run and not be weary;*
*they shall walk and not faint.*

ISAIAH 40:31 ESV

As a mother, you are well acquainted with weariness. You do the same things day in and day out. The laundry doesn't end. Everyone needs to eat, every day. Your children need you all the time. You are not a stranger to being tired. Can you imagine running and never feeling weary? Can you imagine being lifted up with consistently renewed strength? This is what is promised to you as you wait upon the Lord. He will fulfill his promises to you.

Some of the promises you read in Scripture almost sound too good be true. Get lost in those promises. The faithfulness of God will prevail, and you will experience goodness beyond what you can imagine. Let the glory of what is to come motivate you to wait for the Lord. Today, keep your eyes on what he has promised no matter how far that seems from your daily experiences. Let the disparity between life now and what is to come draw you even closer to the Lord in thanksgiving for what he has planned.

God, I know that this earthly life is not what you originally planned. One day I will walk without weariness. One day all things will be made right. Teach me to wait patiently for you to renew my strength.

# PERFECT LOVE

*There is no fear in love, but perfect love casts out fear.*
*For fear has to do with punishment,*
*and whoever fears has not been perfected in love.*

1 JOHN 4:18 ESV

How many times has your presence calmed your child's fears? In thunderstorms, unfamiliar situations, an intense scene in a movie, or when they've had a nightmare, your calming arms and steady love is a shelter. There isn't room for fear when you know that you are secure. This is precisely how you can approach God. Because of his infinite love for you, you can find refuge in his love. You don't need to approach him timidly, afraid of how he might respond to you. You don't need to fear his discipline or guidance because he knows what is best for you. Just as your child runs to you, confident in your love for them, so you can run to the Father.

If you find yourself afraid to share certain parts of your life or heart with God, ask him to renew your understanding of his love for you. Ask him to strengthen you and give you a clear picture of what he thinks of you. He will always be faithful to demonstrate his love for his children.

Thank you, God, for your perfect love. Today, please show me areas where I have not seen you rightly. Show me areas where I have been afraid to approach you. Teach me how to find refuge in your love. I want to walk through each of my days securely rooted in your love without fear.

# NOT OVERWHELMED

*I look up to the hills,*
*but where does my help come from?*
*My help comes from the LORD,*
*who made heaven and earth.*

PSALM 121:1-2 NCV

The book of Psalms provides so many opportunities to validate your humanity. The psalmist doesn't shy away from intense emotions. No matter how raw you feel, you are not too much for God. He doesn't look at you and wish that you had it together. He's not tired of you or exhausted by you. God is not an exasperated father, frustrated that he has to deal with one more tantrum. He is your helper. It's in his very nature which means that he is constant and consistent to help you. He is the maker of the heavens and the earth and he is more than capable of handling your most desperate cries. There is no part of you too dark or too ugly that you cannot call upon him.

As a father who is full of affection for you, he is compassionate, kind and an ever-present help in your time of need. Today, as you take a few minutes to sit still and focus on the Lord, praise him for the gift of the Word that reminds you where to direct your pleas for help.

Thank you, God, that I am not too much for you. The Psalmist teaches me that intense emotions do not disqualify me from your presence. Help me to turn to you as the safest and best source of help. I praise you for who you are—the maker of heaven and earth! Teach me to depend on you more fully.

# BETTER THAN ONE

*Two are better than one,*
*because they have a good return for their labor:*
*If either of them falls down,*
*one can help the other up.*
*But pity anyone who falls*
*and has no one to help them up.*

ECCLESIASTES 4:9-10 NIV

You aren't supposed to be alone. You have not been designed to walk through life on your own. Loneliness can be painful and deceiving, telling you that you are the problem, that you are not worthy of help, or that you aren't wanted. None of this is true. No matter the reason for your loneliness, let the God of comfort hold your heart. Not only does he see you, but he is willing to hold you close. You might not have the deep friendships you crave in this season but that doesn't mean you won't ever have them.

Bring your pleas to your Father. If you are without community, ask him for it. Ask him to open your eyes to how you can bless and serve the body of Christ. Ask him to bring you friendship. If you find yourself in community that is encouraging and safe, thank him for it! Praise him today for the ways he has brought you close to others. He loves it when his children live in harmony with each other.

Thank you, God, that you have not designed me to be alone. Teach me to bless others and to be the kind of friend who lifts others up. Open my eyes to see the lonely, so I might be a blessing and an encouragement.

# A LAMP AND A LIGHT

*Your word is a lamp to guide my feet
and a light for my path.*
PSALM 119:105 NLT

When you are in the dark, turn to the Word. When you are lost, turn to the Word. When you cannot see the right way to go, turn to the Word. It has been given to you to help you navigate your days. You have consistent access to truth that will guide you and keep you steady on the narrow path. If you are walking through the dark, would you keep your flashlight in your pocket, stumbling around, trying to figure out where to go? No, you would let it shine, showing you where there are pitfalls and clear paths.

So it is with the Word. Utilize the tool that has been given to you. Fill your mind with Scripture and it will make its way to your heart, illuminating dark places and revealing truth as you walk. As a mother, you might feel like you don't have time to dive into Scripture. Don't let this discourage you. God is fully capable of working with what you have. If he can raise a man from the dead, then he can take your minutes and multiply them. Don't let your lack of resources limit the ability of God.

Father, thank you for your Word! Thank you for the gift that you've given me in Scripture. Teach me how to apply your truth to my life. You are capable beyond my limitations. Take what I have and draw me closer to you. May your Word find its home in my heart and help me navigate my days.

# COMMUNE WITH GOD

*Are any of you suffering hardships? You should pray. Are any of you happy? You should sing praises. Are any of you sick? You should call for the elders of the church to come and pray over you, anointing you with oil in the name of the Lord. Such a prayer offered in faith will heal the sick, and the Lord will make you well. And if you have committed any sins, you will be forgiven.*

JAMES 5:13-15 NLT

There is no difficult thing that is beyond warranting prayer and thanksgiving. As followers of Christ it can be easy to take prayer for granted. You might find yourself assuming that you seek the Lord, but how much time do you truly spend communicating with him? Bring your trials before him today. Sit in his presence and listen for what the Holy Spirit wants to share with you. You might feel like you've heard, "I'll pray about it" a million times, but truly take advantage of the time you have with your Father.

In all circumstances, whether you are experiencing hardship or happiness, communicate with God. Your heart will be softened toward who you pray to, who you pray for, and what you pray about. The more you commune with your Father, the more you will build up your faith.

Thank you, God, that I can come to you in all circumstances. Teach me how to pray always, whether I am experiencing hardship or happiness. When I am sick, or those around me are sick, may my first response be to pray to you about it. Where my faith is weak, strengthen it, that I might ask you for healing.

# ALPHA AND OMEGA

*He said to me, "It is done! I am the Alpha and the Omega, the beginning and the end. To the thirsty I will give from the spring of the water of life without payment."*

REVELATION 21:6 ESV

He is the beginning and the end. New life began when Christ defeated death on the cross and now here you are in the middle, awaiting the day he comes back. These middle days are painful and full of trials. They require perseverance and great hope. The hope that you have is a gift that you didn't have to pay the price for.

As you eagerly await Christ's return you can fully rely on God's provision. He is aware of the days that you spend here in the middle. He knows the difficulties you face and how hard it is to stay on the narrow path, but he promises that he will be with you every step of the way. He is the beginning and the end; he surrounds you. As a follower of Jesus and a child of God, you are hedged in, safe and secure. Today, praise God that he is the Alpha and the Omega. Nothing came before him and nothing will come after.

God, you are the beginning and the end. As I wait for Christ's return, teach me how to lean on you more fully. I want to honor you with my days because of the price that Jesus paid for my freedom and hope.

# SPIRITUAL RENEWAL

*That is why we never give up.*
*Though our bodies are dying,*
*our spirits are being renewed every day.*

2 CORINTHIANS 4:16 NLT

It doesn't make sense does it? While your body ages and wastes away, your spirit is consistently renewed. The world will tell you to maintain youth at any cost, spending your time, energy, and money on ways to stay looking young. Our culture does not humbly accept the aging process; it actively and fervently fights against it. But you know that this time on earth is not all you are living for. You see the life to come so you can quiet that frantic voice that says to stay young. Each day, as you persevere in faith, your spirit is being renewed. Your spirit, the part of you that will last for eternity, is becoming more youthful each day.

This incredible and backwards way of the kingdom has the power to help you walk in defiant contentedness. You can stand bravely despite what the world tells you and know that the glory of what is to come far surpasses the loss of youth to wrinkles, grey hair, and aching bodies. Your spirit, firmly saved by the blood of Christ, is beautiful and ageless. Today, if the world's plea to fight for youth is weighing heavily upon you, ask God for his perspective. Find peace in the fact that as you persevere in faith, you are being renewed.

Thank you, God, that you renew my spirit. This body is not my forever home. Teach me to value what you are doing over what the world says is valuable. Open my eyes to see beauty beyond what culture says is beautiful.

# MAY

"Be strong and bold; have no fear or
dread of them, because it is the Lord your
God who goes with you; he will not fail
you or forsake you."

DEUTERONOMY 31:6 NRSV

# CREATION DISPLAYS HIS GLORY

*Ask the animals, and they will teach you,*
*or the birds in the sky, and they will tell you;*
*or speak to the earth, and it will teach you,*
*or let the fish in the sea inform you.*
*Which of all these does not know*
*that the hand of the Lord has done this?*
*In his hand is the life of every creature*
*and the breath of all mankind.*

JOB 12:7-10 NIV

Creation, with all of its intricacies, is an incredible gift. So much of it could have been left out, but God is an artist. Do we truly need sunsets and craggy mountains? What about crashing waves on rocky shores or trees that tower to the skies? Is it really necessary for there to be so many types of wildflowers or for clouds to look so fluffy and delightful? God could have created the earth to look like whatever he wanted. It could have been highly efficient, utilitarian, or even chaotic. But he made the earth to be true to his character—all of it perfectly good. All of his creation points to him. It declares his glory and the works of his hands. It teaches us that he values beauty and delight.

In your weariness today, let the majesty of creation refresh your soul. Then, remember that you are the pinnacle of his creation. That is the God that you serve. He is not a tyrant or a harsh king. He is not an angry father. He is an intricate creator, who has done a marvelous thing in creating the world and placing you in it. You are highly valued and perfectly designed.

God, thank you for your creation! I can learn so much about you by looking at what you've made. Help me to be refreshed by what you've made and for it to cause me to come to you in praise and thanksgiving.

# PERFECTER OF FAITH

*Let us run with endurance the race set before us, fixing our eyes on Jesus, the author and perfecter of faith, who for the joy set before him endured the cross, despising shame, and has sat down at the right hand of the throne of God.*

HEBREWS 12:1-2 NASB

Jesus is the author and perfecter of your faith. Not only is he the one who you put your hope in, but he is the one who works in your heart to strengthen your faith. He is the one who teaches you how to live and who promises the good work that was started in you will be completed. He is the perfect teacher.

As a mother, you know full well how difficult it can be to teach something to your children especially when they are distracted, frustrated, or unwilling to learn. Imagine the perfection of patience and goodness that Christ has in order to lead a stubborn humanity to God. He is infinitely good as the perfecter of your faith. He will never stop leading you to the Father, teaching you patiently who he is. He will never tire of glorifying God and drawing you closer to him.

Thank you, God, that you are the author and perfecter of my faith. You are a kind and good teacher! Help me to trust you with the shaping of my faith instead of striving to shape it myself. Teach me how to surrender my Christianity into your hands and focus on following you rather than working for my salvation.

# OPEN YOUR ARMS

*Love each other like brothers and sisters.*
*Give each other more honor than you want for yourselves.*
ROMANS 12:10 NCV

Your family is made up of much more than the people within the walls of your home. Your family isn't limited to the people who share your DNA. Treating others as though they are your brothers and sisters is not just a nice sentiment, it's a command. You are to love and honor the body of Christ in the same way that you love your own flesh and blood. As you lay your life down for your children, lay your life down for each other. As you don't think twice about serving your loved ones, serve your brothers and sisters in Christ. Give them honor, treat them with dignity, and highly esteem them no matter their status, opinion, or way of life.

There are not exceptions made in Romans as to who you should show love to and who you needn't. In order to love like Jesus did, you need to lay down your fears, insecurities, and judgments and humbly open your arms and your heart. You cannot love in this way by yourself. You can love in this selfless way because it is a mirror of how radically you have been loved.

Father, it's hard to love those around me like I love my family. I'm prone to selfishness and frustration, but you don't limit your love to where it is comfortable or convenient. Your love reached down and saved me at my worst; help me to love others like that. Teach me how to honor others more than myself. Forgive me for where I have withheld love.

# THE GENEROUS WILL PROSPER

*A generous person will prosper;*
*whoever refreshes others will be refreshed.*
PROVERBS 11:25 NIV

Certain seasons of motherhood can feel isolating. In times of loneliness, it can be tempting to focus on what you don't have. Maybe you crave connection and community. Maybe you long for that close friendship you can turn to. In those times, instead of turning inward and focusing on what you lack, reach your hands outward. God promises that when you refresh others, you will be refreshed. In your loneliness, encourage others. Pray for those around you. Find out how you can help other mothers.

God is not asking you to spread yourself thin or to give what you don't have. His reminder is that of a gentle father. He knows that when you put others before yourself, you will be rewarded with true rest. He knows that when you are generous, you will prosper. It takes hard work to stop focusing on yourself and to put others before you, but it is worth it. He is faithful to his Word; if he says that you will be refreshed, then you can believe him.

God, thank you that you know what is best for me. When I am lonely and want to focus on what I don't have, help me to find my comfort in you and to encourage others. Teach me how to think of others before I think of myself. As I pour my life out, refresh me! Teach me to be generous and to trust that you are faithful to your Word.

# TENDER CARE

*Warn those who are lazy. Encourage those who are timid. Take tender care of those who are weak. Be patient with everyone. See that no one pays back evil for evil, but always try to do good to each other and to all people. Always be joyful. Never stop praying. Be thankful in all circumstances, for this is God's will for you who belong to Christ Jesus.*

1 Thessalonians 5:14-18 NLT

We live in a culture that values independence. On the contrary, the kingdom of heaven values dependence. We need each other. We need to be aware of each other's weaknesses, not so we might succeed more ourselves but so we can encourage, warn, and care for them. God has designed us to lift each other up and point each other toward Christ. You are reminded to take tender care of those who are weak, just as Christ has cared for you in your weakness.

It can be tempting to value success over sacrifice, but truly the life God has asked you to live is one that is defined by the sacrifice of Christ. If you find yourself more focused on your own success over the tender care of the weak, ask God to soften your heart and teach you how to love like Christ did, unchanged by the behavior of others and always speaking hope into hopeless situations.

Thank you, God, for the example of Christ. Thank you for the reminder to be a woman who is encouraging and supportive of the weak. If there are areas where I have valued my own success over others, teach me how to humbly do good to all people. Give me words of encouragement for those who are discouraged.

# WILDLY IN LOVE

*Brothers and sisters, I do not consider myself yet to have taken hold of it. But one thing I do: Forgetting what is behind and straining toward what is ahead, I press on toward the goal to win the prize for which God has called me heavenward in Christ Jesus.*

PHILIPPIANS 3:13-14 NIV

With a myriad of things calling for your attention every day, it can be hard to stay focused on one thing in particular. You have a to-do list a mile long and constantly changing needs to meet. Maybe you have a habit you've been trying to break or a past mistake that also grabs at your attention. You are reminded here in Philippians to run your race of faith with your eyes fixed forward. Like an athlete running a race, keep your eyes on the finish line. With your past, future, and present held firmly by the Lord, keep your eyes on what he has promised.

Jesus has redeemed you and promises that he is coming back again. When you find yourself distracted or overwhelmed, take a deep breath and focus your gaze on him. Lay your burdens at the cross and with each step move away from what is behind you.

Thank you, God, that no matter what has happened in my past or what I face each day, I can keep my eyes firmly on Jesus. As I look to him, help me to faithfully walk throughout my days, honoring you. Where I have been overwhelmed, help me to lay my cares at the cross and press on toward the goal of eternity with you.

# REFUGE DESPITE NOISE

*He who dwells in the shelter of the Most High*
*will abide in the shadow of the Almighty*
*I will say to the Lord,*
*"My refuge and my fortress, my God, in whom I trust."*
PSALM 91:1-2 ESV

Your home, sturdy and made by man's hands, is not your only shelter. Your surroundings, no matter how quiet, cannot be your main source of peace and refuge. With time, those things are bound to fade. Your home, while built to last, won't stand forever. Your surroundings are not dependable and will leaving you wanting if you've based your peace on them. You know full well that eventually a child will interrupt, a mess will be made, a conflict will break out.

Instead of being tossed about by ever-changing circumstances, find your refuge in that which never changes. While your physical body can by housed by brick, wood, and mortar, let your heart abide in the shadow of the Almighty. This is where true peace comes from: unfading no matter how noisy or chaotic life becomes.

God, you have given me a safe place to find refuge! My peace doesn't need to depend on my circumstances or my surroundings. Help me to run to you when life feels chaotic. Teach me how to dwell with you and trust you more than I did yesterday.

# DESIGNED FOR PEACE

*The wisdom from above is first of all pure. It is also peace loving, gentle at all times, and willing to yield to others. It is full of mercy and the fruit of good deeds. It shows no favoritism and is always sincere.*

JAMES 3:17 NLT

It is normal to be self-centered and concerned with your own well-being. You are not alone in your humanity. You were also created for more. Have you ever longed for a perfect relationship with somebody? This is because in the depths of who you are you know that things are not the way they are supposed to be. We were not designed for impurity, conflict, and selfishness. We were designed to walk fully in perfect love, peace, gentleness, and selflessness.

As you seek the Lord and ask him for wisdom, you can see glimpses of this life that you were designed for. As you become more like Christ, you will walk in greater gentleness and selflessness, yielding to others and being full of mercy and sincere love. Where you know that you are lacking, ask for wisdom. Where you know that things are not as they were meant to be, ask God for guidance. The wisdom from above is reflected in relationships that glorify him.

God, teach me how to ask you for wisdom as I navigate my relationships. I want to honor you and I want my interactions with those around me to be sincere and full of godly love. Forgive me where I have been led by my own wisdom or by ungodliness. Show me how to reflect you more fully.

# NEVER GIVE UP

*Love never gives up, never loses faith, is always hopeful,
and endures through every circumstance.*
1 CORINTHIANS 13:7 NLT

God never gives up. He never loses faith. He is always hopeful. He endures through every circumstance. This is your Father. This is the King you serve. He is the embodiment of love. Through Christ's death and resurrection, God has made a way for you to walk in this love as well. By walking with Jesus, you can be a woman who never gives up, never loses faith, is always hopeful, and endures in every circumstance. That description of love might feel intimidating, but the same power that raised Christ from the dead lives in you to strengthen you to walk in the true love of God.

Where you are lacking, he is strong. There is no need to feel discouraged by your shortcomings in love. Where you are weak, God's strength can be displayed even more. Today, lean into the kind of love that God displays to you and let that motivate you to share it with others. As you experience the unending and enduring love of God, may it overflow to those around you.

Your love is great, God! You never give up or lose faith. Thank you for displaying such perfect love for me. Help me to do the same for others. As you hold me closely, help me to lean on your strength and point others to you.

# DON'T GIVE FEARFULLY

*"Give, and it will be given to you. A good measure, pressed down,
shaken together and running over, will be poured into your lap.
For with the measure you use, it will be measured to you."*

Luke 6:38 NIV

Do you ever fear generosity? Maybe you feel like you just
don't have enough to share. Maybe you worked really hard for
something and it feels like an impossible sacrifice to pass it on.
These mindsets would make sense if you were operating by the
ways of the world. But God's way is contrary to the world's. God
says that when you give, it will be given back to you in abundance.
Generosity of heart is really an act of trust. By giving, you are
trusting that God will be true to his Word. You are trusting that he is
capable of meeting your needs more than you are.

You serve a God who cares deeply not only for the one you are
giving to, but also for you. He won't leave you in want. He won't
leave you helpless. If he was faithful to meet the needs of whoever
you are giving to, then he will clearly be faithful to meet your
needs. You are not the only child of his whom he has called to be
generous. Today, ask him to reveal to you areas where you can
be more generous with your time, money, words, or resources.
Generosity between his children delights him.

Thank you, God, that I can give generously knowing that I
am well cared for. Teach me how to have your perspective in
this area. Forgive me for holding tightly to that which I can
surrender. Show me areas where I can give more generously
and give me the grace to depend on you.

# TELL EVERYONE

*I will sing of the LORD's great love forever;*
*with my mouth I will make your faithfulness known*
*through all generations.*
*I will declare that your love stands firm forever,*
*that you have established your faithfulness in heaven itself.*
PSALM 89:1–2 NIV

No matter what your circumstances are today, you can keep your eyes on heaven by speaking of God's goodness. Tell your children of the things that he has done. Praise him with your words and worship him with songs of thanksgiving. Speak, out loud, of his goodness and faithfulness. Your words have power, and as you physically open your mouth to sing his praise, your spirit will follow suit.

If you are feeling downtrodden or discouraged, talk about the goodness of God. Your heart will soften as you speak the truth. Tell whoever will listen about the thigs that God has done. Your declarations of praise create a path to the presence of God where you can find true rest. Your thanksgiving makes a way for you to experience God's nearness as you focus more on who he is and less on your circumstances. Even if you're in an empty house, with a sleeping baby, sing praise to the one who is worthy. Today, deliberately talk about his perfection and unending love.

Teach me how to praise you in all circumstances, God. When I am stuck, prompt me to open my mouth and use my words to honor you. Your faithfulness and goodness are worthy of my praise. May the words I speak and the songs I sing lead me closer to you.

# FOLLOW YOUR SHEPHERD

*"My sheep listen to my voice;*
*I know them, and they follow me."*
JOHN 10:27 NIV

When Jesus talked about being a good shepherd, he was in conversation with the Pharisees who were insisting that they had favor with God because of how they dutifully adhered to the law. Jesus went on to explain that in fact, the true mark of a believer was that they heard the Shepherd's voice and followed him. Time and time again, Jesus reassures us that abiding is more valuable than striving. Whenever he is challenged with a requirement to please God, he reassures all who listen that all that is required is to follow.

When you are tempted to attach a to-do list to your relationship with God, remember that in following him and knowing his voice, you have accomplished all you need to. The more time you spend with him, the more quickly you will recognize his voice when he speaks to you. The more quickly you recognize the voice of your Shepherd, the more efficiently you weed out other voices, giving you the ability to keep your eyes steadily on him.

Thank you, Jesus, that you are a good shepherd. True life is found in abiding and not in striving. When I am tempted to define my relationship with you by works, help me to instead focus on learning your voice. Teach me to follow more closely and respond more quickly to your voice.

# LET GO OF WRONGS

*[Love] keeps no record of wrongs.*
1 CORINTHIANS 13:5 NIV

Your record of wrongs might feel safe, like a security blanket. It is painful to let go of hurts. As long as you keep a tidy record, you are in control and you get to call the shots. Remember that love keeps no record of wrongs. As you humbly seek forgiveness, you are covered and redeemed by Jesus' death on the cross. Your wrongs are fully paid for and are not brought up again. As others wrong you, seek to love them like Christ loves you. You'll find that the longer you maintain your record of wrongs, the more you build up a wall around your heart. Bitterness will grow and the true victim will be you.

Your lack of forgiveness will make your steps heavy and your spirit weary. God knows this; he knows that as you forgive others, you will walk in freedom. He doesn't ask you to let go of wrongs because they aren't valid but because he doesn't want you to be weighed down. He is capable of handling the wrongs done against you. You can trust him to advocate for you and protect you. You can trust his wisdom in setting boundaries and finding reconciliation. As you pass on the wrongs done to you, you are actively acknowledging his sovereignty in your relationships and trusting him for the healing that you need.

Thank you, God, that I don't need to keep a record of wrongs. Thank you for the example that Christ set for me to walk in forgiveness. Teach me how to give up control where I have held on to wrongs. Help me to trust you for healing and reconciliation because you are truly the only one who can accomplish that.

# THE IMPOSSIBLE

*"Humanly speaking, it is impossible.*
*But with God everything is possible."*
MATTHEW 19:26 NLT

God is the God of the impossible. He opens closed doors, raises the dead, and showers hope on hopeless situations. He is the light in the dark, the rain in dry places, and the Father to the fatherless. Where you cannot see a solution, God is able. Where you feel discouraged, God is able. Where you are exhausted from trying, God is able. As your Father, he wants you to go to him as a child, fully confident that he can do anything.

Like a little girl in awe of her daddy, you can bring your most impossible darkness to him and he will shine light where you didn't think it could exist. He defeated death and he can defeat your darkest moments. There is nothing that you could bring before him that would scare him away or be beyond his ability to fix.

God, you are able to see solutions where I see roadblocks. I know that you are capable of doing the impossible. In areas of my life where I have doubted you or simply not asked, teach me how to step out in faith and thanksgiving. Teach me how to ask you for your help, knowing that you can do the impossible.

# PERFECT PEACE

*You will keep in perfect peace
all who trust in you,
all whose thoughts are fixed on you!*

ISAIAH 26:3 NLT

No matter what happened before you sat down to seek the Lord and no matter what happens afterward, you have the opportunity to fix your thoughts on the Lord. As you do that, he will keep you in perfect peace. His peace is not dependent on any circumstances. It is simply dependent on your trust. Peace stems out of trust. You can trust that God is good, that he is who he says he is and that his love for you is unending. As you keep your thoughts on who he is, you'll find that anxiety cannot thrive.

Today, if you are anxious, full of worry, or stressed about what the future holds, let his peace overwhelm you instead. Run to the Father who cares for you and let him transform your mind with truth as you trust in him. No other source of comfort can provide the peace that God can. When you find yourself turning to other things, listen to the soft voice of the Holy Spirit and turn your attention to what is true.

Thank you, God, that you promise to keep me in perfect peace as I trust in you! Teach me how to focus on you when anxiety creeps in or when I am overwhelmed. Forgive me for the times I have tried to muster up my own peace. Help me to lean on you instead.

# FILLED WITH TRUTH

*"You shall teach them diligently to your sons and shall talk of them when you sit in your house and when you walk by the way and when you lie down and when you rise up."*

DEUTERONOMY 6:7 NASB

Let the Word of God fill your home until the seams are bursting. When you speak to your kids, tell them about who he is and what he has done. Speak to them about how you have experienced the Lord's goodness and redemption. They are never too young to hear about God's work in your life. Tell them about how he pulled you out of sin and placed your feet firmly upon a rock.

Speak about who God is when you wake up, when you're making dinner, and when you're getting ready for bed. When you're in the car, glorify God. When you're walking the dog, praise him. When you're at the grocery store, honor him. You have a million opportunities to teach your children about the Lord. Utilize them with diligence. Let your conversation pour out of a heart that is loved and secure.

Thank you, God, that I have the opportunity to teach my children diligently about who you are and what you've done. Through the Holy Spirit, remind me to speak your words. Help me to see this as a privilege that you have equipped me for and not as a burden. Where I am overwhelmed in raising my kids, teach me how to simply point them to you because you are the one who can love them fully and care for them best.

# COMMAND TO LOVE

*"If you keep my commandments, you will abide in my love,*
*just as I have kept my Father's commandments and abide in his love.*
*These things I have spoken to you, that my joy may be in you,*
*and that your joy may be full."*

JOHN 15:10-11 ESV

Abide in the love of God. This phrase is mentioned several times in Scripture and, while it sounds beautiful, have you ever felt like it's abstract and difficult to obtain? What does that actually look like and how can you apply it to the busy life you lead as a mom? Here in John, you are told that if you keep Christ's commandments you will abide in his love. So, when you feel lost, simply remind yourself of what Christ has said you should do: love each other in the same way that you have been loved.

Abiding in the love of God does not necessarily come from a really spectacular quiet time, it comes from actively displaying love to those around you. By his grace, you can highly esteem those around you and then you will find yourself at home in God's love. Don't let abiding feel like something you don't have time for or cannot obtain in this season of life. Let abiding come from the outpouring of your time, energy, and love to your children and others around you.

Father, I have been greatly loved, so give me the grace to love others. You've said that if I keep your command to love others, then I will abide in your love. Teach me how to do this. Help me to lay my life down for those around me just like you did for me.

# TURN TO THE WORD

*Such things were written in the Scriptures long ago to teach us. And the Scriptures give us hope and encouragement as we wait patiently for God's promises to be fulfilled.*

ROMANS 15:4 NLT

You are able to hold the Word of God in your hands. You can turn the pages and soak up the contents. You are immensely blessed to be able to sift through his thoughts and a record of what he has done. Don't forsake this incredible gift. It has been given to you to teach you, to encourage you, and to give you hope. God knew that waiting for his promises to be fulfilled would be difficult. He knew that time would feel endless as you wait for Jesus to come a second time. In his knowing, he gave you his Word, that it might fill you with hope!

When you feel anxious, bury yourself in truth. When you feel overwhelmed, let God's promises wash over you. He has generously equipped you to walk through your days. He has not left you empty-handed in your battles. You've been given the sword of the Spirit which is the Word of God. Today, ask the Holy Spirit to stir your heart toward the truth and to bring up Scripture when you need it.

God, thank you for your Word! You have not left me empty-handed. Teach me how to read your Word faithfully and to depend upon your truth. Help me to glean hope and encouragement from what you've said. Today, as I go about my day, bring to mind Scripture that will draw me closer to you and help me walk in a more Christ-like manner.

# SERVE EACH OTHER

*"If I then, your Lord and Teacher, has washed your feet,
you also ought to wash one another's feet."*

JOHN 13:14 NKJV

You have been doted upon. You have been lavishly cared for. You have been given an undeserved gift. God's love has been given to you abundantly. Christ's sacrificial death and resurrection was carried out that you might have a way back to the Father. The promise of Christ's return gives you hope that you might gloriously persevere throughout your days. If all of this has been done for you, how great should your love be for those around you?

As Christ served you, serve others. In the same manner that he has laid his life down for you, lay your life down for those around you. As you've been given an undeserved gift, freely love those around you without expectation. This is not asked of you that you might burn out or wither away in your giving. God knows every sacrifice that you make. He sees you and he is preparing a place for you.

Thank you, God, that I can look to Jesus as an example of how to love and serve. Create within me a willingness to pour my life out for others. May your love for me be motivation to love those around me. Teach me how to do this well. Even as I sacrifice, you give me all I need, and you are preparing a place for me.

# NOTHING IS HIDDEN

*Nothing in all creation is hidden from God.*
*Everything is naked and exposed before his eyes,*
*and he is the one to whom we are accountable.*

HEBREWS 4:13 NLT

Do you ever tell your kids that you have eyes in the back of your head? To a degree, you are intuitively aware of what is happening in your home especially if you have young children who still think they can hide their antics from you. Your vantage point as one of the oldest and wisest members of your family gives you a more accurate perspective than your children have.

So, it is with God. In his infinite wisdom, nothing in creation is hidden from him. Even the parts of your heart that you might have barricaded or thought were too broken to even deal with are seen by him. He doesn't observe like a tyrant, shaking his finger at a naughty child, pointing out all of your wrongs with a taunting voice. He sees with loving eyes, gently reassuring you that you are known and cared for. He sees all of you and all of creation, yet he still wants to redeem it to himself. You are fully known and fully loved. There is no point hiding from him; nothing is too big or too small to be placed into his loving hands.

Father, thank you that you see me and yet I am fully loved! Teach me how to trust you with the parts of myself that I don't want seen. I am accountable only to you. Help me to see you as a loving father and not as a haughty tyrant.

# A FLOURISHING TREE

*That person is like a tree planted by streams of water,*
*which yields its fruit in season*
*and whose leaf does not wither—*
*whatever they do prospers.*

PSALM 1:3 NIV

A tree is not meant to bear fruit 100% of the time. Its roots should go deep, it's leaves should not wither, it's branches should reach to the sky, but it should not yield fruit in every single season. The lack of fruit does not mean that the tree is not prospering. It flourishes despite the fact that not every season is made for harvest. There are seasons of motherhood in which your roots will go down deep as you quietly reach for refreshing water. There are seasons of motherhood in which you will be constantly searching for the sun and the life that it gives. There will be seasons of motherhood in which you will bear fruit.

Trusting the guidance of the Lord for which season you are in is necessary to have reasonable and accurate expectations. Maybe you're in a season that requires a lot of sewing seeds but not a lot of harvest. Each day you sow seeds of patience, of steadfastness, of setting boundaries. The fruit seems far off, but it just isn't the right season yet. Lean into the season, knowing that by God's design, it won't last forever. Trust his leading.

Thank you, God, that as I trust in you, my roots will go down deep, and when times of trouble come, I won't be shaken. You prepare me for each season that I walk through. Help me to lean on you when I feel unsure of which season I am in.

# DEPENDED ON

*"If you love me, keep my commands. And I will ask the Father, and he will give you another advocate to help you and be with you forever— the Spirit of truth. The world cannot accept him, because it neither sees him nor knows him. But you know him, for he lives with you and will be in you."*

JOHN 14:15-17 NIV

The Holy Spirit has been given to you as a gift. Jesus himself asked the Father on your behalf and has blessed you with the Spirit as an advocate and an ever-present help. He knew that you would need someone to walk with you. In your desire to follow Jesus and seek the presence of God, don't forget about the resource you've been given in the Spirit. He is the one who points you to truth and guides you in wisdom. Don't leave your time with Jesus and forget that you have one who walks with you throughout your day. Rely on the Holy Spirit to remind you of truth, to help you bear fruit, and to encourage you to persevere when you are weary. His presence is what stirs truth in your heart when you need it most.

As you navigate motherhood, the Holy Spirit is the one who redirects you when you take your eyes off Christ. He dwells in you and enables you to live righteously. He comforts you, intercedes for you, and brings wisdom and fortitude. In the Spirit, you have been fully equipped to walk like Christ did.

God, you have given me the gift of the Holy Spirit. A simple thank you doesn't seem like enough. I praise you for all you've done! In your lovingkindness you have given me a helper and an advocate for all of my days. Thank you for leaving me with someone to guide me and point me toward Jesus.

# ANSWER SOFTLY

*A soft answer turns away wrath,*
*But a harsh word stirs up anger.*
PROVERBS 15:1 NKJV

When everything inside of you is screaming to be heard, to make your point, to defend and to fight back, a soft answer feels contradictory, counterintuitive, and impossible. Yet, quieting the chaos you feel and choosing to communicate with control from a calm spirit has great power. Whether you struggle to speak to your kids with softness or you feel anger stirred within you at the behavior or opinions of others, the best way to respond is always the same. In those moments, the power of your tongue can be on full display. The way that you respond to someone can shift the entire tone of the conversation.

Just like Jesus on the boat with the disciples, you have the ability to calm storms with your words. Through the power of the Holy Spirit you have the ability to be the thermostat for your home and in your relationships. The way you speak can set a precedence of peace, safety, and gentleness. Today, ask the Lord to show you how to speak in a way that promotes peace.

Thank you, God, that the best response to wrath is not to fight back but to speak softly. Teach me how to control my tongue and to love others with the way I speak. I want to be the kind of woman and mother who speaks lifegiving words not words that stir up anger.

# PATIENTLY WAIT

*In this hope we were saved. Now hope that is seen is not hope.*
*For who hopes for what he sees? But if we hope for what we do not see,*
*we wait for it with patience.*

ROMANS 8:24-25 ESV

The hope that you have in Christ cannot be seen. You can't circle a date on your calendar like you might mark a dentist appointment and know that's the day you'll see him. You have to trust that what God promised and planned will occur. Jesus came one time in humility, died in servitude, and said he would come again in majesty. You spend your days waiting for your shepherd king. You've placed your faith in what you cannot see. To walk steadily in this, you have to wait with patience and without a timeline.

God knew this would be hard, so he gave you the Holy Spirit to guide you and point you to Jesus when your hope is wavering. By his grace, he will give you the fortitude to honor him while you wait for what is to come. You know that his Word is true, you know that his promises will come to fruition, but without patience, you'll find yourself frustrated and prone to wander. Today, ask the Lord to renew your patience. He will be faithful to help you wait for what you cannot see.

God, it can be really hard to wait for what I cannot see. I need patience! Help me to rely on you for the patience I need each day as I wait for Jesus. I know that you have promised me eternity with him and sometimes it's hard to remember that when I get lost in daily life. Help me to place my hope in your promises.

# UNDERAPPRECIATED

*"Whoever exalts himself will be humbled,*
*and whoever humbles himself will be exalted."*
MATTHEW 23:12 ESV

In your daily sacrifice for your family you might feel underappreciated or worn too thin. When this is the case, turn to the example of Christ. He is the one to emulate. He humbled himself to the point of death and he will be exalted to the highest point when he comes back as King. Your sacrifice isn't for naught. When you feel discouraged, look at what Jesus has done and follow his example. He didn't minimize his sacrifice, but he didn't do it with bitterness either. He knew exactly what he was getting himself into and he walked through each painful step trusting his Father.

Humbly lay your frustrations at the cross and the let the Holy Spirit point you to truth. Trust that you are seen and cared for by God. He knows all that you give up and he won't leave you empty-handed. In your continuous looking to the cross, God will be faithful to keep your heart soft and to refresh you when you need it most.

God, thank you that as I sacrifice different things as a mother, you see me. Help me to keep my heart soft as I serve my family. When I am struggling with discouragement, help me to lay that down at the cross and keep my eyes on the example of Jesus.

# ASK SEEK KNOCK

*"Ask and it will be given to you; seek and you will find; knock and the door will be opened to you."*

MATTHEW 7:7 NIV

Your quiet times might be anything but quiet. You might struggle to find solitude, and the noise might just never quit. Before having children, you might have developed the habit of spending your time with God peacefully reading Scripture, bringing your needs to him in prayer, and praising him for what he's done. Now, it can feel impossible to connect with him in that way in the midst of pouring yourself out for your children. Your time is limited, your energy is dwindling, and your attention is on a million little things.

Though your time with him might not be as neat and tidy as it used to be, there is no reason for it not to be just as sweet and meaningful. He is fully aware of how having children has changed your life. Jesus reminder to ask, seek, and knock doesn't come with prerequisites. He doesn't say, "Ask after you've sat still for fifteen uninterrupted minutes," or "Knock only after you've memorized a psalm and listened to a worship song." Motherhood is the perfect opportunity for you to learn how to walk steadily leaning on truth, flexing your spiritual muscles as you ask, seek, and knock whenever you can.

Thank you, God, that I can seek you at any time. You are not limited to solitude and quiet. When I am overwhelmed, I can find you. You are not defined by my schedule. Turn my heart toward you in each season: chaos and peace.

# IN HIS STRENGTH

*I can do all things through him who strengthens me.*
PHILIPPIANS 4:13 ESV

In this Scripture, Paul refers to his ability to be content no matter what his circumstances are. Contentedness and satisfaction are not common in our culture. It's completely normal to always want more and to assume that you would be happier if certain things were different. Paul has found the secret to contentedness. He can walk in that way because Christ strengthened him. If that was done for Paul, it can be done for you as well.

Do you ever find yourself discontented in motherhood? Maybe it's not what you thought it would be. Maybe you long for some freedom or independence. Maybe you're in the thick of a really difficult season and it feels unending. You don't need to grit your teeth and get through it. God can soften your heart. As you turn to him with your circumstances, he is fully capable of expanding your ability to be content. If you let him, God can change your heart.

Thank you, God, that no matter what the world says, it is possible to walk in contentedness. Teach me how to do this. Help me to turn to you in thanksgiving as you strengthen me. Turn my discouragement into joy and dissatisfaction into quiet contentedness no matter what my season or circumstances are.

# NOT ALONE

*"Teach them to faithfully follow all that I have commanded you.
And never forget that I am with you every day,
even to the completion of this age."*

MATTHEW 28:20 TPT

In a world that is so full of connection and instant interaction, it is just as easy as ever to feel alone. Your heart craves real and true connection. Relationships that are based on superficial interactions and brief communication will never satisfy you. Instead, turn to the one who is with you always. He has promised to never leave you or forsake you. He goes before you, after you, and is in your midst.

When loneliness threatens to overtake you, go to God for comfort. He will not turn you away. He longs to walk with you. He made you for unhindered communion. You were designed to be with him, and in his presence you will be most satisfied. If you find yourself turning to other things for satisfaction, take time to lay those things down and turn to him.

Thank you, Father, that you are not a God who is far off. You promise to be close to me. Help me to turn to you when I am lonely. Instead of running to other sources for satisfaction, may the Holy Spirit remind me that true rest and satisfaction come from your presence.

# YOU ARE KNOWN

*Search me, God, and know my heart;*
*test me and know my anxious thoughts.*
*See if there is any offensive way in me,*
*and lead me in the way everlasting.*

PSALM 139:23-34 NIV

Have you ever had that lingering feeling that maybe something is askew in a relationship? You can tell the other person is bothered but you don't want to open up the conversation because that would mean a potential conflict. When you discuss offense with other people, you can't guarantee their response or how it will impact your relationship. The conversation, while worth it, could be uncomfortable. As humans, we like to be in control, so it takes concerted effort to humbly approach potential wrongs.

The difference in your relationship with the Lord is that you can guarantee his response. His character never changes. He is the safest place for all of your wrongs because he promises to always forgive, always heal, and always be kind. His love for you doesn't change even when you have done something offensive. You can allow him to search you and know you without fear because you trust in who he says he is. It is always worth it to be vulnerable with God. He knows the depths of your heart and he loves you still. Humbly ask the Lord to search your heart. No matter the contents, you are safe with him.

Thank you, God, that I can depend on you. Help me to trust in your character. Search my heart today and help me to trust that you are worthy of my vulnerability. My anxiety is safe with you. My fears are safe with you. Teach me how to walk humbly before you, not hiding anything.

# LAVISHED WITH LOVE

*See what great love the Father has lavished on us, that we should be called children of God! And that is what we are! The reason the world does not know us is that it did not know him.*

1 JOHN 3:1 NIV

In your constant mothering, don't forget that you too are a greatly loved child. You are learning just like your children are. You, as a child of God, are highly valued. Maybe you tend to see God as a king, a ruler, a tyrant, or a boss. It might seem simplistic but remember that he is your kind and gentle Father. His tenderness is in perfect unity with his power and majesty. He is not more one than the other

In your time with him today, climb up on his lap, acknowledging your childlikeness, and rest in the safety that is found there. In that space, even if just for a minute, you can take a deep breath and let him love you. As your Father, he sees you with mercy. He is delighted by your acknowledgement of who he is. He is eager to carry your burdens and give you peace. Praise him today for the great love he has lavished on you.

Thank you, God, that you have called me your child. Help me to see you as a good father. Hold me where I am tired and broken, and let me find healing in your love. If there are areas where I don't understand the goodness of a kind father, teach me your ways. Heal my heart and help me to see you rightly.

# DESPITE FEELINGS

*Why, my soul, are you downcast?*
*Why so disturbed within me?*
*Put your hope in God,*
*for I will yet praise him,*
*my Savior and my God.*
PSALM 42:11 NIV

As you walk through days that are difficult, sometimes you might be just as discouraged by your reaction as you are by the actual cause of the difficulty. Perhaps you shy away from emotions that feel too big. Remember that you are given multiple examples in Scripture of men and women with passionate and raw reactions. Don't be discouraged by big feelings, put your hope in God. His is big enough for all of you, at your best and your worst. When your soul is downcast, turn to God. He doesn't ask you to come to him politely or sweetly, he just asks you to be close to him.

Instead of being discouraged by how you feel, praise the Lord. It might feel contradictory or out of place in your dark moments but praise him anyway. No matter how weak your praise feels, God sees your heart. He knows that at your worst even the smallest hallelujah feels impossible. He sees you exactly where you are and he isn't intimidated by it or disappointed.

Thank you, God, that in my darkest moments, I can turn to you. When my soul is downcast, I can put my hope in you. You can handle all of my most intense emotions. You don't require me to approach you nicely or politely. I can be honest with you, and as I walk in thanksgiving, you will renew my hope.

# JUNE

Take delight in the LORD,

and he will give you your heart's desires.

Commit everything you do to the LORD.

Trust him, and he will help you.

PSALM 37:4-5 NLT

# HEART HEALTHY

*Praise the LORD, my soul, and forget not all his benefits—*
*who forgives all your sins and heals all your diseases,*
*who redeems your life from the pit*
*and crowns you with love and compassion.*

PSALM 103:2-4 NIV

You know when your child is sick. They might eat less, sleep more, have a fever, or display any number of symptoms. As their mother, you know when something is off because you know what normal is. Just as bodies can get sick, so can hearts. If you watch for symptoms like bitterness, negativity, complaint, or anger, you can monitor your heart health. If you find yourself walking through your days with these symptoms, follow the instruction of the psalmist and praise the Lord, remembering all that he has done.

Practicing thanksgiving can actively move you away from negativity. Remembering the goodness of God can actively stir up affection and love within you. If you can't remember the last time you praised God for the forgiveness of your sins and the redemption of your life, start there. He adores you and crowns you with love and compassion. Don't let your heart stay sick, climb into his arms and let him heal you.

Thank you for all you've done, God! Thank you for healing me and redeeming me. Help me to keep an eye on the symptoms of my heart. Where I have let bitterness or negativity go unchecked, heal me. Help me to turn to you for the health of my body and my heart.

# THE WATCHMAN

*He will not let your foot slip—*
*he who watches over you will not slumber;*
*indeed, he who watches over Israel will neither slumber nor sleep.*
PSALM 121:3-4 NIV

Have you ever watched your child while they sleep? Have you ever watched them sleep while they are sick? You watch their chest rise and fall, you stroke their hair, hoping for healing, and praying for whatever their little bodies are going through. Though you yourself are tired, nothing is as important in that moment as making sure they are okay. Imagine then, how diligently your Father watches over you.

He is the God who neither slumbers or sleeps. He faithfully has his eyes on you, always ensuring that you are okay. He never takes a break, never looks away, and is never distracted. He has not left you alone to stumble through your life. Today, rest knowing that he won't. Rest fully as one who is watched over and guarded by the most capable, most sufficient, most powerful watchman. He is in control, so you don't need to be.

Thank you, Father, for faithfully watching over me. You keep me safe and you make sure that I don't slip. Teach me how to rest fully, knowing that you are in control. May my rest be praise unto you because I trust in you fully.

# RADIANT

*I sought the Lord, and he answered me*
*and delivered me from all my fears.*
*Those who look to him are radiant,*
*and their faces shall never be ashamed.*

Psalm 34:4-5 esv

Think of how you feel when your child, busy and occupied, looks up from their toys for a moment and shouts a quick, "I love you Mom!" Or maybe when they're running out the door they hurry back in for a brief hug and a kind word. In those moments, your heart swells with affection. You're likely not thinking, "That was nice, *but* it wasn't quite good enough." Imagine then, how God must view your brief glances toward him.

Look to him, turn your face to him, seek him. Whether you feel close to him or not, take some time today to quiet your heart and listen. Find even a minute and utter a few words to him. He is bigger than your lack of both time and silence. The Psalmist says that those who look to him are radiant. Each of your small glances add up to a lifetime of turning to him for assurance, guidance, and love. Your small glances, though they might not feel like enough at the time, are valuable. They show a habit directing your attention to God even when there are a million other things trying to occupy your time.

Today, help me to look to you even if I don't feel like I have time. Teach me how to turn my attention toward you when other things are pulling for it. As I offer you even small glances every day, you are drawing me closer to you.

# THE GOOD SHEPHERD

*The Lord is my best friend and my shepherd.*
*I always have more than enough.*
*He offers a resting place for me in his luxurious love.*
*His tracks take me to an oasis of peace, the quiet brook of bliss.*
PSALM 23:1-2 TPT

No matter what happened in your day prior to right now, no matter what the rest of the day holds, for this moment of time let the words of Psalm 23 be a balm to your soul. Where you are tired, let the Holy Spirit minister to you. You serve a God of restoration and incredible kindness. He is the Good Shepherd. His desire to care for you is unchanging and he does not place requirements upon it. He doesn't ask you to give him a solid thirty minutes and then he will bless you. He doesn't ask you to change anything about yourself before you come to him. It's spending time in his presence that will bring about godly change.

Today, right now, you have an opportunity to let the words of Psalm 23 wash over you. You have more than enough. You have a resting place. He restores you and revives you. He leads you to follow him that you might honor his name. Your Good Shepherd is a life giver and he wants you near to him so he can restore your life. As you dwell upon who he is, let that stir you to worship him with thanksgiving.

Thank you, God, that you are a good shepherd! You care for me fully and with kindness. In your presence, you restore my life. Today, help me to see your provision and the ways that you have provided a place for me.

# A RELIABLE NAME

*Those who know your name trust in you,*
*for you, Lord, have never forsaken those who seek you.*
PSALM 9:10 NIV

Have you ever benefited from the reputation of someone else's name? You might get a discount from a referral or maybe you've trusted someone because of the history behind their name. In the same way, God's name can be trusted. Those who know him, know that he is reliable and faithful. He cannot behave any other way. It is in his very nature to be faithful to you. He has never forsaken his children who seek him, and he never will. Anytime you doubt your faith or the validity of your relationship with God, remember that it is one hundred percent dependent on his character and his nature, not yours.

As you seek him, no matter if you think your efforts are enough, he will be faithful to you. He will not forsake his child. His name is reliable. Today, remember that he has promised not to leave you. Let that security impact your everyday moments.

Thank you, God, that you've promised never to leave me. I want to be among those who know your name and trust in you. Teach me how to see you rightly and to depend on your faithfulness. Even when I am unfaithful, you are still there. Thank you for loving me so well when I don't deserve it.

# AN HEIR

*You Gentiles are no longer strangers and foreigners.*
*You are citizens along with all of God's holy people.*
*You are members of God's family.*
EPHESIANS 2:19 NLT

You belong fully and completely to God's family. Where there was once distance between you, you have been brought close because of Christ's work on the cross. As a member of God's family, you are privy to all of the benefits. You are an heir, you are protected, and you are loved. Though your body may fail and your memories might fade, your position in God's family is something that even time cannot take away.

You can cling to what Jesus has done for you and know that as a result you will always be enough, and you will always belong securely in his family. Today, let your belonging spill into every area of your life. Because you belong, you can love others fully. Because you belong, you can walk through trials with a peaceful spirit. Because you belong, you can praise God for what he has done.

Thank you, God, that I am part of your family. I belong and I am loved as a child. Teach me how to walk through my day rooted in belonging. May the way that I think about myself and others come from a deep understanding of who my Father is.

# ENLIGHTENMENT

*With meekness you'll be able to carefully enlighten those who argue with you so they can see God's gracious gift of repentance and be brought to the truth.*
2 TIMOTHY 2:25 TPT

When you think of arguing, you might think of fruitless social media debates or squabbles between friends. Today, as you read the Word of God, think about how it can apply to who you are as a mother. Do you often find yourself joining your child in the boxing ring, speaking back and forth until authority demands respect? Instead of arguing, God says that with meekness you can carefully enlighten. This meekness gives your children eyes to see God's gracious gift of repentance.

As you abide in Christ, walking with the Holy Spirit, you will bear the fruit of meekness. If you struggle to remain calm when emotions are high, God is ever willing to help you. He knows your weaknesses and he desires to strengthen you. Don't be discouraged by your shortcomings. Instead, boldly ask for help and humbly receive what you need. Draw closer to God in repentance as you trust in the work of Christ on the cross.

Thank you, God, that your Word gives good instruction. As I depend on your Word and seek to be more like you, you help me where I am weak. Today, when I am tempted to argue, help me instead to practice meekness. Teach me how to help my children desire repentance and truth.

# A STEADY FATHER

*The LORD directs the steps of the Godly.*
*He delights in every detail of their lives.*
*Though they stumble, they will never fall,*
*for the LORD holds them by the hand.*
PSALM 37:23–24 NLT

Read this verse and imagine it describing a father and a child. Imagine a father walking hand-in-hand with his toddler, his steps steady and even, the toddler wobbly and still a little unsure on her feet. He keeps his eyes on her, making sure she won't fall. She excitedly points out everything that delights her. A leaf! A bug! A rock! And with each minute observation, the father smiles because his delight is in his child. He is not too old, too mature, or too grown to brush past what is important to her in that moment.

This is the type of Father that you have. He delights in every detail of your life. Nothing about your day, even though he has seen millions of days, is too minute for him. Nothing about your life is too insignificant. He delights in every little piece of you. He holds you firmly so you won't fall and he directs your steps because he cares for you. Today, share the mundane and the small with him. He wants to meet you in your big difficult moments, but he also wants to join you in the seemingly insignificant.

Thank you, God, that you care about my whole life. You delight in every detail of my life, no matter how small. Where I have seen you as a far-off God, help me to see you as close and personal, concerned with every detail of my days. Teach me to invite you into every aspect of my life.

# AS YOU ARE

*God, being rich in mercy, because of the great love with which he loved us, even when we were dead in our trespasses, made us alive together with Christ—by grace you have been saved— and raised us up with him and seated us with him in the heavenly places in Christ Jesus, so that in the coming ages he might show the immeasurable riches of his grace in kindness toward us in Christ Jesus.*

EPHESIANS 2:4-7 ESV

When you were at your very worst, Christ died for you. While you were dead in your sins, he brought you back to life. It can be difficult to approach your children in their sin. So often you push for right actions. God does not see you this way, he doesn't wait for you to get it right, withholding life in Christ until you are able to get your act together. He kindly meets you wherever you are.

You don't have to muster up right thinking or check anything else off your list. He will meet you in your joy and in your thanksgiving. He will also meet you in your hiding and your shame. He is the God who rescued humanity when we were most undeserving. He did this because of the great love he has for you. He is the one who raises you up and seats you with him in heavenly places. Come as you are and praise God for what he has done.

Thank you, God, that you don't require me to behave a certain way before I can come to you. While I was dead in my sin, you raised me up. Thank you for saving me by grace, by no doing of my own. When I am too focused on outward actions, turn my heart toward the mercy that you give.

# ALWAYS KNOWN

*O LORD, You have searched me and known me.*
*You know when I sit down and when I rise up;*
*You understand my thoughts from afar.*
PSALM 139:1-2 NASB

Motherhood brings about a lot of changes. There might be parts of you that feel different than they did before you had kids. Your body has changed, your heart has expanded, and the way you view the world has changed. You might have seamlessly navigated all of these changes or you might find yourself floundering or feeling foreign in your own skin. You might have embraced the transition, or you might long for who you were before becoming a mother.

No matter the degree to which you've accepted or struggled against change, know that you are fully known. No matter how you grow or adjust, God never stops knowing you. Even as you struggle to navigate unchartered waters, he understands you. This can be a comfort to you because you can turn to him. When you feel unknown even to yourself, you can let him hold you close and remind you of who he is: the ever constant, never changing God who sees you, knows you, and loves you.

Thank you, God, that you know me. Even when I am walking through something new and unknown, your understanding of me is constant. You see me and you love me full well. Teach me how to lean on your constant love when I am shaken or lost. Help me to navigate new seasons while leaning on your steadfast love.

# ALWAYS NEAR

*"When you walk through the fire of oppression,
you will not be burned up; the flames will not consume you.
For I am the Lord, your God, the Holy One of Israel, your Savior."*

Isaiah 43:2-3 NLT

You serve an ever-present God. He is always with you. When your emotions are frazzled, he is with you. When you feel swallowed up in disappointment, you will not drown. When you experience trauma, it will not consume you. His promises are good and true, and he promises to always uphold you. What are the deep waters that you are wading through right now? Trust that he is near you. He has not left you alone to navigate treacherous waters. He sees you, knows you, and longs to meet you exactly where you are. It's part of his very nature to rescue you.

He is the Holy One of Israel, your Savior. He cannot act in a way that is contradictory to his character and it is fully within his character to walk with you through whatever trial you might face. Today, if you are navigating difficulty or walking smoothly, praise him that he is close to you at all time. Exalt his name that no matter your circumstances, he never changes. Nothing can separate you from his love.

Thank you, God, that you are ever-present! If I feel alone in what I am facing, remind me of your nearness. You never leave me. I praise you for your ability to save me and rescue me. Help me to see your goodness even when I am going through hard times.

# GOD GIVES ENDURANCE

*May the God who gives endurance and encouragement give you the*
*same attitude of mind toward each other that Christ Jesus had.*
ROMANS 15:5 NIV

You know that you need endurance to get through the day. Your physical, emotional, and spiritual muscles get tired. You might have seasons of peace and rest but it's likely that the majority of the time you can easily list something in your life that causes weariness. You need endurance and God is the one who can provide you with it. He will strengthen you exactly where you need to be strengthened in order to navigate what's in front of you.

There are times when the answer to prayer will include a situation being altered by the Lord, but more often than not, he moves in your heart. While your circumstances might not change, you can trust that when you follow him, he will consistently equip you to walk with peace. Today, think about areas where you need strength or endurance and ask the Lord to equip you.

Thank you, Father, that you give me the endurance that I need to get through my day. Teach me how to rely upon you more fully. Fill me with peace and joy as I walk through difficult things.

# HOLD FAST

*Let us hold unswervingly to the hope we profess,*
*for he who promised is faithful.*

HEBREWS 10:23 NIV

Think about where you have placed your hope. The things of this earth will fade, so if your hope is in your job, your spouse's job, your security, or even your relationships, you will be disappointed. If you have placed your hope firmly in the promises of God, then you can trust that it is secure. Your foundation of Christ's work on the cross and God's promise that Jesus will return again can never be shaken. Those things are steady, unchanging, and able to withstand even the fiercest storms.

You are reminded in Hebrews to hold unswervingly to that hope because it is the most secure anchor you'll ever find. Nothing will hold you steadfast like the love of the Lord. If you find yourself wavering today because of trials, emotions, stress, or weariness, remember that when you place your hope in Christ, it cannot be moved. Setting your eyes upon Jesus allows you to look beyond what you are currently facing. It doesn't make your trials illegitimate or easy, but it does put them in perspective.

Thank you, God, for the great hope that I have in Jesus! Today, help me to hold firmly to that hope and to persevere. As I wait upon Christ, help me to trust in your promises and walk through my days in a way that honors you.

# LOVE GOD AND OTHERS

*Now that you have purified yourselves by obeying the truth so that you have sincere love for each other, love one another deeply, from the heart.*
1 PETER 1:22 NIV

Do you ever sit down to spend time with God and somehow you end up feeling like you're just not enough, like you need to add a few things to your good-Christian check list? If you are feeling worn out by motherhood and all that it demands, it can be overwhelming to add even one more thing to your to-do list. Take a deep breath and know that there is no such list for you to be accepted and loved by God. His requirements of you are simple: love God and love others.

If you feel stressed thinking about all that you need to do, pass your list through the sieve of what God wants from you. Is what you're doing demonstrating a love for God and for his people? If not, happily cross it off your list and move on. You can be confident that you have accomplished more than enough if your actions are rooted in love. Let your love for God and others be the only standard that you hold yourself to today.

Help me to value love for others over my task list, Lord. Teach me how to love like you and to lay my life down joyfully for those around me. Show me practical ways to display your love in a way that blesses others. I want to love deeply, not superficially.

# HE GENTLY LEADS

*He takes care of his people like a shepherd.*
*He gathers them like lambs in his arms*
*and carries them close to him.*
*He gently leads the mothers of the lambs.*

ISAIAH 40:11 NCV

Since becoming a mother, no matter how long it's been, have you ever felt like your relationship with God has changed? Where you used to have time to read the Word or dive into theology, perhaps now you are overwhelmed with changing diapers and the many other constant demands of motherhood. Where you used to engage in ministry wholeheartedly perhaps now you're simply too tired.

Know that in this season of your life, when you are pouring yourself out for your children, the Lord is leading you gently. He knows exactly what this season demands of you and he is compassionate toward you. He sees how tired you are. He sees how you worry and care for your children. He gathers them close like lambs in his arms and he leads you gently. Let this take a weight off you today. You can rest while he holds your children close. As their mother, you are the one that bears the weight of their care. Let God carry that burden. Let him hold them as he leads you.

Thank you, God, that you are a good shepherd. Let me rest as I trust my children to you. You see me, you have compassion on me, and you lead me gently. Today, where I have unnecessarily carried burdens, help me to surrender them to you. You are a better caregiver for my children than I will ever be. I trust you.

# IMITATE GOD

*Be imitators of God, as beloved children.*
EPHESIANS 5:1 ESV

You know that you should aspire to be like God. His perfection is not a surprise. You can likely make an extensive list of the ways that you succeed in imitation and the ways you've failed. You should model your life after his character and seek to have his perspective in all you do. In your imitation, don't forget the second part of this Scripture. It's pivotal and life changing when you read this command as a whole.

You are his beloved child. This means that your imitation of him comes from a secure place of belonging. If your imitation is rooted in a works mindset or a fear of disobedience, then you've misplaced the heart of this command. Knowing that you are a beloved child takes you from a place of seeing God as a master to seeing him as your kind and gentle Father. Imitate him as your child might imitate you, full of wonder and affection. If you find yourself working to gain his favor, ask him to soften your heart and remind you of how he really sees you.

God, you are such a kind father! Teach me how to imitate you because I am secure and loved. May my reflection of you come out of a place of belonging and not of striving. I want my life to look like you because I am greatly loved and desire to love you more. Protect me from the mindset that I need to work to gain your favor.

# SERVE ONE ANOTHER

*You have been called to live in freedom, my brothers and sisters.*
*But don't use your freedom to satisfy your sinful nature.*
*Instead, use your freedom to serve one another in love.*

GALATIANS 5:13 NLT

You live in a culture that constantly tells you to look out for yourself. Your personal rights are the most important. If your freedom is infringed upon you should desperately fight for it to be restored. In contrast, Jesus says that you have not been set free to satisfy yourself but instead to serve each other. True freedom comes from living the way Christ did, joyfully laying your life down for those around you.

Instead of thinking about how you are being impacted by something, take a moment to ask your neighbor what their experience is. Value the opinions of others above your own. Make space at your table for the unloved. This type of service and generosity is life giving and life changing, for both the giver and the receiver. After all, your freedom comes from a well that never runs dry, so you never have to worry about sharing too much. It's an impossibility!

Thank you for the freedom that I have in you, Jesus! Teach me how to serve others in love over serving myself. I know that I am prone to elevate my own needs above those around me. Teach me how to give generously, love abundantly, and trust in my security in you.

# HE GIVES ABUNDANTLY

*God is able to bless you abundantly, so that in all things at all times,
having all that you need, you will abound in every good work.*

2 CORINTHIANS 9:8 NIV

As your Father, God is aware of what you need. Not only that, but none of your needs are beyond him. He is fully capable of blessing you abundantly. You can trust him because his ability backs up his promises. When you think about your needs, you might be tempted to think about the material. You might wonder why God hasn't given you certain things when he says he will bless you abundantly.

Today, focus instead on the immaterial. He says that he will give you all that you need so you will abound in every good work. What does your heart need today? Is your soul crying out for rest, peace, joy, or belonging? While your material needs are important and valid, they can sometimes crowd out what your heart needs. Today, let him speak to your heart and give you good gifts that you might not be able to see or touch.

Thank you, God, that my needs go far beyond material. Today, help me to see past my physical needs and to also trust you for what my soul needs. You see me fully and you know exactly what I need to abound in every good work.

# SAVED BY GRACE

*By grace you have been saved through faith.*
*And this is not your own doing; it is the gift of God.*
EPHESIANS 2:8 ESV

Take a break from the consistent requirements of motherhood and focus on the basics of your faith. Let the simplicity of the gospel wash over you. Let the work that Christ has done on your behalf flood your entire being. Receive wholeheartedly what has been done for you, free of charge. There is nothing in your life right now that can diminish the validity of the gospel, God's gift for you.

Whether you're reading this while you sip hot coffee in a cozy chair or your tears are staining the page, there is comfort to be found in the fact that nothing you can do, think, or feel that will change what God has done for you. The gospel of grace is the same for you during times of painful trial and rejoicing. By no merit of your own, you have been saved. Today, no matter your circumstances, receive that gift from God. He gives it to you freely, abundantly, and consistently.

Thank you, God, that there is nothing I can do to earn your love. No matter how chaotic life feels right now, help me to focus on the beautiful simplicity of the gospel. Help me to receive what you've given with thanksgiving and praise. What you have done is incredible! Thank you for the gift of Jesus and the saving grace that you've given me.

# HOPE IN JESUS

*"I have told you all this so that you may have peace in me.*
*Here on earth you will have many trials and sorrows.*
*But take heart, because I have overcome the world."*
JOHN 16:33 NLT

Maybe your journey to and through motherhood was well planned and smooth. Maybe it's been chaotic. Maybe it's been marked by loss and longing. So much of life isn't what it was imagined to be. If you find yourself overwhelmed by the trials you've faced, God tells you to take heart for he has overcome the world. He doesn't ever promise that your life will be breezy. He knows that you will have seasons when sorrow washes over you like a wave. He knows that your life on this earth will be marked by trials. What he is asking is that you put your confidence and trust in him.

Despite what you walk through, peace can be found in Christ. He has overcome the world and the day is coming when trials will cease. You cannot place your hope in the absence of trials but firmly in the fact that Christ will return and establish his kingdom. At that day, your sorrows will cease. Instead of being discouraged by what life looks like now, look forward to that day when all things are made right.

Thank you, God, that you promise peace in Christ. You know my life isn't always easy and you walk me through it with kindness and comfort. You have overcome the world and your plan is greater than my trials. Help me to turn to you and keep my eyes focused on what is to come.

# BOAST IN THE CROSS

*May I never boast about anything except the cross of our Lord Jesus Christ. Because of that cross, my interest in this world has been crucified, and the world's interest in me has also died.*

GALATIANS 6:14 NLT

You have more resources and more access to comparison than any previous generation. It can be tempting to boast in what you have or what you are capable of. Instead, if you must boast, boast about the cross of Christ. Elevate his glorious work above anything you might accomplish. Glorify his name over your own and you'll find that your interest in the world will fade. If you are overly concerned with the ways of the world and looking a certain way or being perceived a certain way, do the work of directing your gaze toward what Christ has done.

As you focus on the cross, you'll find that your earthly worries will diminish. Instead of dwelling on your successes and failures, place your confidence in what God has done. The sacrificial work of Christ on the cross has redeemed you and made a way for you to be with the Father for eternity.

Father, help me to take the focus off myself and to elevate your name instead. You have done great things, you are doing great things, and you will do great things! Help me to boast not of myself but of Christ's work on the cross that I might develop the perseverance I need to remain faithful until his return.

# SMALL FAITH

*"Truly, I say to you, if you have faith like a grain of mustard seed, you will say to this mountain, 'Move from here to there,' and it will move, and nothing will be impossible for you."*

MATTHEW 17:20 ESV

You might feel like your faith doesn't quite measure up. Especially in the midst of a season when you are tired and weary from the mundane, you might feel like you just don't have what it takes to cultivate great faith. You might find yourself comparing your relationship with God to those around you or even to examples in the Bible. Phrases like, "I'm just too tired" or "I can't handle this right now" might run through your mind as your arms are heavy from carrying a fussy baby and your mind feels frazzled from juggling everyone's needs.

Without fail, you'll find examples in the Word where God works powerfully in situations just like that. He constantly uses the weak, inadequate, and broken to display his glory. He doesn't ask for big faith or well executed works. He asks you for mustard-seed faith. He knows exactly what burdens you and exactly what hurdles are in your path. Remember today, that your small glance, your tiny but true belief in who he is, can move mountains. He is the mountain mover, not you. If there are mountains in your way, you can calmly rest in his arms, asking him to move them.

Thank you, God, that you are the mountain mover! Teach me how to depend on you and your power. My faith might feel small, but you say that it is enough. Today, I place my confidence not in my ability but in who you are.

# LIFEGIVING WORDS

*The words of a good person give life, like a fountain of water,*
*but the words of the wicked contain nothing but violence.*
PROVERBS 10:11 NCV

You're walking through the grocery store and your toddler is sitting in the cart screaming because you won't buy the giant jug of chocolate milk. The six-year-old is whining because she doesn't like how her shoes fit, and the baby is crying because she needs to eat. A few people give you knowing smiles, some roll their eyes and look annoyed, but one person looks you in the eye, offers to help, and whispers, "You're doing great, Mama. Keep it up!" Those simple words lift a burden off your shoulders, comfort you like a warm blanket, and give you strength to make it through the rest of your grocery trip.

Words are powerful, and despite the negative reaction of anyone else in that store, those few good words were like a fountain of water. Today, remember that your words can shift the entire day for someone. They can lift up your children and bring life to dry places. Even if they are simple and small, let your words be encouraging and kind.

Thank you, God, for the reminder that my words are powerful. Teach me to be sensitive to the Holy Spirit and to speak words that are life giving. May the things I say be like a fountain of water for people who are thirsty.

# YOU WILL FIND HIM

*"You will seek me and find me,
when you seek me with all your heart."*
JEREMIAH 29:13 ESV

Have you ever lost something you desperately need? If you're getting ready to leave for a dentist appointment and you can't find your keys or your scarf, you're going to pour all of your energy and resources into finding the keys because they are vital to the success of your day. The scarf, while nice, isn't completely necessary and you know that you don't need to waste your time searching for it. You'll likely find your keys because you've given all of your attention to figuring out where they are.

Seek God in the same way—as though he is a vital necessity. When you pour everything you have to give, no matter if you think it is enough or not, you will find him. He promises that you will not be left wanting. Some days your heart might be stronger than others. The strength of your heart is irrelevant, just give him what you have. He is the most necessary part of your day; treat him as such and you will find him easily. He is not hiding from you.

Thank you, God, that you are not hard to find. You are not hiding, waiting for me to get myself together. Instead, all you ask is that I give you what I have. Help me to prioritize you above everything else. Teach me how to seek you over other things that call for my attention.

# BRAVE AND STRONG

*"Remember that I commanded you to be strong and brave. Don't be afraid, because the LORD your God will be with you everywhere you go."*

JOSHUA 1:9 NCV

When your child calls out for you, afraid, the first thing you might say to them is, "It's okay, I'm here. Don't worry, Mommy's here." Your presence is their comfort. Their fear stems from the thought that maybe they have been left without help, without comfort, to figure everything out on their own. But you know the truth. You know that all they need is to call for you, to turn to you, and you will run, ready to comfort with just the right words.

No matter how many times your child doubts it, you know that you will never leave them alone. Their doubt could never change the fact that you will always be there when they need you. So it is with the Lord; he promises his presence to you. He reminds you not to fear because he knows that he will always be there. He cannot go back on his Word no matter how big your doubts are. Like a good father he will never leave you alone to manage on your own.

Thank you, God, for your unchanging presence! Show me areas where I have doubted your nearness and walked in fear. Teach me how to trust that you are with me always. Thank you for being such a kind and dependable father.

# TENDER LOVE

*Give thanks to the Creator who made the heavens with wisdom!*
*His tender love for us continues on forever!*
PSALM 136:5 TPT

God's love for you is tender. He sees you with affection. He speaks to you gently. He doesn't tease you or poke at your wounds. He knows your weaknesses and strengthens you. He knows your strengths and is proud of you. He is not disappointed in you. He is nurturing and kind. He knows your hurts and wants to comfort you. He is not intimidated by your doubts or angry about your failures.

His love for you is tender. He is the most attentive father you will ever know. His love for you is never-ending, and there will never be a day that you reach its limit. If you sit and think about how God sees you and your thoughts sound something like, "I know God loves me but…" stop there. Remove your conditions and preconceived notions of what his love looks like. Take a moment and let him speak to you about it. Rest in his presence and ask him to teach you. He will not refuse you. If all you do today is contemplate what his love for you looks like, that is more than enough.

Thank you for your tender love, God. Teach me what your love looks like. Where I don't understand your kindness, show me the ways that you have cared for and nurtured me. You are a loving father and not a God who is distant. Help me to rest in your love because that is more than enough.

# GOOD WORKS

*They should be rich in good works and generous to those in need,*
*always being ready to share with others. By doing this they will be*
*storing up their treasure as a good foundation for the future so that*
*they may experience true life.*

1 TIMOTHY 6:18-19 NLT

There will always be someone whose needs exceed your own. If you feel overwhelmed by what you don't have, the quickest path out of that mindset is generosity. Generosity is a discipline and it takes practice to consistently be ready to share with others. If you have extra room at your table, invite someone to dinner. If you have a spare minute when you're running errands, grab coffee for a friend. If you know someone is sad, drop of a bouquet of flowers and a note. Send a text and be generous with your words. Buy someone's groceries and be generous with your money. Don't fret over the guest who stays late and be generous with your time.

Being selfless is not about what you give but about the attitude of your heart in the middle of giving. You have more to share than you think. Today, ask the Lord how you can practice generosity. He will be faithful to direct you, and in your giving you'll find that you are laying a firm foundation for yourself as you bless others.

Thank you for what I have, Lord. In seasons of want and seasons of plenty, help me to hold everything with a loose grasp. Teach me how to be generous with all you've given me. Lead me to opportunities for giving to those in need.

# THINGS ABOVE

*Set your minds on things above, not on earthly things.*
*For you died, and your life is now hidden with Christ in God.*
COLOSSIANS 3:2-3 NIV

Are you a past dweller or a future wisher? It can be tempting to focus your thoughts on what has already happened or what might happen in the days to come. Being fixated on things that you cannot change will never result in peace or contentment. You are reminded in Colossians not to look behind, not to look ahead, but to look up. Set your mind on things *above*.

While you physically walk through your days, your spirit is alive in Christ who is seated on the throne with his Father. Let your focus be who he is and what he is doing rather than on earthly things. As you set your mind on things above, you'll find that you will be more firmly rooted in truth and less prone to being swayed or unearthed when storms come. Your attention being fixed on the Lord shows that you know where your help comes from. You know who he is and that his character is proven, so you keep your eyes focused on that which is worthy of your attention.

Lord, keep me focused on you. Where I am prone to dwell on the past or worry about the future, help me instead to turn my eyes to you. You are worthy of all of my attention. You are worthy of my praise! Teach me how to set my mind on things above and not on earthly things.

# HEAL YOUR HEART

*A cheerful heart is a good medicine,*
*but a downcast spirit dries up the bones.*
PROVERBS 17:22 NRSV

You probably tell your kids all the time, "Change your attitude." You know that their attitude impacts not only those around them but their heart as well. You know that the state of their heart allows them to love well but also allows them to feel good from the inside out. This is God's desire for you. He wants your health to go beyond the physical. He knows what you need to have a healthy spirit, and in Proverbs you are reminded to cultivate a cheerful heart.

If your spirit feels downcast, don't let it continue to dry up your bones. Ask God how you can move from being downcast to cheerful. Maybe you need a moment to yourself, a cup of tea, some time outside, or a joyful family memory. Whatever it is, ask the Lord to direct you and then commit your steps to him.

Thank you, Lord, that you know what is best for me. You know that a cheerful heart positively impacts those around me but is healthy for me too. Teach me to cultivate a healthy spirit. I commit to you the state of my heart and I ask for your help.

# PLEASE GOD

*Our purpose is to please God, not people.*
*He alone examines the motives of our hearts.*

1 THESSALONIANS 2:4 NLT

As a follower of Christ, you are called to serve those around you. You are called to lay your life down and to selflessly give of yourself in order to lift others up. You are not called to make everyone else happy. The only standard that you can hold yourself to is the Lord's. If you are living each day trying to please everyone, you will burn out. It just isn't sustainable.

Today, let the burden of managing everyone else's happiness go and rest in the sovereignty of God. He is the only one who is supposed to manage hearts. Even if you have taken on the weight of pleasing your children, you cannot keep walking that way. Surrender to the Lord and let him do what he does best. Release your control to God and ask him how you can please him instead of seeking to please those around you.

Thank you, Father, that I can live first and foremost to please you. I don't need to walk under the weight of pleasing others. Where I am tied to the happiness of people around me, teach me to walk in freedom. Show me areas in my life where I am seeking to please people above you. I want to honor you and worship you with my actions instead of pridefully thinking that I need to be in control.

# JULY

If anyone belongs to Christ,
there is a new creation.
The old things have gone;
everything is made new!

2 Corinthians 5:17 NCV

# FOCUS

*On the glorious splendor of your majesty,*
*and on your wondrous works, I will meditate.*
PSALM 145:5 NRSV

Take a moment to dwell upon the glorious splendor of God's majesty. It can be easy to spend your time with God focusing on what you have or what you lack. You try to quiet your heart and you're immediately consumed with what you need and how you're failing. Instead of dwelling on yourself, find refreshment in thinking about the wonderful things that he has done.

Sit before him in praise and thanksgiving. Look at how he has provided for you, look at how he has healed your heart, look at how he has painted the sky for you and made the sun shine for you. His works are wonderous. As you practice the discipline of thanksgiving and praise, you'll find that even the smallest blessings can shape and define your day. As you dwell less on yourself and more on what God has done, you'll find that your trust in his faithfulness will grow. Even if you can only muster up one thing that you are thankful for, that one thing can soften your heart toward the Lord.

Thank you for your glorious splendor, God! Teach me to have eyes to see your majesty even in the smallest ways. Where I am tempted to focus on myself, turn my eyes toward you. I want to meditate on your works instead of being anxious about what I need.

# A QUIET PLACE

*Jesus withdrew again to the mountain by himself.*
JOHN 6:15 ESV

As impossible as it might seem, you need time by yourself. You need time that is quiet and uninterrupted. You need time with just you and the Lord. You likely don't have the luxury of days or even hours away from your everyday life, but God knows that and he can move just as mightily in five minutes of hiding in the laundry room as he can during a weekend in the woods. No matter what your options are, you can find a moment or two to quiet your heart.

Jesus withdrew to the mountain by himself, and you can figure out where your mountain can be. Maybe it's a few moments of peace with your morning coffee, maybe it's a walk to the mailbox while the kids play in the house. It might feel impossible and like it's never enough but know that as you deliberately seek the Lord, he will honor that and meet you where you are.

Thank you, God, that you are more powerful than time. You are not limited by my lack of it. You know exactly what I need to meet with you, and you are capable of meeting me where I am. Teach me how to find moments with you when life feels chaotic. Teach me the discipline of turning to you whenever I can, no matter how brief.

# FAITHLESSNESS

*The LORD is my light and my salvation—*
*whom shall I fear?*
*The LORD is the stronghold of my life—*
*of whom shall I be afraid?*

PSALM 27:1 NIV

Because of your faith in Jesus Christ, you have a guaranteed light to illuminate your days and keep you safe. You have been brought out of darkness and into marvelous light. Where the light of Christ shines, darkness cannot exist. Even the most secret and hidden parts of your heart can be made bright because of Jesus.

There is nothing for you to fear in being vulnerable or fully surrendered to the Lord. He is your stronghold and your salvation. Your lack of fear isn't about you mustering up courage but about understanding who he is and trusting his character. He is light despite your fear. He offers salvation despite your faithlessness. He is your stronghold regardless of your courage or lack thereof. Today, focus not on what you lack, but on who God is and what he promises you.

Thank you, God, that I don't need to walk in darkness anymore! You are my light and my salvation. Teach me how to focus not on my lack of courage but on how your ability to keep me safe never changes. Thank you for protecting me in all that I do.

# FREEDOM

*The Lord is the Spirit,
and wherever the Spirit of the Lord is,
there is freedom.*

2 CORINTHIANS 3:17 NLT

When you chose to follow Jesus, you were offered freedom unlike anything you've ever experienced. If there are areas of your life that feel burdensome, remember that Jesus offers you lightness and peace. The parts of your heart that feel imprisoned have already been paid for. You were not designed to walk in darkness, bound to brokenness and stuck in discouragement. You have been set free.

Today, think of areas where you are not walking in freedom and ask God to open your eyes to what he wants for you and what he has already accomplished. Earnestly ask him to heal your heart. As your loving Father, his desire for you to walk in freedom stems from never-ending kindness and gentleness. He will be faithful to teach you how to be free; it is his great joy for you live that way.

Thank you that I have freedom in you, Jesus. Show me areas of my life where I am not walking in the freedom that was purchased for me. Show me how to surrender my whole heart to you and to trust your leading. Thank you for your lovingkindness; you desire for me to be free as much as I do.

# HEART VIEWED

*We live by faith,*
*not by sight.*
2 CORINTHIANS 5:7 NIV

You cannot see Jesus. You can't literally run into his physical arms when you are afraid or sit at his feet and listen to his wisdom. You cannot feel him wiping away your tears while he looks you in the eye and tells you to persevere and trust him. You don't see with your eyes; you see with your heart. Your trust in God is based on a belief that what he has promised is true. While the disciples had the honor of literally following Jesus, you have the honor of trusting what you cannot see. This delights God!

Each time you turn to Jesus, without being able to actually see him, your faith grows, and you honor the Lord. God knows exactly how hard it is to stay on the narrow path, putting your faith in Christ when the world is screaming at you to look away. God knows how hard it is to keep your eyes steady on what you cannot see. He is proud of you for each step of faith you take. Today, as you sit still for even a moment, know that your smallest steps of faith are seen by the Lord.

Thank you, Lord, that you see my faith! You know the hurdles that I face and that sometimes it's hard that I can't physically see you. You see me, and you help me walk with my eyes on you despite the distractions around me. Keep me steady until the day I can be with you face-to-face.

# SURRENDERED WORRIES

*Give all your worries to him,*
*because he cares about you.*
1 PETER 5:7 NCV

When you bring your worries to God, you can have full confidence that not only are you heard and seen, but that he is the most equipped to deal with them. As his child, you have full access to him. He is the safest and best place to cast your fears. It can be easy as a mom to become burdened with worry. As your child's primary caregiver and advocate, you might find yourself overwhelmed with all the things they struggle with or experience in life. Do they sleep enough? Are they healthy? Will they be bullied in school? What if they are different from their peers and life is just harder for them?

Instead of dwelling on these things, find the freedom that comes from casting your cares on the Lord. You care so deeply for your children; to that same degree, throw your worries upon the one who can manage them best. This doesn't need to be a polite, well-mannered transaction. Cast, pitch, hurl your anxiety upon the Lord. He doesn't want you to carry it and he is more than capable of shouldering it all for you.

Thank you, God, that you care for me so abundantly. You can manage my worry. You desire for me to walk in freedom and dependence upon you. Show me where I am needlessly carrying burdens. Help me to trust you more fully today than I did yesterday.

# JUST AND TRUE

*He is the Rock, his works are perfect, and all his ways are just.*
*A faithful God who does no wrong, upright and just is he.*

DEUTERONOMY 32:4 NIV

There is so much happening in the world right now. It is difficult to know where you can put your trust. You are met each day with a deluge of information from a myriad of different sources. Everyone has an opinion and is convinced that theirs is the right one. When you feel overwhelmed by all of those voices, take a moment to quiet your heart and praise the one who is faithful, who does no wrong.

You serve a God who is just and true. Instead of feeling battered and swayed by all the noise around you, turn to him. Let him be your true source, your standard, your example, and your sieve. He can and will help you navigate the days you are in. He knows that you are constantly deciding which voices to listen to. If you ask, he will give you wisdom and discernment. As you trust his voice, he will give you peace. As you praise him for his steady and perfect ways, your heart will find rest.

Thank you, God, that you are perfect. In a time when everyone has an opinion, I can turn to you for wisdom. I praise you for you are just and always good! Help me to quiet my heart to hear your opinion. I want to peacefully and confidently follow you instead of being panicked by all that's going on around me. Give me your perspective today, Lord.

# TURN TO JESUS

*"I am the way, the truth, and the life.*
*No one can come to the Father except through me."*
JOHN 14:6 NLT

Let your inadequacy point you to Christ. As you're tempted to dwell on your failures, instead let them push you closer to Jesus. If your thoughts are overwhelmed by whispers of "I just don't have anything to bring to the table," redirect your heart to say, "Christ brings to the table all that I lack." He is the only way to the Father. He is the way, the truth, and the life. Your thoughts of inadequacy and self-doubt might be true, but they are incomplete. In your lacking, turn to Jesus. Let the ways that you don't measure up be a catalyst to displaying the love and glory of God. You don't need to become better, fix your problems, or master a new habit.

True freedom comes not from mastering your weakness but in letting God be glorified through it. He knows how you lack, and he covers you with his love. He doesn't wait for you to better yourself before you're allowed an audience with him. He sent Christ to die for you while you were a sinner. He doesn't hold your weakness against you; he comforts you in it and offers you redemption.

Jesus, you are the way, the truth, and the life. The way to the Father is through you, not through my own betterment. Where I am overwhelmed by thoughts of my own failures, help me to redirect my thoughts to you. Where I am tempted to spend my time mastering my sin, help me instead to trust that you have redeemed me from its power.

# REAP WHAT YOU SOW

*Do not be deceived: God cannot be mocked. A man reaps what he sows*
*Whoever sows to please their flesh will reap destruction; whoever sows*
*to please the Spirit, from the spirit will reap eternal life.*

JAMES 3:5-6 NIV

When you plant tomatoes in your backyard, you won't find peppers at harvest time. When you plant a row of sunflowers, you won't be surprised to look out the window one day and see snapdragons. You reap what you sow. This should bring you freedom, not condemnation. If you sow impatience and anger, that is what you will reap. When you collect a harvest of negativity, take notice and plan to sow differently. If you sow patience and kindness, that is the harvest that you will reap. Thank God that it's not a guessing game.

Trust in the growing process when it comes to yourself and also when it comes to your kids. Motherhood can feel thankless but know that each small act of love and kindness will reap a harvest in due time. What you are doing counts. God will be faithful to lead your children and to draw them close to himself. As you teach them to keep their eyes on him, even on your worst days, he will honor what you have sowed.

Thank you, Father, that life doesn't have to be a guessing game. If I am reaping a harvest that I am unhappy with, I can change what I am sowing. Teach me how to sow the fruit of your Spirit into my home that I might reap a harvest full of life and freedom.

# LITTLE THINGS COUNT

*"The master said, 'Well done, my good and faithful servant. You have been faithful in handling this small amount, so now I will give you many more responsibilities. Let's celebrate together!'"*

MATTHEW 25:23 NLT

When your child masters a new skill, they receive the reward of being able to tackle something even bigger. They also receive the reward of celebration. They start by bravely dunking their head under water and are eventually trusted to jump off the side of the pool. That simple act of trusting their swim instructor as their face gets all wet for the first time is pretty basic but you cheer from the bench because you know that while small, it was a personal victory and you're proud. Eventually you'll cheer as they dive off the diving board or swim laps with ease, but for now, step one is enough and you happily encourage your child.

Know that God also celebrates your small faith victories. What might seem trite to you is a big deal to him. He is proud of you. He knows exactly how much effort you put into that difficult conversation, or how your resisted temptation, or how you didn't say that harsh word but instead practiced gentleness. He sees each of your seemingly little steps and he celebrates with you. He knows that eventually that little step might seem like a drop in the ocean as you grow in him but for now he is a proud father.

Thank you, God, that you see me. You know and acknowledge each step of faith I take. As I am entrusted with more, you encourage me each step of the way. Thank you for your faithful encouragement. I need your voice to remind me that I'm doing the right thing. Keep guiding me and I will keep trusting you!

# DRY PLACES

*The LORD will guide you always;*
*he will satisfy your needs in a sun-scorched land*
*and will strengthen your frame.*
*You will be like a well-watered garden,*
*like a spring whose waters never fail.*

ISAIAH 58:11 NIV

God will satisfy your needs in a sun-scorched land. He will make it rain where the land is dry and parched. He will refresh you and create new life where you have felt desperate and depleted. Does this year feel sun-scorched to you? Do you feel like in the midst of a chaotic world, you are struggling to find peace and abundant life?

God promises to give you what you need. Turn to him in your weariness and choose to believe that he can make it rain. Continue to lean on him and ask for what you need, knowing that he is your kind Father who not only delights in caring for you but also cannot go against his own Word. If he has promised renewal and freshness, then it will come to pass. You can place your hope firmly in what he has said he will do. Today, rest in his promise for restoration.

Thank you for your promises, God. When I feel depleted and weary, you promise that you will bring rain and restoration. You alone can make new life grow where it is dry. Thank you for strength, power, and your lovingkindness.

# DWELL WITH HIM

*One thing I ask from the Lord, this only do I seek:*
*that I may dwell in the house of the Lord all the days of my life,*
*to gaze on the beauty of the Lord and to seek him in his temple.*

PSALM 27:4 NIV

The Psalmist knew the immense value of dwelling with God. He knew that wherever God was, that's where he needed to be. God's home needed to be his home. Today, sit before the Lord and ask him to draw you in like a beloved child coming home. May his presence bring stability and security to your heart in the same way you feel warmly embraced when you walk into your own home.

May the house of the Lord be where you feel most at home. May you walk through the front door and immediately feel tension release. May you delight in the comfort that he gives. May your time in his presence be where you find the truest rest as you gaze on his beauty and praise him for all that he has done. Even when everything around you feels chaotic or broken, you can find life in the house of the Lord.

Thank you, God, for the ability to seek you and find you. I want to spend all my days with you, at home with you, soaking in your presence. May your presence be my truest home, where I run to first for comfort and restoration.

# PRODUCING PERSEVERANCE

*We glory in our sufferings, because we know that suffering produces perseverance; perseverance character; and character, hope.*

ROMANS 5:3-4 NIV

The best things come out of suffering. Babies come after a painful labor. Rainbows come after storms. Diamonds occur under immense pressure. Muscles grow after they are stretched and pushed. The examples are endless. Often, difficulty is needed to produce good things. This is true in your own life as well. Suffering produces perseverance because once you've experienced something difficult, you know you'll be able to get through it again. When that storm comes, instead of wavering, you can say, "I have already done this. I will survive. I'm not as afraid as I was last time." Then, as your perseverance grows, you'll gain character.

As you are able to weather the storm, you'll find that fear is replaced with confidence, and sorrow is replaced with joy. As your character is strengthened, you'll gain hope. You've been through storms before, so you're no longer unsure of the future. You know that you'll make it. Do you see the pattern? Suffering begets perseverance which begets character which begets hope. You can rejoice when hard things happen because you are being refined and strengthened.

Thank you for suffering, God. Even though it's hard, even though I want to quit, thank you that my suffering isn't for nothing. Help me to see how you are producing perseverance, character, and hope within me. Help me to see the beautiful things that can come from hardships. Change my perspective to the way that you see things.

# A CONTRITE SPIRIT

*You are not pleased by sacrifices, or I would give them.*
*You don't want burnt offerings.*
*The sacrifice God wants is a broken spirit.*
*God, you will not reject a heart that is broken and sorry for sin.*

PSALM 51:16-17 NCV

There is freedom in the fact that there is nothing you can do to please God. He doesn't want any material or physical thing you have. He doesn't want your striving or your works. What he wants is a contrite spirit. What he wants is fully within your means to give. He simply asks for you to come to him, aware of your brokenness and your need for his redeeming love. This is not a one-and-done transaction. You need renewal on a daily basis. When you continuously approach God with humility and softness, you'll find yourself approaching those around you the same way.

Walking in humility before God doesn't leave any room for pride. A contrite and broken spirit cannot demand its own way, insist that it is right, or diminish the needs of others. Today, as you bring your contrite spirit before God and he washes you with the truth of his Word, trust that he is pleased with you. As you come to him in humility, you can have confidence that he will not reject you.

Thank you, God, that you don't ask for something I cannot give. All you ask of me is to come to you in humility, aware of my immense need for you. Teach me to walk in awareness of who I am and of your greatness. Today, renew my spirit and show me where I can become more like you.

# FIND YOUR HAVEN

*Then they cried to the Lord in their trouble,*
*and he delivered them from their distress.*
*He made the storm be still,*
*and the waves of the sea were hushed.*
*Then they were glad that the waters were quiet,*
*and he brought them to their desired haven.*
PSALM 107:28-30 ESV

When storms come, your children know where their haven is. They crawl onto your lap and let you calm the winds and the rains. As you stroke their hair or rub their back, you reassure them that you will keep them safe, that you are the steady one when they feel frantic. Likewise, in their trouble, the people of Israel cried to the Lord. They were distressed, frantic, overwhelmed, and wild with emotion.

God makes storms still. He is not ever distressed, frantic, or overwhelmed. He is the God who hushes the waves. There isn't a storm fierce enough that he cannot calm it. There aren't waves high enough or waters rough enough that he cannot deliver you from. Trust in him the same way your child trusts you. Let him calm your frantic thoughts and bring you the haven you need. Your child knows that togetherness brings peace. The same is true for you. Togetherness with your Father is what your heart needs most.

Thank you, Father, that you are capable of calming my worst storms. Help me to turn to you for shelter, peace, and safety when everything around me feels chaotic. I trust you to bring stillness and peace. Thank you for being close to me when I need you. Help me to call on you when I am overwhelmed.

# DWELL ON GOODNESS

*Sing to him, sing praise to him;*
*tell of all his wonderful acts.*
1 CHRONICLES 16:9 NIV

If your heart is not focused on what God has done, you'll find yourself prone to focus on the negativity around you. As you dwell on his goodness, you'll be less swayed by discontentedness and frustration. Proclaiming his wonderful acts is both life giving and life sustaining. If you find yourself feeling anxious, annoyed, or discouraged, turn your eyes toward the Lord.

A good indication your perspective is off is when you are more focused on the actions of others than you are on the work of the Lord. Sing praises to him and he will be faithful to change your heart. Keeping your eyes steadily on him is what will give you the strength to walk through your days in a time when the world is full of conflict, strife, and brokenness. He is always moving. Even when all seems hopeless, God is still doing wonderful things.

I praise you, God! Your goodness is without measure and your love is never-ending. Teach me how to focus on you when everything around me feels negative. As I keep my eyes on you, I know I will be content no matter what I am lacking. Help me to see all the wonderful things you are doing.

# CARRYING BURDENS

*Carry each other's burdens,*
*and in this way you will fulfill the law of Christ.*
GALATIANS 6:2 NIV

Imagine a friend trying to carry a heavy box from their car to their house. They struggle to get a good grip on it but start to inch toward the door anyway. Once they get there, they don't have a free hand to open the door so they try to balance the box with one arm and they stumble through the door, dropping the box in the foyer. They're out of breath, frustrated that they may have broken what was inside, and there you are standing and watching. You could have easily jumped in and helped, but instead you sat and wondered why they were carrying the box, if they were strong enough to do it the right way, or if they did something to deserve toting a heavy package around.

Don't be the friend who analyzes a situation while it's unfolding before your eyes. Jump in, no questions asked, and offer help. Carry burdens for your friends. Lighten their load and earnestly walk beside them in their pain. Strong friendships require sacrifice. If you are without deep friendships that you long for, ask yourself when the last time was that you carried someone else's burden.

God, thank you for the reminder to carry each other's burdens. Show me ways that I can support those around me. I want to love others the way that you love me. Teach me how to be selfless in how I offer my time, money, and energy.

# FEAR OF THE LORD

*She is clothed with strength and dignity;*
*she can laugh at the days to come.*
PROVERBS 31:25 NIV

Read that Scripture again. Can you imagine being this woman? Can these words be used to describe who you are? Think about what clothes you. When do others see? You can be clothed in anxiety and stress or you can be clothed in strength and dignity because you know that the one who clothes you is a good father who cares for each of his children. You can laugh at the days to come because you know in the depths of your soul that you are held firmly by the Creator of the universe.

The Proverbs 31 woman laughs at what is to come because she has replaced a fear of the future with fear of the Lord. She does not fret what she cannot see because she knows that each of her days are seen clearly and are orchestrated by a God who is immensely powerful and loving. He's got it under control. You also can laugh at the days to come. You can refuse to be intimidated by what is out of your control.

Thank you, God, that you control my future. You see my days clearly. Teach me to depend on you so I might live in freedom. Where the world tells me to fret, help me to laugh at the days to come. I want to trust you. Help me to walk in strength and dignity because of who you are and how you've made me.

# HE BRINGS COMFORT

*"As a mother comforts her child,*
*so I will comfort you."*
ISAIAH 66:13 NIV

You comfort your child based on what they need. You assess situations and you know whether or not to provide a snack, a hug, a nap, a distraction, or laughter. You typically know the best way to help. In an even more thorough way, God comforts you out of a complete understanding of your needs. He is fully capable of helping you exactly how you need to be helped. He is the one who can decipher your thoughts and your heart.

You can go to him without needing to explain yourself or even ask for specific things. Even when you feel lost in grief, pain, or sorrow, there is no need for you to understand what you are muddling through before you go to God for comfort. Let him hold you close especially in times of discomfort and confusion. Let him minister to your spirit when you feel lost and unsure of what to do next. When your emotions overcome you and your path feels unclear, let him be the one to make sense of tangled or broken things. All you need to do is rest in his presence.

Thank you that you are the greatest comfort I could ever need, Father. You know my needs before I ask. In times when I don't know how to feel or behave, teach me how to come to you first, trusting that you see more thoroughly than I do.

# YOU ARE CHOSEN

*You are a chosen race, a royal priesthood, a holy nation, a people for his own possession, that you may proclaim the excellencies of him who called you out of darkness into his marvelous light.*

1 PETER 2:9 ESV

Has your child ever made the wrong choice and in a discussion about it you ask, "Do you understand what you did?" You want to help your child see the choice they've made. If they don't understand the situation, they won't be able to move forward. So, you gently walk them through it, helping them to understand why their actions were wrong and you teach them how to make it right.

You too, must understand who you are what you've done. You have been called out of darkness and into a marvelous light. If you don't know what you've been saved from, how can you proclaim the goodness of God to others? Knowing who you were, lost in your own sin, only strengthens your understanding of who you are now: chosen and dearly beloved. Let it be known deep in your heart that you have been rescued, redeemed, healed, and held. Let your somber understanding of who you were cause you to proclaim the excellencies of God. He has done incredible things!

Thank you, God, for who you've made me to be. Help me to always see who I was in relation to what you've done. May I always praise you for how you've called me from darkness to light. Help me to always see your works as wonderful.

# HE EMPOWERS

*I pray that from his glorious, unlimited resources*
*he will empower you with inner strength through his Spirit.*
EPHESIANS 3:16 NLT

No matter how much patience, courage, or devotion you try to muster up, you need God to strengthen you from the inside out. You can't train for a marathon by running the right number of miles and eating junk food all day. It doesn't matter what you do on the outside if the inside is weak. May God in his great mercy strengthen you from the inside out. May you be filled with the Spirit and walk as a new creation. May you find your strength in abiding and not in striving.

The more you struggle to make your life look a certain way, the more exasperated you will become. You need the power of God and his glorious unlimited resources to strengthen your heart. Only then will the fruit you bear be authentic and glorifying to him. You need his lovingkindness to move powerfully on the inside before his character can be displayed on the outside. Today, let go of the control you hold and stop your striving. Rest in God's presence and ask him to strengthen you.

Thank you, God, that I have access to your unlimited resources! Teach me to rely on you to strengthen me instead of fighting to make my life look a certain way. I need you to take control. I want to trust you with my life.

# STRONGER THAN MOUNTAINS

*"Though the mountains be shaken and the hills be removed,
yet my unfailing love for you will not be shaken nor my covenant
of peace be removed," says the Lord, who has compassion on you.*

ISAIAH 54:10 NIV

In your humanity it's difficult to understand the concept of forever or that something could be unfailing. There is nothing under the sun that can last forever. Even the mountains in their splendor and grandness can be shaken. The very landscape of the earth can be shifted and altered, but God's love for you won't ever end. Even a small glimpse of this can cause your heart to draw closer to him in thanksgiving and affection.

Think today about the ways you need to experience God's love. He has incredible compassion on you. He wants your heart to be whole, healthy, and at rest. There is never a time when you cannot access his unending love. His covenant of peace with you is eternal. Because of what Christ has done, you live under a binding contract that cannot be broken. It's never too late to find rest in the unfailing love of God. This is true about your life as a whole but also about your day in particular. It's never too late to turn to him in humble thanksgiving for his eternal love.

God, thank you for your unfailing love. It is unending and even though I can't understand it, it is stronger than mountains and always available to me. I am in awe of your compassion and peace!

# COMFORT IN MOURNING

*"Blessed are those who mourn,
for they shall be comforted."*

MATTHEW 5:4 ESV

Nobody expects to mourn. Grief isn't planned and we aren't taught how to do it well. For whatever reason you find yourself in a season of grieving, you might feel vastly unprepared to navigate it. God designed you to feel deeply and loss is no exception. Your heart is broken, and you might not know how to get through each day. For you, these waters are uncharted, scary, and potentially very lonely.

With whatever meager glance you have, you can look to God and trust that he will provide you with comfort. He will hold you close in your loss and be gentle and kind. No matter how overcome you feel, he will sustain you. His faithfulness to comfort the mourning is true for you and for those around you. He holds those who mourn gently. If you aren't in a difficult season, let the words of Jesus serve as a reminder of how to treat those who are mourning. Choose kindness, comfort, and quiet compassion over opinions, quick fixes, or judgments. Seek to be like Jesus, who sat with the broken for as long as needed.

Thank you, Jesus, that you comfort the mourning. You hold me close in my pain and grief. Help me to navigate seasons of grief and to provide quiet comfort when those around me grieving. Teach me to comfort as you do, laying your life down to provide peace and gentleness.

# TRUE REST

*In repentance and rest is your salvation,*
*in quietness and trust is your strength.*
ISAIAH 30:15 NIV

No amount of striving will make you better. No amount of checking things off a list will make you productive and successful. True strength and salvation are found in repentance, rest, quietness, and trust. Notice that these things require very little of you. God's expectation for you is to let him do the hard work. This means letting go of control and trusting his leading. When everything inside you tells you to try harder, do better, or work longer, God is telling you to rest and repent.

Say no to anxiety because true productivity is found in humble repentance. Even if you only have a moment today, deliberately take that moment and sit quietly before the Lord. Declare that you trust him. Declare your weakness and praise his strength. His presence is the one place that requires nothing of you. There is room at the table for you.

God, I am so tempted to just keep trying harder. The anxiety to do better is me putting my trust in my own ability. Forgive me for elevating my ability above yours. Teach me how to truly rest in your presence, letting go of my anxieties and letting you be in control.

# THE WAY

*"I am the gate. Those who come in through me will be saved. They will come and go freely and will find good pastures. The thief's purpose is to steal and kill and destroy. My purpose is to give them a rich and satisfying life."*

JOHN 10:9-10 NLT

Jesus is the gate into the presence of the Father. He is the one who has made a way for you to be free and to find good pasture. His death on the cross is the reason you have access. When you were separated from the perfection of God, Jesus died and was the propitiation for your sins. When you experience the freedom and satisfaction of the presence of God, remember that it is Christ's death that has made that possible. Jesus is the only one death bows to. His incredible sacrifice is what has brought you life everlasting. There is no way to be close to God other than through Jesus.

Today, let your heart rejoice in what has been done for you. Let it cause you to sit at the foot of the cross in humility and thanksgiving. Don't let the mundane tasks of motherhood numb your spirit to the miracle that you are privy to. No matter how normal your days are, may you consistently be in awe of what Jesus has done.

Thank you for your sacrifice, Jesus. I don't ever want to forget what you have done. You have made a way where there wasn't one. When I was lost in sin, you became the gate into the perfect presence of God. Help me to see you rightly and to draw closer to you in thanksgiving and humility.

# DO YOUR WORK WELL

*Whatever your hand finds to do,*
*do it with all your might.*
ECCLESIASTES 9:10 NIV

With each task that is set before you, you have the opportunity to do it with great care and love. There is no act of love that is too small to have an impact. As you put your hands to even the most mundane work, you can show your children that diligent love is what moves mountains. If you have a pile of laundry to put away, do it well. If you have a difficult conversation to have with a teenager, do it well. If you have a sleepless night ahead of you, do it well. Lean securely on the strength of the Lord and let him hold you as you pour yourself into each task.

Depend on God and let his love flow through in even the simplest ways. As you view your work as a means of glorifying him, you'll find that there will be less room for grumbling and frustration. Instead of viewing your day as an endless and wearisome task list, seek to view it as opportunity after opportunity to depend on a strength that is mightier than your own. Each shoelace you tie, each meal you make, each car ride is an opportunity to love well.

Father, help me to see my day as full of opportunities to trust in you. When I am burdened by my task list, help me to turn to you for strength. I want to do each little task with love. Help me to see big and small opportunities to bless my family. Turn my heart toward you and teach me how to do my job well.

# ADOPTED AND BELONGING

*All who are being led by the Spirit of God, these are sons of God.*
*For you have not received a spirit of slavery leading to fear again,*
*but you have received a spirit of adoption as sons by which we cry out,*
*"Abba! Father!"*

ROMANS 8:14-15 NASB

We have a broken picture of God. We know that he is good, we know that he is a kind father, but our own broken families and strained relationships paint a picture that is hard to see past. Today, sit in whatever measure of understanding you have and let yourself imagine for a moment that God's lovingkindness goes infinitely beyond anything you know now. Even if you have beautiful, whole relationships, God's love for you is still beyond anything you can fathom.

You have been adopted into his family and are safe and secure in his love. Understanding that aspect of his heart might come easily to you, or it might be incredibly painful. Let yourself sit in that place, whatever it is, and receive the kindness and acceptance that God longs to give you. You are his child and as you turn to him, he is delighted by you.

Thank you, Father, that you have called me your child. You have adopted me into your family. You are not far away or impersonal. You are the God who delights in his children. You are attentive and you have said that I belong. Teach me how to rest in your love and to marvel at how unfathomable it is.

# UNFATHOMABLE WORKS

*As you do not know the path of the wind,*
*or how the body is formed in a mother's womb,*
*so you cannot understand the work of God,*
*the Maker of all things.*

ECCLESIASTES 11:5 NIV

It might feel trite if you are struggling to find joy but take a look at your child and remember the miracle they are. They were formed by God in the womb. They were intricately and purposefully made. When the weight of motherhood feels heavy, it can be easy to forget how miraculous your children are. Each hair on their head, the intricacies of their heart, and their very life was perfectly made and is fully sustained by God. He is the maker of life and the one who upholds it every day.

Take a moment to stand in awe before God, the Maker of all things. Let yourself worship him for what he has done. If you are stumbling through your days or have been struggling to see God's hand in your life, open your eyes. What he has done is right in front of you. Your praise and recognition of his goodness can soften your heart.

God, your works are far beyond my understanding! You have made everything, and you sustain life. Help me to see my children as the work of your hand and to walk in consistent thanksgiving for all you have done. When I am overwhelmed by the weight of motherhood, let praise and thankfulness soften my heart.

# CALL ON HIM

*I call on you, my God, for you will answer me;*
*turn your ear to me and hear my prayer.*
*Show me the wonders of your great love.*
PSALM 17:6–7 NIV

God is always available to you. There isn't any situation in which you cannot call on him. He longs to lead you through your days. He longs to guide you with his gentle hand. You calling on him is an act of humility as you recognize that you need his help. Do you ever have days when you get tired of your kids calling out your name? You hear "Mom!" over and over, and eventually you'd rather hide in the pantry than answer one more time. In contrast, God never tires of you calling on him. In your own weariness, ask him for help. Let him renew your spirit as you face another day of mothering.

As you look to him, he'll reveal his character to you. He is gentle and kind and his love for you never ends. His resources are vast, and he gives you abundant grace when you ask for it. He is not bothered by your cries for help or exasperated by your constant need. He is a patient and kind father, always ready to help you.

Thank you, God, for your constant help! You never tire of me needing you. As I come to you with my needs, show me more of your character. As you pour grace upon me, open my eyes to the wonders of your great love.

# ETERNAL HOPE

*There is surely a future hope for you,*
*and your hope will not be cut off.*

PROVERBS 23:18 NIV

You cannot guarantee the circumstances of your future. You cannot be 100% sure that things will work out the way you want or the way you've planned. However, your hope in what God has done is guaranteed. You can be 100% sure that your hope will not be in vain or be disappointed. There will be a day when Jesus comes back and makes all things new. He will right wrongs, lift up the oppressed, and dry tears.

This is the hope that is assured for you. You are never promised ease of life or worldly success, but you are promised an eternal hope in the work of Christ. If you have placed your hope in anything else, you will be disappointed. Don't hang onto that which won't last: monetary gain or the plans of men. Instead, anchor yourself in what God has promised.

God, thank you for the eternal hope that you have given me. I can trust what you've promised. I know that if my hope is in Jesus, it will not be disappointed. You will make the wrong things right and I want to wait in eager anticipation for that day. I praise you for what you have done and what you have promised to do.

# NO CONDEMNATION

*There is therefore now no condemnation*
*for those who are in Christ Jesus.*
ROMANS 8:1 ESV

You are fully covered by the blood of Jesus. His work on the cross is sufficient for covering your sins. There is no condemnation for you because it's been carried by Jesus unto death. He defeated death so you wouldn't have to. He sacrificed his life so you wouldn't have to. He carried your burdens, your shame, and your trespasses on the cross. When he rose to life again, so did you.

Today, take inventory of your heart. Think about areas of your life where you are hanging on to sin or shame. Lay those things at the cross and let yourself wake up in the freedom that Christ bought for you. There is no reason for you to live as though you are bound to sin. Lay down your heaviest burdens and let he who gave his Son to free you hold you in his love. Now, because of what Jesus did, God's abundant mercy is available to you. He cast judgment upon Christ so you could be lavished with mercy.

Thank you, Jesus, for the freedom that I have in you! Because you defeated death when you rose again, help me to walk in freedom and not shame. Help me to depend upon what you did on the cross instead of walking in my own condemnation. You are the true and perfect judge and you do not condemn me. Help me to see your perspective when it comes my sin.

# AUGUST

God gave us a spirit not of fear
but of power and love and self-control.

2 TIMOTHY 1:7 ESV

# FULLY KNOWN

*My frame was not hidden from you
when I was made in the secret place,
when I was woven together in the depths of the earth.
Your eyes saw my unformed body;
all the days ordained for me were written in your book
before one of them came to be.*

PSALM 139:15-16 NIV

When life feels like it's just too much, you can rest in the fact that all your days are numbered and known. Your loving Father knows everything about you. He is the one who weaved you together, bit by bit, with great care and infinite wisdom. Breathe deep, close your eyes, and remember that you can move freely through your days because you are not the one who ordained them. You are not the one who orchestrates or sustains your life.

Let the understanding that you were created and are held by a great God cause your heart to be light and your steps to be confident. He is the one who made you and who guides you. As his child, lovingly and fully known, you can trust him to help you navigate each season you encounter. He has known about each one since before they happened. He has prepared you in ways you'll never understand, and he has held you securely even when you were unaware.

Thank you, God, that you are the one who made me and who orchestrates my days. May my understanding of your sovereignty cause me to rest in you and to trust you more fully. As I relinquish control to you, teach me to praise you and walk confidently through each season. You are the one who knows all my days, so I trust you, knowing that you are holding me and equipping me for each one.

# ASK FOR WISDOM

*If any of you lacks wisdom, you should ask God,*
*who gives generously to all without finding fault,*
*and it will be given to you.*

JAMES 1:5 NIV

There are a multitude of things in life that you probably don't understand. The way people behave, the path you've ended up on, the trials you face—all of these can easily leave you with more questions than answers. The ability to ask for wisdom in the midst of uncertainty can be like an anchor in a storm. God promises that he will give wisdom generously. He does not lie, so you know if you seek wisdom, you will be given it.

Gaining wisdom doesn't necessarily mean that you'll be given direct answers to your questions. Instead, it can alter your perspective and help you see your situation the way God does. Godly wisdom will strengthen your resolve and help produce steadfastness over frustration and impatience. Today, if you have a situation that needs attention, ask God for wisdom. Entrust the details to him and believe that he is capable of changing your perspective if need be. Ask him for strength and perseverance while you wait for answers or resolution.

Thank you, God, that you give wisdom to those who ask for it! Please, give me wisdom as I walk through this situation. Help me trust in you. I want to have perseverance over impatience. I want to have a quiet heart instead of one that feels frantic when things are uncertain. Help me to turn to you for help.

# CONTROLLED BY WHAT

*If people's thinking is controlled by the sinful self, there is death.*
*But if their thinking is controlled by the Spirit, there is life and peace.*
ROMANS 8:6 NCV

There are many instances in which you tell your child to trust you simply because you know better. As you lovingly parent them, they learn that you are worth trusting because your age generates a perspective they just don't have. Their perspective is limited while yours has more experience, knowledge, and understanding. When you live trusting in the Spirit, you will have peace. Trusting in yourself leads to death because your humanity limits you. You simply cannot compare your perspective to that of the Lord's.

Leaning on the Spirit is an act of trust that says that his thoughts are higher than your own. His ways are greater than yours and his understanding is infinitely deeper. Just like you expect your child to trust you in your experience and wisdom, so you should depend upon the Spirit. Today, ask the Lord to show you areas where your thinking is controlled by yourself rather than the Spirit. As he reveals those areas, seek to humbly repent and move forward in surrender. It's worth it for the peace that you will find.

Holy Spirit, thank you that I can lean on you for life and peace. I know that your ways are higher than mine and I trust you to teach me how to think. I don't want to think so highly of myself that I don't acknowledge your greatness. Help me to see where I can further depend on you.

# UNDESERVED GRACE

*The grace of God has appeared that offers salvation to all people.*
*It teaches us to say "No" to ungodliness and worldly passions,*
*and to live self-controlled, upright and Godly lives in this present age.*
TITUS 2:11-12 NIV

It would be completely just for God to leave you on your own to navigate life. Afterall, he has already given you redemption through Christ's work on the cross. You didn't deserve the grace you were given, and you don't deserve the grace that he lavishes on you as you walk through your days. He has generously given you the Holy Spirit to help you. If you ever feel overwhelmed by following Jesus, remember that you have been lovingly given a helper.

Just like you cannot earn your salvation, you also have not earned the gift you've been given in God's grace. He lovingly teaches you to say no to things he knows will not benefit you. He teaches you how to have fortitude and to refuse things that will harm you in the long run. You can trust that your Father knows what is best. Today, thank him for his guidance and the grace he has given you freely.

Father, thank you for your grace! Help me to see your direction as a kind act of mercy. You could have left me on my own but instead you teach me how to live because you love me and you know what's best for me. Help me to see your grace as a gift.

# ALWAYS WITH YOU

*"When you pass through the waters,*
*I will be with you;*
*and when you pass through the rivers,*
*they will not sweep over you.*
*When you walk through the fire,*
*you will not be burned;*
*the flames will not set you ablaze."*

ISAIAH 43:2 NIV

Have you ever walked through something difficult and felt the sting that comes from a friend or loved one who isn't faithful to remain by your side? Sometimes life's circumstances reveal the perseverance of those around you. You navigate unexpected and painful things and not everyone around you will understand how or be willing to walk with you through them. God promises you consistent help. He promises that he goes before you and after you.

There is no trial that you could face during which God would decide to leave you on your own. He promises you that he will remain near you no matter what. Not only will he remain close to you, but he will protect and keep you safe. He is reliable and faithful to walk with you. Today, let his nearness bring you comfort. Where you have felt left alone or forgotten, he has never left. Let him bring healing to those areas of your heart with his presence.

Thank you, God, that you never leave me. You are always near. You cannot be scared away or intimidated by my circumstances. Where I feel like I have been alone or forgotten, show me how you have been present. You are mighty enough to walk with me intimately! Today help me to see your nearness as I walk through my day.

# THE STAR COUNTER

*He determines the number of the stars;*
*he calls them each by name.*

PSALM 147:4 NASB

The God you serve is not some far-off creator who has left his creation to manage on its own. He has gone so far as to name the stars in all of their multitudes. If he puts that much effort into that which cannot love him back, imagine the care and great affection he has for you his beloved daughter.

You are infinitely more valuable to him than the stars. You are his likeness, his masterpiece, the crescendo of creation. You are his delight. The way he cares for you is intricate. If he knows the name of every single star, imagine how he knows each part of you. He knows the corners you think you're hiding and the parts of your heart you have never shared. He sees all of you and he loves you as a dear child. Today, let your heart be drawn to him as you think about how a poetically beautiful, infinitely powerful God loves you fully.

Father, you are great and beautiful! Your majesty is infinite and yet you are close to me. You have made me your child. You know me fully and you love me well. Help me to walk in awe of who you are today.

# GUARD YOUR HEART

*Above all else, guard your heart,*
*for everything you do flows from it.*
PROVERBS 4:23 NIV

A lot of people don't correlate their small habits with the daily attitude of their heart. As a mother, you can see how certain habits impact your child's behavior. If they spend too much time in front of a screen, they might be anxious or overly energetic. If they eat a lot of sugar, they might be fidgety or hyperactive. When they play with certain friends you might notice a change in behavior or a tendency to pick up certain mannerisms. You can observe those things in your children but are you mindful of them in your own life?

If you are constantly anxious, tired, or short-tempered, take a moment to think about what you are consuming and surrounding yourself with. Maybe you need to readjust the media you absorb on a daily basis. Maybe you need to deliberately soak up the sun when you can or surround yourself with friends who encourage you and point you to Jesus. Guard your heart, treat it with kindness, being aware of protecting it and keeping it healthy.

Teach me how to guard my heart, Lord. Show me areas where I have fallen into unhealthy habits that have affected my daily life. Teach me how to protect my heart. I commit my day to you. May everything I consume honor you.

# ROOTED IN LOVE

*Christ will make his home in your hearts as you trust in him. Your roots will grow down into God's love and keep you strong. And may you have the power to understand, as all God's people should, how wide, how long, how high, and how deep his love is. May you experience the love of Christ, though it is too great to understand fully.*

EPHESIANS 3:17-19 NLT

A strong tree has deep roots. Picture a towering maple or a craggy oak. Their root systems are more extensive than the limbs and foliage you see on the surface. Those roots keep it steady in the midst of storms and they find water to keep the tree alive. Right now, as you spend this time seeking God, know that your roots are growing deeper.

As you reach your hands toward the Lord in worship and thanksgiving, just a tree reaches its limbs to the sun, your roots are digging deeper to keep you steady. As you focus your mind on him and on his Word, you will become stronger no matter the storms. As you actively trust him today, with the big or small, you will become cemented in his love. Then, as your roots go down deep, sustaining you and keeping you steady, you'll begin to understand just how vast, and lifegiving, and unimaginable his love is.

Thank you for your love, God. As I spend time with you, I am being strengthened. When storms come, your love will sustain me. Teach me how to grow my roots deep into your love. I want to experience more of your love. Make your home in my heart. Teach me how to make space in my heart for you.

# KEPT FROM SLIPPING

*When I said, "My foot is slipping,"*
*your unfailing love, Lord, supported me.*
PSALM 94:18 NIV

In the same way you support and guide your children, helping them navigate difficult situations, the Lord guides and supports you. He goes before you and he goes after you. He upholds you when your footing is rocky, and he carries you when the path seems impassable. His love is strong enough for you always. He keeps you from falling and he gives you the help that you need. He sees you with eyes of mercy because you are his beloved child.

God made a way for you to be with him forever through Jesus. His love knows no bounds. His love for his creation is extensive, sufficient, and beyond any limit that death, sorrow, or darkness might create. Today, walk steadily in that love. When you feel yourself wavering, turn your attention outward and ask for help. Instead of turning inward and feeling shame for your shortcomings, let God be the one you depend on. He already knows where you are weak, and he does not condemn you for it. Let his love support you.

Thank you, God, that you always support me! I will not fall so long as I lean on you. Teach me how to depend on you in a deeper way today. Help me not to focus on my weakness but to dwell on your strength and unfailing love.

# PLANS PROSPER

*Many are the plans in the mind of a man,*
*but it is the purpose of the LORD that will stand.*
PROVERBS 19:21 ESV

Have you ever tried to do something fun with your kids and it just doesn't work out? It doesn't matter how well you plan; you can't control their reactions, moods, or perspective. You can put as much energy, money, and time into the day but there are things that are just beyond your ability to predict. Your best laid plans won't always succeed. This is true when it comes to parenting and also in regard to the rest of your life. You can plan all you want, but the purpose of the Lord will stand.

Instead of being constantly overwhelmed when things don't work out, you can practice the discipline of holding things loosely and humbly following the Lord. When something you planned doesn't work out, you can maintain a quiet heart and keep your eyes steady. While your human plans might not succeed, God's way always will.

Thank you, Lord, that even my best plans don't compare to what you have planned for me. Teach me how to hold my plans loosely so I can elevate your plans above my own. Teach me how to stay steady and confident in you when things don't work out. By your grace, help me to be flexible when it comes to things I cannot control.

# SIT WITH THE BROKEN

*Then they sat on the ground with him*
*for seven days and seven nights.*
*No one said a word to him,*
*because they saw how great his suffering was.*
JOB 2:13 NIV

One of the greatest things you can learn from reading about Job is how to deal with the hurting. From his friend's behavior, you can learn the value of presence over solution. Job was in such pain that his friends knew words wouldn't help. They met him where he was and remained there. Think about some of your darkest moments. The knowledge that someone is willing to be with you in your grief can be life changing.

Think about the people in your life that you know are hurting. Maybe you feel intimidated by their situation or like you are inadequate to help them. Letting them know that you are close by is probably more valuable than saying just the right thing. Keeping someone company in their pain can make a way for encouragement and comfort when it's able to be received.

Thank you, God, for the example of grief that I see in the book of Job. Teach me how to love this way, to be a person who sits with others in their suffering. Teach me how to value presence over solutions. Give me the perseverance to be the kind of friend who doesn't leave when things are difficult.

# PROTECTION

*The LORD is gracious and righteous;*
*our God is full of compassion.*
*The LORD protects the unwary;*
*when I was brought low, he saved me.*

PSALM 116:5-6 NIV

No one will ever care for you like God does. He delights in showering you with tender compassion. He protects you even when you are unwary. When you are not cautious, when you aren't aware of danger or harm, his care for you is steady and unwavering. His care for you is all knowing, all-encompassing, and full of wisdom. He cares for you out of an infinite storehouse of knowledge about your life.

No matter where you find yourself today—calmly walking through your day, struggling to keep your head above water, lost in discouragement, or joyful and triumphant—God's love for you is constant and his eyes are on you. His compassion for you goes beyond human understanding. His ability to care for you and guide your steps goes beyond how you feel or what your current circumstances are. When you are low, he is faithful to meet you where you are and lift you up.

Thank you, God, for your unending compassion. You care for me all of the time even when I am unwary. Teach me how to see the ways that you've cared for me. Thank you for your gracious leading and for saving me when I am low.

# A SAFE PLACE

*The name of the Lord is a fortified tower;*
*the righteous run to it and are safe.*
PROVERBS 18:10 NIV

Where you turn in times of distress tells you where your trust lies. Do you find yourself searching for comfort in media, friends, food, or money? If you've ever run to those things in times of need, then you know that the comfort they provide isn't long lasting. Soon enough you'll find yourself wanting and feeling like you still haven't found that safe haven your soul longs for. Instead of chasing after that which won't satisfy, remember that you serve a God whose name is a fortified tower. You can find true safety in the shelter that he provides. Those who take refuge in him will not be shaken or overcome.

Today, let the Lord reveal areas of your life where you have sought safety in things other than him. As he reveals those areas, humbly repent and run to him. Deliberately seek shelter and safety in his arms when you are overwhelmed. You are his child and he longs to protect you.

Thank you, God, that your name is a fortified tower. I can run to you in my distress and trust you to keep me safe. Help me to depend on you and not on other things for comfort when I am overwhelmed. Teach me how to seek you first. As I turn to you in my distress, may my children learn that you are a safe place to run to.

# ALWAYS FAITHFUL

*If we are faithless, he remains faithful,*
*for he cannot disown himself.*
2 TIMOTHY 2:13 NIV

One of the greatest lies you can believe is that your unfaithfulness disqualifies you from a life of freedom in Christ, fully loved and redeemed. His ability to redeem you and to be faithful to you has never had anything to do with your own merit. You have been saved only by grace. This is true whether you have sought to serve the Lord for a week or a lifetime. His grace is and always will be sufficient for you.

There will never be a time when God's faithfulness is dependent upon you. You have been saved by grace and so you will walk by grace. You will never reach a point in your life when your salvation is dependent upon anything other than the grace of God. He will always be faithful because it's who he is. He cannot go against his character or change his ways. He is the same yesterday, today, and always. Today, you can trust in his redemption and find freedom in the great gift that you've been given.

Thank you for your faithfulness, God. I know that there is nothing I can do that will change how you see me or how you respond to me. You are faithful because it's who you are. Teach me to be confident in your faithfulness.

# LOVE YOUR ENEMIES

*"I say, love your enemies!*
*Pray for those who persecute you!"*
MATTHEW 5:44 NLT

The kingdom of God is often contradictory to the world. The last is first and the first is last. When you are weak you are strong, and in losing your life you will gain it. God says to love your enemies. This might feel unnatural. In this command to pray for those who hate you, God is mindful of both your heart and the hearts of those against you. He knows that hate is like a poison. He knows if you carry around animosity, it will eat away at you, causing bitterness to grow a deep root in your heart. His call to love your enemies is not an indictment and it is not done with a lack of awareness. He asks because he knows what is truly best for your heart.

Not only will those against you get a glimpse of the love of God and experience his character, but you will become more like Jesus as you walk in humble submission, full of love. The Holy Spirit is quick to come to your aid when you ask. Today, ask him to reveal areas where you are not loving your enemies. God is faithful to turn our hearts in love when we ask humbly.

Thank you, God, that you ask me to love my enemies both for their sake and also for mine. You see what is best for me and you help me where I am weak. You know that it isn't easy to love my enemies, but I commit this area to you, and I know that you will equip me with what I need. Soften my heart and help me to love like you do.

# GODLY EXAMPLES

*Teach the young women to love their husbands, to love their children,*
*to be wise and pure, to be good workers at home, to be kind.*
TITUS 2:4-5 NCV

If you are a young mom, you have a great resource in women who have already raised their children. Don't look to the world for how to live. Look to older, wiser, godly women who have already experienced the trials you are facing. They have made it through the sleepless nights, the screaming toddlers, and the newfound independence of the teenager. Ask the Lord to direct your attention toward such a woman who can fight alongside you through the trenches of motherhood. As you seek wisdom, he will be faithful to provide it.

Being loving, wise, pure, kind, and a good worker are not skills that you are expected to have immediately upon becoming a mother. They can be cultivated and taught. If you find yourself lacking in an area, don't respond with shame or embarrassment, seek out a godly example who can help you to learn. If you are a mom who has older children, ask the Lord to direct your attention to a young mom who needs encouragement and direction. You have much more to offer than you probably think.

Thank you, God, for the example that you've given in Titus. Teach me to turn to those wiser than me for help. Bring to mind someone who can encourage me or whom I can encourage. Help me to seek wisdom when I am unsure of what to do. In my shortcomings as a mom, help me ask for help instead of sitting in shame.

# WEARY REFRESHED

*I will refresh the weary and satisfy the faint.*
JEREMIAH 31:25 NIV

As a mother you know what it's like to feel desperate for rest. You're not a stranger to exhaustion and you're not unfamiliar with what it's like to navigate your days with a foggy brain and weary limbs. As you depend upon the Lord for true rest, realize that in your weariness you have the opportunity to teach your children about the value of rest.

In a culture that values productivity, it is revolutionary to value rest and stillness. Needing to quiet your heart in the middle of the chaos that motherhood can bring is not a weakness. It is an opportunity to depend on the Lord for strength and show your children that Christ is worthy of your trust. He is the only one who can satisfy your weariness. As you practice the discipline of resting in him, your children will see that strength is found in slowing down not striving.

Thank you, God, that you are the one who refreshes me and satisfies me. Teach me how to depend upon you for true rest even when I am exhausted. When I am tired, you are the one I can turn to. May my children see the way you bring rest to my soul.

# GOD HEALS

*He heals the brokenhearted*
*and binds up their wounds.*
PSALM 147:3 NIV

As a mother, you've seen your fair share of wounds. You've placed Band-Aids, made emergency room visits, and done your best to keep your children physically safe. You also know that some wounds you cannot heal. Some wounds are deeper and much harder to access let alone fix. God is the healer of those wounds. He is fully capable of healing your body, yes, but he also binds up your broken heart. That is something no human can do.

God doesn't just fix what is visibly broken. He brings full healing from the inside out. He holds you gently and mends what seems to be beyond repair. You can trust him with your most sensitive wounds. He knows what he is doing. He won't make the wrong diagnosis or put you through unnecessary procedures. He knows exactly how to attend to your hurts. Today, if there are parts of your heart that you've been hiding, afraid of what might happen if you expose them, let God in his gentleness and power hold you close.

God, I know that you are fully capable of healing me. You say that you can bind up wounds and I trust that your words are true. Help me to trust you where I've been trying to protect myself. I want to put my faith in your healing hands. Please hold me close in this area where I am hurting.

# REJOICE OVER TODAY

*This is the day the LORD has made;*
*We will rejoice and be glad in it.*
PSALM 118:24 NKJV

This specific day has been designed by the Creator of the universe. This specific day and everything in it have been ordained and seen by God. He sees you in your waking and in your sleeping. He knows what will happen and how the day will play out. He has made the sun to rise and the world to be illuminated one more time.

As you settle into your day, no matter the time, take a moment and rejoice in who God is. Praise him for sustaining you. Praise him for all he has created and all he has done. He crafted this day, and as you look for him in it, you are trusting him further and deepening your dependence on him. Today, as you recognize him as Creator, you're acknowledging that he is the one in charge of your days.

Thank you, God, that you are my glorious Creator. I can look to you and praise you for all you have done. Today, help me to elevate your name above my own. Give me an attitude of thanksgiving. Help me to rejoice in this day you have given me.

# GOD GIVES REST

*My soul, find rest in God;*
*my hope comes from him.*
PSALM 62:5 ESV

You may have never experienced a tiredness quite like what motherhood has brought to your life. God knows that you are tired. He knows that you are weary and that your eyes are heavy. He has made you that way: to need sleep and rest. Your tiredness displays need that can only be met by resting in who God is. Maybe you are desperate for a break or maybe you struggle to practice rest.

True rest comes only from God and requires reliance on him. This means that you need to give up control and let your heaviness fade away as you sink into truth. Let him hold you close, give you hope, and speak to you of your value to him. You have access to this rest because of what Christ did on the cross. His sacrifice means that you can approach God as a father. He is the Father who will carry your burdens and bring restoration where it is needed.

I am tired, Lord. Teach me how to truly rest. Help me to lean on you and rely on who you are. As I quiet my heart in your presence, give me hope and restore my soul. I can be near you because of your work on the cross. Teach me how to rely on you for true restoration.

# VICTORY THROUGH CHRIST

*Thanks be to God!*
*He gives us the victory*
*through our Lord Jesus Christ.*
1 CORINTHIANS 15:57 NIV

We all have things in our lives that feel impossible. Maybe you have an incredible financial need or a relationship that seems beyond repair. Maybe you have experienced trauma and can't imagine what healing would even look like. Where you don't see solutions, God is capable of making a way. Where you see impossibilities, he is able. If Jesus can defeat death, then he can conquer the armies that you face.

Continually turning to him and surrendering your most impossible struggles is a means of walking in faith. As you trust in him to do the things that you cannot, you'll find yourself drawn closer to him as you allow him to carry your burdens. He has defeated death for you, so in your weakness you can allow his strength to be magnified.

Thank you, God, for defeating death on my behalf. Help me to depend on you for the impossible things in my life. Instead of being intimidated by solutions I cannot see, I want to trust in you. Help me to cast my cares upon you and trust in your power.

# BLESSED TO BE WEAK

*I am happy when I have weaknesses, insults,*
*hard times, sufferings, and all kinds of troubles for Christ.*
*Because when I am weak, then I am truly strong.*
2 CORINTHIANS 12:10 NCV

Nothing reveals weakness quite like motherhood. When you are teetering on your last nerve, someone will ask for a glass of water for the millionth time. When you are rushed and desperate to get to that appointment on time, someone will have a bathroom emergency. When you are tired and overwhelmed, there will always be more asked of you. Motherhood reveals weakness exceptionally well. When you are laid bare, remember that God's grace is enough for you. In fact, where you lack, his power can be perfected. You are blessed to be weak.

As weakness is revealed in your life, you have greater opportunity to depend on the power of Christ. How you respond to your shortcomings says more about you than the shortcomings themselves. Turn to Christ; let him be exalted. Let your life be a collection of moments where you leaned fully on Jesus. Let your days be defined by the fortitude that comes from consistently saying, "I can't do it Lord, but I trust your strength!"

Thank you, Lord, that your strength is enough for me. Where I am weak, your power can be exalted. Teach me to turn to you when I am discouraged and to view my weakness as opportunities for your power to be displayed.

# GOD OF RENEWAL

*Create in me a pure heart, O God,*
*and renew a steadfast spirit within me.*
PSALM 51:10 NIV

Let this simple prayer be the cry of your heart today. Let go of whatever happened yesterday or this morning and ask God for renewal. He is capable of doing that for you. He is the God of second chances and do-overs. You will never run out of opportunities to ask him to purify your heart or renew your spirit. He knows that you are prone to wander, and he isn't intimidated by that. He isn't frustrated that you need a do-over again.

As you continuously run to him, instead of focusing on your continual need or failure, focus on his grace and faithfulness. Let him teach you how to be steadfast, so your hope remains in him no matter how many times you need to start again. In your moments with him today, you have the opportunity to be still and find the newness that you need.

Thank you, God, that you never turn me away. No matter how many times I need to ask for the same things, you always help me. Renew my spirit today, Lord. I need your restoration and I need your mercy. You give it freely and abundantly!

# AT THE CORE

*She speaks wise words*
*and teaches others to be kind.*
*She watches over her family*
*and never wastes her time.*
*Her children speak well of her.*

PROVERBS 31:26-28 NCV

When you read the description of the Proverbs 31 woman it can be tempting to feel intimidated, like you don't measure up. She is noble and virtuous. She is honored by those around her, and she seems to be the epitome of godly character. A beautiful picture is painted, and it might seem impossible to attain. When you compare her life to yours, there are likely vast discrepancies. Remember that at the core of this woman's life is the fear of the Lord. Each of her admirable traits flow out of a wellspring of understanding who God is.

Today, where you feel inadequate, turn to God. Let your life be a reflection of who he is instead of a comparison of what you think it should be. Trust in your Creator's leading and shaping of your life. He will be faithful to complete the good work in you that he began when you started following him.

Thank you, God, for the example of the Proverbs 31 woman. Thank you for the inspiring picture of someone who fears you and follows you well. Teach me to fear you, that every aspect of my life would flow out of my security in you. Lead me where I am lacking.

# PROCLAIM HIS GOODNESS

*I have not kept the good news of your justice hidden in my heart;*
*I have talked about your faithfulness and saving power.*
*I have told everyone in the great assembly*
*of your unfailing love and faithfulness.*

PSALM 40:10 NLT

If you feel like your relationship with God has hit a wall, talk to someone about his faithfulness and saving power. Speak about the things that he has done in your life. Praise him, to others, like you would brag about a friend or your child's accomplishments. Let the everyday language in your home be defined by consistent praise and talking about what God has done. The more you proclaim his character and his goodness, the more you will see it.

As you crown him Lord with your words, your lens will begin to change. You'll see his goodness in a million small ways that you didn't before. Praise opens your eyes to his presence and reveals his hand in your life in intricate ways. Praise softens the hard places of your heart and makes room for peace. Today, say out loud the ways God has moved in your life. Talk with your kids about his character and tell a friend about something he has done.

God, I know that thanksgiving draws me closer to you. Where I am weary or stuck, help me to praise you. You have done great things and you are always moving. I want to see the work of your hands. Open my eyes to what you are doing and help me to talk to those around me about you.

# EMPOWERED TO FORGIVE

*Be kind to one another, tenderhearted, forgiving one another,*
*as God in Christ forgave you.*
EPHESIANS 4:32 ESV

Tenderhearted forgiveness is not the same as moving on, hardening your heart, and doing your best to forget the issue. We are asked to forgive each other in the same manner that God has forgiven us. He doesn't hold our sins against us, remind us of them, or treat us differently because of what we've done. He sees us in a completely different manner. When you seek his forgiveness, the transgressions cease to exist. He casts them away, as far as the east is to the west. This is how you are being asked to forgive others, with a soft heart and a fresh perspective. It's not easy work. In fact, it's impossible. This is why you cannot do it on your own.

In order to truly forgive others, you must operate with the power of the Holy Spirit. He is the one with the ability to change hearts and bring healing to impossible situations. Today, if you have a situation that you have deemed unfixable, humbly ask the Lord to lead you in forgiveness. He is faithful to hold you close, bring healing, and give you wisdom about how to handle it.

God, teach me how to be tenderhearted to those around me. Because Christ has forgiven me, I can forgive others. Show me areas where I have not walked in true forgiveness and help me to honor you. You see the hurts I've experienced, and you promise you are near me when I'm brokenhearted.

# ALL THINGS NEW

*He has made everything beautiful in its time. He has also set eternity in the human heart; yet no one can fathom what God has done from beginning to end. I know that there is nothing better for people than to be happy and to do good while they live.*

ECCLESIASTES 3:11-12 NIV

Each time you experience pain, stress, brokenness, or difficulty, let it remind you that things are not the way they are supposed to be. God has set eternity in the human heart, so you live with a longing for perfection that can only be met in God. One day, he will make all things new. One day, you'll walk with him in the cool of the day just like Adam and Eve did in Eden. As you wait for that day, as you walk through the broken world, let your anticipation give you hope and draw you closer to your Father. He has promised to make everything beautiful in its time, so you can trust all he is doing even when you don't understand it.

Today, in your quiet moments with him, think about the perfection and eternity with him that you were designed for. It's okay to recognize that things are not as they are supposed to be. Instead of letting that disparity burden you, let it cause you to wait expectantly and joyfully because what God has planned is worth waiting for.

Jesus, I was not made for brokenness. I was made for an eternity with you. Help me to look toward your coming with expectancy and joy. You've promised to make everything beautiful and I trust that you will. May my hope be securely in what you have done even when I don't understand it.

# FORGOTTEN SINS

*"I—yes, I alone—will blot out your sins for my own sake and will never think of them again."*

ISAIAH 43:25 NLT

God's ability to forget our sins is not something that we can easily wrap our minds around. In our humanity, we don't naturally possess the ability to forgive or forget. When you confess your sins to God, he blots them out. He wipes them from existence. He never thinks about them again. This is mind blowing and incredibly freeing. No matter how often you think about that transgression, God never does. He sees you as though it never happened. Can you imagine that kind of mercy?

Think about a time when someone sinned against you. Whether your pain was great or not, you know how difficult it is to look at that person with fresh eyes after a transgression has occurred. Today, let God's ability to wipe away your sins cause you to draw closer to him in affection and thanksgiving. Praise him for the personal and kind God that he is and let his forgiveness draw you to him in awe and wonder.

God, I don't understand how you blot out my sins! Thank you for your forgiveness and that you never again think of my sins. Teach me how to walk in forgiveness and not condemnation. Your mercy is incredible!

# QUIET FEARS

*When I am afraid,*
*I will put my trust in you.*
*I praise God for what he has promised.*
*I trust in God, so why should I be afraid?*
PSALM 56:3-4 NLT

Fear can be so deceptive. It can not only rule the obvious or big moments, but it can also quietly rule your thoughts and the everyday parts of your life. You might not be afraid of heights, an obvious enemy, the dark, or getting into a car accident but you might still be walking in fear. Your anxiety might be quiet, "Am I enough?" "How will we pay our bills?" "Is my child smart enough?" "What if no one wants to be my friend?" Your fears don't have to be big or obvious to rule your life. You aren't limited to trusting in God for the obvious. He wants to deliver you from your quiet fears as well.

In those moments you can't let go of a persistent thought that is based in fear, he wants you to trust him. Even in those seemingly normal or small doubts, he wants you to praise him and let him handle the fear. His desire is for you to walk in freedom and praise, knowing who your Father is. There is no fear too small that he doesn't want you to be free from it. Today, let him search your heart and show you where you can trust him even more than you have.

Thank you, God, that I can turn to you with my big fears and with my seemingly small anxieties. I don't want to be ruled by anxiety, so help me to praise you and put my trust in you. Teach me how to ask you for help rather than sit in worry.

# SOLUTION FOR ANXIETY

*Don't worry about anything; instead, pray about everything. Tell God what you need, and thank him for all he has done. Then you will experience God's peace, which exceeds anything we can understand. His peace will guard your hearts and minds as you live in Christ Jesus.*

PHILIPPIANS 4:6-7 NLT

The solution for anxiety is not to gain confidence in yourself or your circumstances. It is to know the one who displaces anxiety with peace, fully and completely. God doesn't tell you not to worry because you are capable of handling it. He tells you not to be anxious because he can handle it. As you go to him in confidence of who he is and thanking him for what he has done, you will gain a contentedness that could never be found through your own attempts.

The peace that God offers to you goes beyond human understanding. He is the one who calms storms and quiets the seas. If the wild winds will submit to him, then he is mighty enough to calm your heart. As you turn to him instead of choosing to worry, you will find that his ability to meet your needs far surpasses anything you can imagine.

Teach me, Lord, how to choose prayer over worry. Where I am prone to anxiety, remind me of who you are and how you care for me. Forgive me for being anxious and forgetting that I can turn to you. Thank you for the peace that you give when I submit my needs to you.

# SLOW TO ANGER

*Everyone should be quick to listen,*
*slow to speak and slow to become angry,*
*because human anger does not produce*
*the righteousness that God desires.*

JAMES 1:19–20 NIV

In the reminder to be quick to listen and slow to anger, remember that your Father is also quick to listen and slow to anger. As you seek to be a reflection of him, let it spring forth from a deep well of love and acceptance. You can be slow to anger because your Father, who created you in his image, is slow to anger, and he equips his children to be like him. Your Father is good and kind; he is the best listener.

Take your burdens to God today; let him hear you as you deliberately talk to him about all that is on your heart. No one will ever care for you like he does. As you experience his gentle care and faithful patience, mother out of that love. As you begin to more fully understand God's character and his delight in caring for you, mother out of that deep sense of belonging. You are heard, known, accepted, and loved.

God, thank you that you hear me. You are quick to listen and slow to anger. Your goodness and kindness draw me closer to you. As I learn more about my belonging in you, may my mothering reflect your kindness. Teach me how to be quick to listen. May the Holy Spirit convict me where I am not honoring you and may I humbly change the way I act in order to reflect you more fully.

# SEPTEMBER

All Scripture is inspired by God and
profitable for teaching, for reproof, for
correction, for training in righteousness.

2 Timothy 3:16 NASB

# ABOUT TOMORROW

*"Don't worry about tomorrow,*
*because tomorrow will have its own worries.*
*Each day has enough trouble of its own."*
MATTHEW 6:34 NCV

Motherhood gives you plenty of opportunities to worry about tomorrow. As you are nurturing your children, of course you are considering their future and what is to come. Don't let those thoughts overtake you. Focus instead on what is right in front of you. Do the next right thing. Sew faithfully today. Ask the Holy Spirit to give you wisdom in what to prioritize and then confidently pursue those things.

Tomorrow your priorities might be different and that's okay. When tomorrow comes, you will be given the grace to confront whatever it might bring. Getting lost in the worries of tomorrow will cause you to sacrifice the joy that you might experience today. As you spend time with the Lord, ask him to give you eyes for what is in front of you. Ask for wisdom to know what needs your full attention today and what can wait until tomorrow. Trust him with the details that you cannot control.

Thank you, God, that you know how much my spirit can carry. You know that worry about tomorrow will wear me thin and won't add to my life. Teach me how to focus on what's in front of me. When I am anxious beyond today, help me to surrender those things to you. I want to trust you more today than I did yesterday.

# A TRUE FRIEND

*A friend loves at all times,
and a brother is born for adversity.*
PROVERBS 17:17 NIV

A true friend loves at all times. This is quite the challenge. When you disagree, when you're tired, when you have conflict, when you don't understand, love your friends. Your longest lasting friends will be ones that you welcome into the messy reality of your life and who invite you into theirs. The most valuable friendships aren't always easy and require mutual sacrifice. If you find yourself longing for a deep friendship, start asking yourself how you love those around you even when it isn't easy.

Motherhood, especially in the early years, isn't an incredibly convenient time to nurture friendships, but there is always an opportunity to encourage someone, to show up in small ways, and to love faithfully. Today, in your time with the Lord, ask him to show you how you can love someone in your life. No matter how abundant or meagre your resources, you have something to offer. Ask God to reveal to you who needs the faithful love of a true friend.

Thank you, Father, for the reminder to love well, even when it isn't easy. I want to be a true friend to those around me. Help me to see who needs encouragement and who needs the comfort of a friend. Teach me how to love well in comfort and in adversity.

# SHARPENING

*As iron sharpens iron,*
*so one person sharpens another.*
PROVERBS 27:17 NIV

It is good for you to be around people who make you better. Instead of surrounding yourself with people who think exactly like you do, remember that it is good to be challenged and sharpened. Likewise, seek to be that person for others, calling each other to higher standards and loving each other with the merciful love of Christ. This can be difficult in the trenches of motherhood, as you might not feel like you have the time to develop deep friendships.

Remember that this Scripture can just as easily apply to life within the wall of your home. You can have a challenging, sharpening, and wisdom-filled relationship with your children. You can teach them how to ask questions with kindness and to always be challenging each other to be better. Your children, even in their youth, can point you to Christ and you can do the same for them. As you nurture them, remember that your relationship with them evolves. They will have their own relationship with God, and in their uniqueness they can teach you about him in a way that might surprise you.

Thank you, God, that my children can sharpen me and I them. Teach me how to see them not only as my children but as unique people, having their own relationships with you. I want to humbly learn from them and also teach them in humility. May we sharpen each other daily in a way that honors you.

# HE IS ABLE

*To him who is able to do far more abundantly than all that we ask or think, according to the power at work within us, to him be glory in the church and in Christ Jesus throughout all generations, forever and ever. Amen.*

EPHESIANS 3:20-21 ESV

Today as you sit in the stillness, dwell on the ability of God. He is your infinitely good Father who is eternally able. There is nothing that is impossible for him. For a moment, imagine the scope of his capability. There is nothing under the sun that is as perfect as he is. However, you imagine your life at its best, he can do better. Our perception of perfection doesn't even come close to his.

From his position, high and mighty, he loves you with tender compassion. His majestic perfection is perfectly and intricately coupled with his gentle lovingkindness. Let this sink in for a moment. His power does not make him prideful, selfish, or a tyrant; instead, he showers his perfection and love on you. Praise him today for his vast ability and his abundant love.

Father, your perfection amazes me. I praise you because you are able to do abundantly more than I can imagine. You are good and you are kind. Your ways are higher than mine and you deserve the glory.

# WISE FOLLY

*The foolishness of God is wiser than human wisdom,*
*and the weakness of God is stronger than human strength.*
1 CORINTHIANS 1:25 NIV

You can likely write an extensive list of things that you want to improve about yourself. It's not hard to focus on your weaknesses. You want to be a better mom, a more patient mom, a more fun mom. You want to have a cleaner house. You want to balance your life more efficiently. You want to be a better friend. If you start dwelling on these things, you'll find yourself with your eyes fixed inward, sitting in negativity and insecurity. Instead, fix your gaze upward. Look to God whose folly is wiser than the most impressive human intelligence. If there is something in your life that you feel needs improvement, bring it to him. He will be faithful to guide you, correct you, and love you.

You are likely a far harsher critic than necessary. Ask your Father, who is wise, strong, and compassionate, where your attention should be. He will be faithful to lead you to repentance with kindness. He does not lead his children to repentance by handing them a list of flaws. That is contrary to his Word and his character. No matter how you perceive your flaws, instead of looking at yourself, look to him.

Thank you, God, that your understanding, wisdom, and strength are far greater than anything I can understand. Help me to look to you for guidance, trusting your lead. I feel overwhelmed when I start thinking about my flaws. Teach me to see myself like you see me and to value your wisdom above my own.

# A LEGACY

*I am reminded of your sincere faith, which first lived in your grandmother Lois and in your mother Eunice and, I am persuaded, now lives in you also.*

2 TIMOTHY 1:5 NIV

Paul is commending Lois and Eunice for the way they instilled their sincere faith into Timothy. They are the ones who displayed for him what it looked like to love the Lord with all of their hearts. As a result, Timothy would become one of the most influential people in the New Testament. As a mother, you have an incredible opportunity to daily show your children who Jesus is. You don't have to be a skilled or trained teacher to equip them in their relationship with Jesus. Let them see your praise, your failure, your trust, and your repentance, and they will learn who Jesus is.

As a mother, you get to leave a legacy for your children. This is a privilege and not a burden. Let the Holy Spirit equip you and continuously point you to the Lord for help when you need it. He is just as concerned with your children's relationship with him as you are. While they are looking at you, the goal is for them to see Christ. You do not have to be perfect; you need to point them to the one who is.

Thank you, God, for the opportunity to lead my children to you. Help me to instill a sincere faith within them. As I fail in front of them, help me to model repentance and forgiveness. As I succeed, help me to model thanksgiving, praise, and humility. Thank you for the gift and responsibility of raising children.

# NEW THINGS

*"Forget what happened before,*
*and do not think about the past.*
*Look at the new thing I am going to do.*
*It is already happening. Don't you see it?*
*I will make a road in the desert*
*and rivers in the dry land."*
ISAIAH 43:18-19 NCV

God's ways are perfect, unlike our own. He can do all of the things that we cannot do in our limited humanity. Today, instead of focusing on what the past held, turn your eyes toward how great he is. He can make roads in deserts and rivers in dry land. He provides manna from heaven and new mercy every morning. He is ever present in whatever desert you might find yourself. He does not abandon his children in the wilderness; he makes a road. He does not leave you parched in dry land; he creates a river. He delights in renewing your hope and in meeting you where you are. His vast ability is coupled with his infinite compassion and unending love.

Dwelling on God's greatness does not diminish your difficulties because not only is he powerful, he is a caring father who never belittles, glazes over, or diminishes his children. Turning your eyes toward him when you are in the wilderness is an act of faith. He is faithful to honor even the smallest act of faith.

Thank you, God, that you are infinitely capable and also full of unending love. You make a way for me when I am lost. Help me to turn my eyes to what you are doing, to put my faith in you, and to focus on who you say you are. Thank you for roads in deserts and rivers in dry land. I put my hope in you.

# RETURN TO THE BASICS

*Be joyful in hope,*
*patient in affliction,*
*faithful in prayer.*
ROMANS 12:12 NIV

If you're lacking direction or struggling to find purpose in your days, let what you read in Romans help bring definition. Be joyful in hope: as you eagerly wait for the hope of the gospel to be fulfilled in the return of Christ, let your heart be glad. Let your hope bring you joy because you know that what is coming is better than anything you've left behind. Be patient in affliction: there will always be struggles. With the grace of God, you can walk through each trial with a steadfast heart, knowing that God will be faithful to deliver you. Be faithful in prayer: your willingness to continuously commune with God shows that you trust in him and that you believe he is who he says he is.

In the midst of motherhood, it can be easy to get lost in the mundane, repeating the same basic things day in and day out. If the repetition has you feeling as though your relationship with God is also stale, return humbly to these three things: joyous hope, patience in affliction, and faithfulness in prayer.

Thank you, Father, that I can find refreshment in your Word when I am lost in the repetition of motherhood. Help me to return to the foundations of my faith in a way that will bring rest and peace. I want to honor you and I want your Word to sink deep into my heart, impacting my daily life. Teach me how to be joyful in hope, patient in affliction, and faithful in prayer.

# THE HEALING WORD

*My child, pay attention to what I say.*
*Listen carefully to my words.*
*Don't lose sight of them.*
*Let them penetrate deep into your heart,*
*for they bring life to those who find them,*
*and healing to their whole body.*
PROVERBS 4:20–22 NLT

Have you ever had one of your children come you frustrated or not feeling well? You talk with them for a moment and you know precisely what they need. Maybe it's a glass of water, a few moments of quiet, or a snack. While you can make suggestions all day long, it's still up to them to follow your advice. They have to be willing to admit that you know best and to walk in the way that you've advised.

As your Father, God knows what is best for you. His is infinitely kind toward you and directs you with gentleness to the fullness of life that is available. He knows that in reading the Word, you'll find encouragement and guidance. If you let it sink into your heart, it will bring you life and healing. Today, follow his instructions. Remember that he cares for you tenderly and he is infinitely wise. Let his good, true, and perfect Word find its home in your heart and transform you. Let it encourage you, draw you closer to him, fill you with humility, and remind you of his love.

Thank you, God, for the gift of your Word. Thank you for the reminder to let it fill my heart. I know that it will bring me life and healing, but I sometimes struggle to make the time to read it. Help me where I am weak and lacking. Give me the grace to listen to your words.

# PRIORITIZE REST

*In six days the LORD made the heavens and the earth, the sea,*
*and all that is in them, but he rested on the seventh day.*
*Therefore the LORD blessed the Sabbath day and made it holy.*

EXODUS 20:11 NIV

You value the rest that your children receive. You can see when they are overtired and overwhelmed, needing a nap or an early bedtime. You recognize how their attitude changes and how they're less able to manage their emotions. You know that the level of peace in your home is often dependent on the rest they receive, so you fight for it, doing the best you can to help them get the sleep they need.

Likewise, you *need* rest. God has ordained it and even partakes of his own prescription. If God in all of his infinite power and glory needs to rest, then there isn't any room for you to refuse rest on the altar of productivity. At some point, as a culture, we began to devalue sleep and rest. We've become too busy, too frantic, and too focused on success that we've lost the ability to truly rest. As difficult as it is as a mom, take steps toward prioritizing times of rest. Ask the Lord what you can do to take a break from the things that wear you down, even the good ones.

Father, even you needed to rest after creating the world. Teach me how to prioritize it. It's really hard to take a break sometimes but I know that it is lifegiving. Teach me how to depend on you for my rest. Bring renewal to my heart, Lord.

# MORNING WILL COME

*Weeping may last through the night,*
*but joy comes with the morning.*

PSALM 30:5 NLT

The night can be deceptive and lonely; it can feel never-ending and disorienting. Even a few hours of darkness can make you forget the days of light that you've walked in. God knows that you are prone to forget his goodness. There is a consistent theme in Scripture to hold on, persevere, and wait for what is coming. Here, the Psalmist uses the night and the morning to display that theme.

As a mom, you know the relief and joy that can come with a new day. There is new coffee, new chances, and new mercy. Don't despair thinking about what has happened in the night, set your eyes upon Jesus and let his mercy wash over you afresh each morning. Soak up the relief that comes from walking through something difficult and coming out on the other side still breathing. Much joy can be found in persevering and keeping your eyes set on the horizon, confident that the sun will rise again no matter how far away it seems.

Thank you, God, that though I weep, joy comes in the morning. Even though in the dark I might forget about your goodness, the sun still rises and reminds me of your new mercy. Teach me how to keep my eyes on what is coming instead of being discouraged by what surrounds me. Help me to persevere through each day, trusting your goodness and putting my hope in what is to come.

# DELIGHT IN WEAKNESS

*"My grace is sufficient for you,*
*for My strength is made perfect in weakness.*
*"Therefore most gladly I will rather boast in my infirmities,*
*that the power of Christ may rest upon me.*
2 CORINTHIANS 12:9 NKJV

You are blessed to have weakness. Otherwise, you would find yourself lost in your own pride. Even so, it is so hard to boast in infirmities. You live in a culture that places high value on success, image, worldly gain, and prestige. Each day you are bombarded with messages that support independence and strength. In contrast, the gospel is for the weak and dependent. As a follower of Jesus, you are asked to delight in your own weakness. Instead of fighting against it, hiding it in shame, or denying its existence, you are given the opportunity to let your weakness glorify the Lord.

In your weakness you can depend on Jesus in a way that isn't possible when you are stubbornly walking in your own strength. Today, instead of letting your infirmities cause you to compare yourself to others or feel less than, let them push you toward Christ. Thank him for the ways that you don't measure up because they can serve as a reminder to let him be the source of your strength.

Thank you, Father, that I am weak. My weakness can serve to magnify your glory and your goodness. Help me to always find a home among the weak and weary that I might show others your mercy. I will never be beyond your mercy. May I always see myself as one in desperate need of your great redemption.

# A NEW CREATION

*If anyone is in Christ, he is a new creation.*
*The old has passed away;*
*behold, the new has come.*
2 CORINTHIANS 5:17 ESV

As a mother, have you ever wished for an opportunity to do something differently? Maybe you've lost your temper or taken a moment for granted. Maybe you didn't give your full attention when it was needed or maybe you've done hurtful things to the people you love. There are many times that a do-over would be so nice. If only it worked that way. This is precisely how the kingdom of heaven works. In Christ, you have been declared new. When you confess your sins and repent, relying on what Jesus has done on the cross, you are declared new. You are one hundred percent a new creation.

It can be nearly impossible to forget the things you wish you hadn't done. Those memories stick with you for better or for worse. That is not the case with God. He sees you only through the blood of Jesus as you are made more and more like him. Today, instead of beating yourself up for your failures, gratefully thank God for the transformation you've been given through Jesus. Let that bring you freedom and joy today.

Father, thank you that I am made new. It's so hard for me to comprehend but I am thankful for the miracle of being a new creation. Teach me how to walk in the full knowledge of what Christ has done for me. Instead of dwelling on my failures, help me to learn from them and walk in love more each day.

# THANKFUL FOR EVERYTHING

*Give thanks for everything to God the Father
in the name of our Lord Jesus Christ.*
EPHESIANS 5:20 NLT

Thankfulness breeds joy. Thankfulness extinguishes bitterness and comparison. It can seem cliché to say, "What are you thankful for?" but in fact, it is warfare. Thankfulness can move you out of self-centeredness and shift your focus onto what is good. Sometimes, walking in thanksgiving is incredibly hard work. It's okay for it to be hard and to acknowledge that, but don't let it keep you from doing it. Deliberately choose to be thankful. If you need to write out a list, do that. If you need to weep before the Lord as one or two things come to mind, do that.

Let God soften your heart as you humbly take notice of what is good in your life. Whether it is a little or a lot, obvious or hidden, there are always reasons to praise him. He is forever worthy of your praise, no matter your circumstances. As you go to him in thanksgiving, he will be faithful to meet you and draw you close.

God, help me to be thankful. Where I am feeling focused on myself, help me to focus on what you've done. Show me ways that you are working, big and small, so I can praise you. Teach me how to walk in deliberate thanksgiving no matter what my circumstances are. I don't want to carry a heavy heart, burdened with anxiety or comparison. Teach me how to trust you with my burdens and give thanks to you for everything.

# YOUR HIDING PLACE

*You are my hiding place;*
*you protect me from trouble.*
*You surround me with songs of victory.*

PSALM 32:7 NLT

Whether you need a safe place from external threats and troubles or from internal turmoil, God can provide it. Let him comfort you, in the truest sense, like a heavy warm blanket or a mug of hot tea. Go to him when the storm is raging and the rains are steady. Go to him when you're wrought with anxiety and when you're dragging with weariness. He promises that he will protect you and surround you. He will hedge you in, providing safety and comfort.

No matter where your trouble comes from, he can be your hiding place. Just as you wrap your arms around your children to provide comfort in their fear, so does God for you. He provides space for you, he provides protection, and he promises victory. Not only does he give you what you need right now, but he promises that he will continuously provide for you into eternity. He is not a God of one-time or short-term promises. What he promises you today will be true for all of your days.

Thank you for your comfort, Lord. Teach me to see you as my hiding place and my protector. I praise you for your goodness and your ability to keep me safe. You alone are worthy of my praise! Thank you for the songs you sing over me; help me to hear them when I am overwhelmed.

# THE AFFLICTED

*You, Lord, hear the desire of the afflicted;*
*you encourage them, and you listen to their cry.*
PSALM 10:17 NIV

During Jesus' time on earth he was consistent to lift up the afflicted and oppressed and elevate their needs above the haughty and the proud. If you want to live your life following Jesus and reflecting the heart of God, you'll need to learn to see the oppressed with incredible love and concern. If God encourages and listens to the cries of the hurting, then that should be your priority as well.

As a mother, you have the unique opportunity to teach this kind of compassion to your children. You have been saved from a great depth, so it is your debt to extend grace to those you encounter. If you elevate yourself above the hurting and the broken, ask the Lord to show you the depravity that you were saved from. He is tender and gentle with those who are in the most pain; let him soften your heart to act in that way as well.

Thank you that you are kind, God, and you hear the desires of the afflicted. You don't turn away the hurting or abandon the oppressed. Teach me to love in this way as well. I want my actions and words to reflect your heart and be an example for my children. Where I have been hard-hearted or have ignored the oppressed, soften my heart.

# GOOD TO YOU

*Return to your rest, my soul,*
*for the Lord has been good to you.*

PSALM 116:7 NIV

Today, take a break from thinking about all the things you feel the Lord hasn't done yet, and instead focus on what he has done. Remember specific times when he has provided for you. Think of exact times when he has proved his faithfulness. While he gives you new manna each day, the passing of time doesn't make yesterday's manna any less miraculous. Praise him for all that he has done and let it remind you of his goodness.

Let this motivate you to walk with a steadfast heart. He is not a one-time God, being kind one time, loving you one time, providing for you one time. He is the God who works always with infinite power and love. He has sustained you all of the days of your life thus far and will not quit anytime soon. You can find true rest because you know that the Lord has been good to you. Remember his works like you would remember a sweet time with a loved one. Smile at what he's done and let your heart be stirred in affection toward him.

Thank you, God, for all you've done. Help me to remember specific ways that you've shown me your goodness, and let it draw me closer to you. I have experienced your mercy and love. Let the remembering motivate me toward faithfulness in the future. Help me to find rest in praising you for all you've done.

# A PROUD FATHER

*I have no greater joy than to hear that my children
are walking in the truth.*

3 JOHN 1:4 NIV

Have you ever watched your kids make the right choices when
they don't know you've seen? You catch a moment of tenderness
between them or they stand up for someone on the playground.
In those moments, your heart swells with pride. You feel joyful that
they did something well on their own. If you are able to feel that
level of pride for your child, imagine how God sees you. He delights
in seeing you walk in truth. Each small step of faith makes him
proud. Each time you walk in truth, no matter how big or small, he
is joyous! He is not disappointed in you.

Maybe you're not used to encouragement and the concept of
someone being on your side is foreign. Know that God is for you. He
is not against you. He delights in you and is proud of you. Even the
small things that you might deem insignificant are important to him.
Today, as you spend time with him, ask him to reveal his heart to you.
Ask him to encourage you and show you why he is proud of you.

Thank you, Father, that you take joy in my life. You are a
personal God who encourages and is proud of his children.
Teach me to see myself the way you do. Lead me throughout
my day to honor you in big and small ways.

# PERFECTION IN BROKENNESS

*We now have this light shining in our hearts,*
*but we ourselves are like fragile clay jars containing this great treasure.*
*This makes it clear that our great power is from God,*
*not from ourselves.*

2 CORINTHIANS 4:7 NLT

The treasure that you hold within your broken frame is the bright and glorious hope of the gospel. God has entrusted this great treasure to the weak and unreliable. He has given the most valuable thing in existence to the frail and to those who are prone to stray. Imagine trusting your children with your most valuable possession. Imagine passing it on to them knowing that they are likely to destroy it, use it incorrectly, or do a poor job caring for it.

In his great love for you, God has given you a treasure so his power might be displayed. In your weakness, you are being renewed and made to look more like Christ. In the ways that you are unreliable, you have the opportunity to glorify the one who is not. In your brokenness, the goodness of God is made even more tangible. Today, seek to praise him for his power. Don't focus on your own failings or inability to succeed, instead glorify God.

Thank you, God, for entrusting me with the gospel. I can use my brokenness to glorify you. Teach me to see brokenness not as weakness but as a chance to display your power to the world. Help me see myself rightly and to turn to you in my lacking.

# DELIVERED

*He has delivered us from the domain of darkness*
*and transferred us to the kingdom of his beloved Son,*
*in whom we have redemption, the forgiveness of sins.*

COLOSSIANS 1:13-14 ESV

The love of Jesus changes everything. Without him, you would be lost in your sin. When you've done the wrong thing, whether you've been mean-spirited toward your children, harbored bitterness, or completely lost your patience, the weightiness of sin can be great. The feeling of guilt that can overcome you is too much for you to bear on your own. Without Christ, that impossible weight would be yours to carry. No matter your sin of choice, no matter how lost your day feels, you have been given redemption through Jesus. Don't carry around that guilt and weight. Don't let shame keep you from Jesus.

There is no such thing a perfect mother. God knows the difficulty of your days and he wants to walk with you through them. He has delivered you, and will continue to deliver you, from the domain of darkness. As a dearly beloved child, run to him in your desperation. Instead of being controlled by shame, deliberately throw yourself upon his mercy.

God, you know I am not a perfect mom. I make mistakes and I choose the wrong things. Help me to depend upon your redemption. Help me to run to you instead of hiding in shame. When I walk in frustration or anger, help me to depend upon your mercy.

# BE COURAGEOUS

*"Be strong and courageous, and act; do not fear nor be dismayed, for the LORD God, my God, is with you. He will not fail you nor forsake you until all the work for the service of the house of the LORD is finished."*

1 CHRONICLES 28:20 NASB

There is no reason for you to walk in fear because you are safely held and wholly sustained. You are never left alone, never forsaken, and never abandoned. Your fears, whether they've been manifested before your eyes or they're based in things that haven't happened yet, don't need to dictate your life. You can walk through them, knowing that your Father is by your side, fully capable of leading you. You can trust his presence in the same way that your children trust in you. Your steadiness brings them peace, even when storms are raging.

Saying no to fear has nothing to do with your own capability to handle things and everything to do with knowing who God is. Like a wide-eyed child, trust your Father with your fears and in the midst of your fears. He is good, faithful, and present no matter how afraid you are.

Thank you, Father, that you are always with me. You've promised not to forsake me. When I am afraid, help me to turn to you and remember your command to be courageous. Give me the grace to draw strength from how much you love me and how faithful you are.

# IN HIS PRESENCE

*Lord, I love the house where you live,
the place where your glory dwells.*

PSALM 26:8 NIV

Have you ever been away from home and found yourself anxious and longing for the familiar? You've traveled away, you've done the outings you planned, you've visited the friends or family, and at the end of the day you find yourself longing for the security and comfort of home. You want to curl up in your own bed and feel comfortable and safe.

Think about God's presence in this same way. He is your safe place. He is where you can find true comfort and belonging. Wherever he is, that is where you are truly at home. Let your soul be most alive, most yourself, in his presence. Let his presence be the place that you long for when you are tired, weary, and stressed. When you've walked through your day and done your best and you have nothing left to give, let his presence be what you long for.

Thank you, Father, for being my home. In your presence I am most myself, and I am so thankful that I can be comfortable with you. I want to long for your presence above all else. May I long for the place that your glory dwells in the same way that I long for home when I am away.

# HOPE ANCHORS YOU

*We have this hope as an anchor for the soul,*
*firm and secure.*
HEBREWS 6:19 NIV

Monday you might be drowning in laundry. Tuesday you may be operating on little sleep. Wednesday you could have a sick child. Thursday you might fumble through your work schedule. Friday you may feel the pain of a broken relationship. Saturday you could be tossed about by your own emotions. Sunday you might have to navigate a new parenting challenge. You cannot possibly predict all of the hardships you may face this week or next. Surely, each day will bring some sort of challenge.

You can't always prepare yourself for what is to come but you can ensure that no matter the storms you face, your soul can be anchored, firm, and secure. You can guarantee that life will be unpredictable, but you can also guarantee that your hope can be unwavering. Your hope will be steadfast when you place it in that which can never change: God's love for you is vast, and Jesus' death brought redemption for all who trust in him. When the changes in your life feel impossible to navigate, remember that the hope you have in Christ can keep you steady.

Thank you, God, for the hope you've given me. No matter how up and down my days feel, help me to remain secure and firm in that hope. When life feels chaotic or unpredictable, give me the grace to depend on your steadfast love.

# USE YOUR GIFTS

*Each of you should use whatever gift you have received to serve others, as faithful stewards of God's grace in its various forms.*

1 PETER 4:10 NIV

You are not asked to operate in a way that you can't. You are not shamed for what you have available to you and what you don't. God asks you to simply use what you have. Use what you have to serve others because of your faithfulness to him. Whether you have a lot or a little, you can be a good steward of what you've been undeservedly given. In feast and in famine, seek to have a generous heart. There will likely always be someone who has less than you.

In your time with the Lord today, ask him to reveal to you someone you can bless with your time, money, or energy. Not every act of generosity needs to have dollar signs attached to it. He will always be faithful to show you areas where you can encourage, help, or love someone. This is heartwarming to him, and he delights in it just as you delight in watching your children be kind and generous toward each other. Whatever gift you have, use it for the benefit of those around you.

Thank you, God, for the gifts and resources you've given me. Help me to hold them loosely and use them to serve others generously. Teach me specific ways to displace your grace to others. Show me someone who needs encouragement or help and then give me practical ways to help. I want to be someone who is aware of your grace and bestows it abundantly upon others.

# GREATER THAN YOURSELF

*The Lord is good;*
*his steadfast love endures forever,*
*and his faithfulness to all generations.*
PSALM 100:4–5 NRSV

His steadfast love for you is never-ending. It is like a banner over you, declaring truth about who you are to all who see it. He declares that you are loved, you are chosen, you belong in his family. His goodness was abundant before you and it will not end with you. He has promised that he will be faithful to all generations. This is the legacy that you are part of. You are a specific and important piece, part of Christ's family, knit together by God throughout all of history. You are part of something miraculous because of the love that covers you.

While on the earth you might not always feel as though you belong, know that you are indeed part of something much bigger than yourself. There will be a day when you will see clearly and with all believers you'll kneel at the throne of God. On that day, you will feel and know that you are intricately connected to the body of Christ. Imagine what it will be like to worship with all of the generations who have trusted God. If you are feeling lost in the repetition and weariness that can come from motherhood, remember that you are part of something much greater than yourself.

God, your faithfulness has no end. Your love endures forever. Today, help me to see the greatness of your love spanning across all generations. When I don't feel like I belong, help me to see that I belong to your family.

# CORRECTION EQUALS GROWTH

*To learn, you must love discipline;*
*it is stupid to hate correction.*
PROVERBS 12:1 NLT

Perfection is unattainable. You will never reach a point in your life when you are free of weakness and without room for growth. If Christ is your standard, you could spend your lifetime becoming more and more like him. As you humbly admit to your own faults, it only makes sense to develop a love for correction. Truly, correction is a form of mercy. You are too loved, too valuable, and too cared for to be left in your brokenness. It is better to have a soft heart toward correction and to keep moving forward than to stubbornly balk every time there is resistance in your life.

As a mother, you know this is true. You correct and teach your children in order to keep them safe, to ensure they reach their potential, and make sure they are properly equipped to navigate life. Leaving them alone in their childishness would be neglectful. You know that effective discipline is an act of love and of kindness when done well. Take this knowledge that you've gained as a mother and apply it to your own life. Seek to be someone who doesn't prickle at correction but who sees it as an opportunity for growth.

Thank you, God, for correction. Soften my heart and teach me to see the value in it. Forgive me for the times I have pridefully refused discipline. Please show me areas where my heart is hard and give me the grace to repent. When I am frustrated at correction, soften my heart and remind me of how you are a kind and gentle teacher.

# TELL OF HIS GOODNESS

*Let each generation tell its children of your mighty acts;*
*let them proclaim your power.*

PSALM 145:4 NLT

Gather your children close and speak to them about what God has done. He has done miracles in your life. He has sustained you. He has overseen each intricate part of your life. Look back and take note of how he has moved and then share those things with your children. Speak to them about his goodness and about how he has impacted you in big and small ways. When they ask you for a story, tell them how he changed your heart, how he made you new, how he drew you close.

Tell them about the skies he's painted for you and the stars that he knows by name. Describe for them how he knows the number of hairs on their heads and how he sees them wherever they come and go. Proclaim the good news of the gospel and tell them parables like Jesus told his disciples. You have an endless narrative at your disposal. Today, no matter if you feel awkward or confident, take some time to tell your kids what God has done.

Thank you, God, for the opportunity to tell my children of your mighty acts. Give me words to say that will proclaim your power to them. May your Holy Spirit stir my heart to speak of you. You have done great things in my life. Help me to share them with my children that one day they might pass them on to their children.

# UPLIFTED IN HUMILITY

*Humble yourselves before the Lord,*
*and he will lift you up.*
JAMES 4:10 NIV

Humility might seem like an act of weakness but actually it's the only appropriate response to trusting in the true character of God. Submission to God's will and ways can only come out of heart that knows who he is. Your humility shows strength and wisdom. You know that God is worthy because of his majesty and power but you also know that you are safe in his love and kindness. When you humble yourself before the Lord, you don't do it out of fear or forced submission to authority. You humble yourself because you know that his love for you is great and he is worthy of all you have to give.

Today, if there are areas in your life where you have been afraid to walk in humility because it means a loss of control or you see it as weakness, ask yourself if you are seeing God rightly. He promises to love you and he promises to lift you up.

Thank you, Father, that though your power is great so is your love. I don't have to see humility as weakness because you promise to lift me up. Show me areas where I have walked in pride instead of humility and give me the grace to repent and see you rightly.

# INFLUENCE TO ADVOCATE

*"Every plant not planted by my heavenly Father will be uprooted, so ignore them. They are blind guides leading the blind, and if one blind person guides another, they will both fall into a ditch."*

MATTHEW 15:13-14 NLT

Especially in motherhood, there are a million voices trying to tell you what to do. The only voice that you need to give your attention to is the Lord's. If you ask, he will give you the discernment and wisdom you need to raise your children. Let him speak to you gently and learn to listen to his voice. As your roots grow deep in his love and your arms reach out in surrender and trust, you'll find that you won't be uprooted when storms come.

When you are planted in his love, you'll remain steady. You can ignore the myriad of influences around you that aren't rooted in God's love. Words have power and if you listen to everything that's said to you, you'll find yourself drowning, with eyes constantly moving from source to source. Instead, keep your eyes on him and trust his leading.

God, in a world where everything is presented as truth, it can feel overwhelming to hear so many opinions. Help me to seek you first. I want to be firmly planted in your love, unwavering when that which isn't from you is presented to me. Help me to ignore the voices that I don't need to listen to and instead focus on what you are saying and where you are leading me.

# PURPOSE OF TRIALS

*Consider it pure joy, my brothers and sisters, whenever you face trials of many kinds, because you know that the testing of your faith produces perseverance. Let perseverance finish its work so that you may be mature and complete, not lacking anything.*

JAMES 1:2-4 NIV

When you face trials, you have the opportunity to encounter them with joy or with bitterness and frustration. This is not an easy thing to do and you cannot do it on your own, but God knows that. Nothing in Scripture is arbitrary. The admonition in Scripture to find joy in trials is there because God knows that it won't always be easy and that you'll need the gentle and kind reminder found in James.

He doesn't expect you to numbly walk through life, with a smile pasted on your face that never falters despite hardship, pain, or trauma. No, you aren't asked to set aside pain; you are reminded not to glaze over trials but to see them rightly. Even the worst circumstances can serve a purpose in your life and you can walk through them depending on the Lord. You don't depend on him because you are a really excellent Christian; you depend on him because he is an incredibly excellent God, worthy of your trust.

Thank you, God, for the ability to lean on you through trials. Help me to see the pain in my life as a means of trusting you more. It's really hard to shift my attitude in the midst of trials but I believe that you are good and that you hold my brokenness gently. When I am broken, you carry me. May I see trials as an opportunity to be carried by you.

# OCTOBER

Surely your goodness and unfailing love

will pursue me all the days of my life,

and I will live in the

house of the Lord forever.

PSALM 23:6 NLT

# EYES ON YOU

*"Are not five sparrows sold for two pennies? Yet not one of them is forgotten by God. Indeed, the very hairs of your head are all numbered. Don't be afraid; you are worth more than many sparrows."*

LUKE 12:6-7 NIV

You have infinite value to God. He created you in his image. When sin separated you from him, he sent his own Son to die so you could be close to him again. How could he possibly forget about you? In your deepest sorrow, you are never alone. On your worst day, you aren't abandoned. While you constantly have your eyes on the needs of everyone around you, God has his eyes on you. His tender care for you isn't dependent upon your attention or your faithfulness.

Even as you focus on mothering and all it demands, God is focused on you. He is aware of you and could never forget you; it is impossible. Today, let your worth in Christ infiltrate everything you do. Let it be the foundation from which you pour out to your children. Let his care for you refresh you in your weariness.

Thank you, God, for the way you value me. Today, help me to see my worth. As I understand that you could never forget me, let that love motivate me to love those around me. Thank you for your constant care as I am caring for others.

# DELAYED GRATIFICATION

*"Do not store up for yourselves treasures on earth, where moth and rust destroy, and where thieves break in and steal. But store up for yourselves treasures in heaven, where neither moth nor rust destroys, and where thieves do not break in or steal; for where your treasure is, there your heart will be also."*

MATTHEW 6:19-21 NASB

There are good things to be stored up during your life on earth. There are beautiful, delightful, and satisfying things. Yet, God reminds you that even better things are to come. What you gather during your days here will not last. God, in his great love for you, doesn't want to see you wasting your time collecting that which will fade. He knows that the true treasure lies in heaven and he wants you to partake of it. Delayed gratification is not always bad.

Have you ever tried to get a toddler to wait for something good? You can see the value in waiting but their little minds can focus only on one thing: getting what they want and getting it now. In your time with the Lord today, ask him how you might have been that impatient child. Ask him to show you areas where you have sought earthly satisfaction instead of heavenly gratification. As he points out those areas, repent and ask for the grace to move in a different direction.

God, you know what is best for me. Show me areas where I have focused too much on things that fade when I should be directing my attention to treasures that will last forever. Teach me how to store up the right kind of treasures. I am thankful for your mercy. You won't leave me lacking in days to come.

# ABOUNDING IN GRACE

*"The LORD, the LORD,*
*a God merciful and gracious,*
*slow to anger,*
*and abounding in steadfast love and faithfulness."*

EXODUS 34:6 NRSV

It's a little bit unfathomable that God is slow to anger. If anyone has a justified reason to be angry, it's God. He is witness to a world of provocation. We constantly whine, ruin his favorite things, and could easily grate on his nerves, but he is always slow to anger; it's part of who he is. Have you ever seen a frazzled mom in the grocery store? She loses it as soon as her child complains. Then there's the mom who walks steadily despite the constant questions, the crying over candy, or the tiny hands knocking things down in each aisle.

While you have likely been both moms at one point or another, God is consistently filled with grace for you. He walks with you through your very worst moments, and yes, he is slow to anger. He is merciful and gracious, abounding in love and faithfulness.

Thank you, God, that you are slow to anger. I don't deserve your patience, yet you lavish it on me. I don't deserve your faithfulness, yet you promise you will always be with me. I praise you for your mercy! Help me to feel secure in your love and teach me how to be slow to anger like you are.

# SKILLFULLY MADE

*You formed my inward parts;*
*you knitted me together in my mother's womb.*
*I praise you, for I am fearfully and wonderfully made.*
*Wonderful are your works;*
*my soul knows it very well.*

PSALM 139:13-14 ESV

Think of a project you've done. Maybe you strung words together into works of art, carefully pieced together a quilt, or faithfully tended to a garden. Perhaps you've poured your time and heart into a career. In whatever you've set your hands to, think about how you feel about what you've created. It's a part of you. It houses your energy, your sacrifice, your creativity, and your hard work. What you've made is of great value to you. It's yours.

On the days you feel unloved or undervalued, remember the value of that work and think of how it only dimly mirrors God's feeling toward you. He has knit you together, faithfully and diligently. You are of great value to him because you are his. You are his greatest work. If you have ever felt even remotely proud of something you have done, imagine how he feels about you—his most precious creation made in his image. As you seek him, let his pride and admiration wash over you.

Father, thank you for the way you've created me. Help me to see myself from your perspective and to praise you fully for what you've done. Your works are wonderful! Teach me how to see others in this way as well: highly valued and loved by you.

# LOVE COVERS

*Above all, love each other deeply,*
*because love covers over a multitude of sins.*
1 Peter 4:8 NIV

The entire book of 1 Peter sits upon this one verse. The command to love each other above all is the culmination of everything else that Peter speaks of. It's a reminder that even if you succeed in every other area of life, if you are without love, you have not succeeded at all. Your gauge for how to love is Jesus. How did he love? He sacrificed himself unto death. He died that you might have life. Your love is meant to cover the sins of others because Christ's love fully covered yours.

When you were in the midst of your sin, lost in darkness and under the rule of death, Christ died for you. His love reached into the depths and pulled you out. So then, don't love timidly or conditionally. Love those around you with fervor, sacrifice, and selflessness. Ask the Lord to reveal areas of your life where love has not been your top priority. Perhaps you've prioritized rules, lists, or worldly success over true love. As he shows you those areas, humbly repent and ask him to renew your love for those around you.

Thank you, God, for the command to love like Jesus loved. Help me to humbly sacrifice like he did without condition. Show me areas of my life where I can love more fully. Renew my love for those around me. Help me to see them as you do.

# WITH ALL YOU HAVE

*"You shall love the Lord your God with all your heart and with all your soul and with all your might. These words, which I am commanding you today, shall be on your heart."*

DEUTERONOMY 6:5-6 NASB

As you run the race of following Jesus, you will come across things that hinder your love for God. Maybe out of fear you don't give him your whole heart, afraid of what he might ask you to do or how he will see you. Maybe you deal with a specific temptation and it has worn down part of your heart. Maybe you've faced a certain trial that has caused you so much pain you've distanced yourself from God in frustration and resentment.

Prayerfully consider areas of your life that you have kept from God. Let him gently speak to you and show you how you can love him with your whole heart, soul, and might. No matter what has made you feel as though you cannot fully love him, know that nothing can separate you from his love for you. While you might feel far away and unable to give him your entire life, he is not far from you. No matter the obstacles in your way, he is near. Let him draw you close and heal what is broken. Let him show you how faithful he is.

God, I want to love you with my whole heart, soul, and might. If there are areas where I have not let myself be fully surrendered to you, please show them to me. Help me to see how kind you are and how your love for me is faithful and true.

# HEART VIEW

*"The LORD does not look at the things people look at.*
*People look at the outward appearance,*
*but the LORD looks at the heart."*

1 SAMUEL 16:7 NIV

As you sit in the stillness today, rest in the fact that God sees your heart clearly and fully. If you've ever been misunderstood, you know the pain that can come from being misrepresented. God will never misunderstand you. He will never jump to conclusions, make assumptions, or judge wrongly. He knows your intentions, your most hidden secrets, your deepest hurts, and your greatest joys. The relationship you have with him is more intimate and personal than you can understand.

Be blessed by the security that you have in him because he knows you perfectly. Praise him that he is close, that he knows your heart, and that he is not a cold God. Trust that as he can see you clearly, he knows exactly how to lead you, comfort you, guide you to conviction, and teach you to love.

Father, thank you that you see me perfectly. Your perspective isn't altered by outward appearances. Help me to trust you knowing that you have perfect judgment and can lead me better than anyone else.

# AT YOUR WORST

*God shows his love for us in that while we were still sinners,
Christ died for us.*

ROMANS 5:8 ESV

You did not earn your salvation. You didn't meet any special requirements or check items off a list. You didn't fit the right description or accidentally stumble upon it. You weren't in the right place at the right time, nor did you use any merit of your own. Not only that, but when you were at your very worst, Christ died for you. In the midst of sin, brokenness, and death, Christ accomplished a miracle for you. Knowing that your salvation could not be worked for, don't change the way you view your walk with God. Don't fall into the habit of checking items off a list or meeting certain requirements.

Don't view other people this way either. You were not too far lost for Christ to save, and neither are any of his other children. Extend to yourself and others the same undeserved mercy that was extended to you. You will never be good enough to earn what was given to you. This should cause you to look upon God with wonder and thanksgiving as you humbly love those around you in the same sacrificial way.

Thank you, God, for reaching down and saving me when I least deserved it. Salvation is not my burden to carry. Show me areas where I have tried to earn your love and remind me that I am fully secure in you because of Jesus not because of my own skills. Help me to see others how you see them, not expecting perfection but bestowing upon them abundant mercy like you did for me.

# THE HUMBLE WILL SEE

*The humble will see their God at work and be glad.*
*Let all who seek God's help be encouraged.*
PSALM 69:32 NLT

In humility you will see God at work. Humility means seeing less of yourself and more of him. Humility magnifies God above yourself because you know who he is, and you know who you are. When this is the way you walk, your eyes will be opened to the ways that he is working around you. Your perspective will be changed as you focus on the work of his hands instead of your own.

If you've been struggling to see what God is doing, kneel at the cross and ask for renewed humility. Ask God to show where you have let pride, a critical spirit, or conceit rule your thoughts and actions. He is a safe place for your doubt and cynicism. He will not look down on you like a frustrated father, refusing to let you feel your emotions because they're inconvenient. He is gentle, kind, and more than capable of receiving even your most intense emotions with mercy and patience. Ask him to open your eyes and you will be glad to see all that he has done and will do.

God, I want to see how you are working. Open my eyes to see what you are doing and help me to walk in humility. Show me where I have let pride or cynicism guide me. Teach me about true humility, so I might see you rightly.

# NOT ARBITRARY

*No discipline is enjoyable while it is happening—it's painful!*
*But afterward there will be a peaceful harvest of right living*
*for those who are trained in this way.*

HEBREWS 12:11 NLT

A good gardener knows that pruning is necessary for the fullness of growth to happen. A good gardener knows that while pruning looks like death, it is actually making room for more abundant life. A good gardener knows that proper pruning brings the harvest that you envision. God is the very best gardener.

Just as you discipline and guide your children for their gain, God knows exactly what you need in order to reap the harvest of peaceful and right living. His work in your life, though you might not like it at the time, is rooted in mercy, love, and great expectation. He can see exactly how you will blossom when one branch is trimmed, and exactly how you flourish when another is removed. He does not arbitrarily discipline his children. You can fully trust his purpose and his skill. Knowing that discipline is for your betterment, you can walk through it with a quiet heart and a trusting spirit.

Thank you, God, for your discipline. Help me to see it as merciful and kind. Reveal to me areas of my life that you want to discipline and help me to trust you. I know that I can trust you because you are kind. You see what I cannot see. Help me to trust you through seasons of pruning so I might have a fuller life in you.

# BUILD UP

*Encourage one another and build one another up,*
*just as you are doing.*
1 THESSALONIANS 5:11 ESV

Your words have great power. You also live in a world where you have constant access to everyone's opinions and voices. In a time when there is a lot of noise and an abundance of conflict, seek to be a voice who encourages and lifts up rather than one who tears down. You have the ability to change the trajectory of someone's day with what you say and how you say it. The right words can change everything.

Not everyone is gifted with the ability to communicate well, but this commandment isn't given to only those with literary skills. It's given to everyone. Everyone has the ability to say something kind and lifegiving. This has the ability to breathe life into your children and into the body of Christ with your words. Today, may the Holy Spirit give you discernment to know what to say to each person you encounter.

God, thank you for the reminder to speak life. I want to be a woman whose words are encouraging and not harsh or argumentative. Teach me how to build others up with what I say. Forgive me for the times I have not controlled my tongue. Help me to speak with the same lovingkindness that you do.

# IN THE MORNING

*In the morning, Lord, you hear my voice;*
*in the morning I lay my requests before you and wait expectantly.*

PSALM 5:3 NIV

How you start your morning sets the tone for your entire day. Resist the temptation to spend your first moments scrolling through your phone and instead sit before the Lord. Commit your ways to him, praise him, and lay your requests before him. He is listening to you and his mercies are new. There is something fresh to be found in your waking moments. Even if you only have a moment before going to pick up a crying baby, you can meet with God.

The expectation that you sit in tranquility with God for hours is not placed on you by anyone but yourself. Days will come again when you have the time for extended quiet and peace, but for now, humbly and deliberately give God what you have. Even a minute spent seeking God is valuable.

God, I want to seek you in the morning. I want my day to start with time devoted to you. That's not always easy, so please give me the grace to give you what I have. When my time is limited, help me to trust that you see me. When I'm tired and overwhelmed, help me to know that my time with you is not limited to quiet spaces.

# WINNING APPROVAL

*Am I now trying to win the approval of human beings, or of God?*
*Or am I trying to please people?*
*If I were still trying to please people,*
*I would not be a servant of Christ.*

GALATIANS 1:10 NIV

Motherhood seems to instantly open you up to a litany of unwanted opinions. Everyone has an idea of what's best and it can be overwhelming to try and navigate the difference between helpful advice and too many voices. Remember that in each part of your life, mothering included, you have the freedom to value God's opinion over anyone else's. As you seek to love your children the best you can, know that the only standard you need to meet is the one set by him.

If you are feeling frazzled trying to listen to everyone around you, take a moment and commit your stress to God. Let him give you peace and confidence in you who are as a mother. He will not leave you wanting when you ask him for wisdom. He loves to give good gifts to his children. Today, prayerfully seek his approval as you move throughout your day.

God, I want to serve you well. Help me to value your approval over anyone else's. Give me wisdom when I am overwhelmed and teach me how to seek you when there are too many voices around me. I want to honor you and commit my ways to you instead of being worried about what others think.

# TO BE GRACIOUS

*The Lord longs to be gracious to you;*
*therefore he will rise up to show you compassion.*
ISAIAH 30:18 NIV

You are not an inconvenience to God. He doesn't look at you in frustration when you fail. At your best or at your worst, he longs to be gracious to you. He *wants* to. Do you hear that truly, deep in your soul? He doesn't have to be kind and compassionate toward you, he wants to. He promises to have compassion on you in the middle of your sin. The death of Christ is the proof of God's ability to have compassion when you are at your worst. He will not turn you away or respond to you in irritation. His arms are open, and his eyes are full of love.

Let his desire to be gracious to you draw you closer to him in thanksgiving and praise. Let his desire to welcome you with kindness change the way you view those around you. As you let the truth of God's compassion toward you sink deep into your heart, let it transform the way you love others.

God, thank you not only for your graciousness but for the fact that you long to give it! You want to be compassionate and you long to be gracious. Help me to truly see how loving and kind you are. Heal the parts of my heart that see you incorrectly. Teach me how to love like you love.

# DON'T BUILD IN VAIN

*Unless the Lord builds the house,*
*the builders labor in vain.*
PSALM 127:1 NIV

What have you tried to build without trusting the Lord's guidance? Maybe you've navigated motherhood depending on your own strength. Maybe you have a relationship that needs healing and you've assumed that you know best how to fix it. Maybe you carry deep pain, thinking that one day you'll heal yourself. Ask God if there are areas of your life that you've left him out of and commit them to him. Let him instruct you, let him speak to you, and let him carry your burdens. You have limitless resources available to you through God.

Rest in the peace that is found when he is the builder. To go about your life without letting him be in control is like eating a peanut butter sandwich when you have access to a top chef who really wants to make dinner for you. Recommit your ways to God. He longs to lead you with kindness and perfection. He is the only one who can build something that will last forever.

Father, thank you that you are infinitely more capable than I am. Help me to depend on you. You are the one who can lead me well and orchestrate my life perfectly. I want to lean on you. Show me areas of my life where I have assumed control when I should relinquish it to you.

# EQUIPPED

*The weapons we fight with are not the weapons of the world.*
*On the contrary, they have divine power to demolish strongholds.*
2 CORINTHIANS 10:4 NIV

As a mother, you are familiar with equipping your child. You ensure they have the right tools for whatever they are going to encounter. You daily equip them physically, making sure they are dressed appropriately for the weather or giving them the right school supplies to get through their day. You also equip them emotionally, loving them well so that they feel secure. You equip them socially, teaching them how to manage conflict and be a good friend.

In the same way, God has equipped you to fight your battles. He has given you the same power that raised Christ from the dead. When you face trials or obstacles, are you waging war with worldly weapons or are you leaning on the divine power of Christ which has the ability to demolish strongholds? Today, as you sit in the stillness of his presence, be blessed by the knowledge that God can give you what you need to fight your battles.

Father, thank you that I don't need to use worldly weapons that will fade. Teach me how to wield the weapons you've given me. Teach me how to turn to prayer, depending on your power to demolish strongholds. You are mighty God and I want to depend on your resources not my own.

# HOLY SPIRIT LED

*They delight in the law of the Lord,*
*meditating on it day and night.*
PSALM 1:2 NLT

In the thick of motherhood, the idea of meditating might make you roll your eyes. How could you possibly meditate on the Word day and night? With your attention being pulled in a million directions and your energy being spent before you even greet the day, it might feel impossible to give the Word that kind of attention. This is why you have been given the Holy Spirit. He is the one who reminds you of truth throughout the day. When you can't literally sit with your Bible open for long periods of time, remember that you have the Spirit who guides you into truth.

As you spend a few moments with Lord right now, ask him to reveal a specific Scripture or truth to dwell on throughout the day. Quiet your heart and ask the Holy Spirit to remind you of that truth when you need it. He will be faithful to point you to God despite the constraints on your time and energy. When he does put a Scripture on your heart, take delight in his leading!

God, thank you for your Word! I know it brings me life and I want my heart to be full of truth. Sometimes it feels overwhelming to think about meditating on Scripture. Show me something that I can focus on today. Holy Spirit, point me to truth throughout my day. Thank you for your leading!

# HUMBLY ACCEPTED

*Those who accept correction gain understanding.*
*Respect for the LORD will teach you wisdom.*
*If you want to be honored, you must be humble.*
**PROVERBS 15:32–33 NCV**

Think about the times you've corrected your child. You watch them fight against what you are saying, knowing that if they just calmly agreed, things would be much less complicated. They expend unnecessary energy fighting with you when it would be easier for everyone if they accepted your wisdom and listened to your words.

Likewise, you can choose to humbly accept correction or you can wear yourself out fighting against God. As you listen to him and respect his guidance, you gain understanding and wisdom. If you insist on your own way, you'll find yourself weary and you'll be choosing stubbornness over peace. The choice is yours. His correction is never harsh, unjust, or angry. He is gentle, kind, and faithful to give you the grace you need. He truly knows what is best for you and your acknowledgement of that shows a trust in his character and an understanding of who he is.

God, thank you for your correction. I know that it will bring me understanding and wisdom as I listen to you. Give me the grace to hear your voice and respond in humility. I know that you are kind and gentle; forgive me for the times I have seen you as harsh or unforgiving. You are my compassionate Father and I want to trust you.

# QUIET CONFIDENCE

*Make it your ambition to lead a quiet life:*
*You should mind your own business*
*and work with your hands,*
*just as we told you.*

1 THESSALONIANS 4:11 NIV

The way other people live is constantly available to you. It can be tempting to compare your life to theirs, becoming more dissatisfied with what you have no matter how beautiful it is. Fight the battle of minding your own business. Ask the Lord what your priorities should be and confidently focus on those things. Don't worry about what everyone around you is doing. If you are following the Lord's leading, you'll find satisfaction in your days. Trust that he knows what is best for you and for those around you. Their priorities might be different than yours but that doesn't make them better or worse.

Today, in your time with the Lord, ask him to direct you. Let him direct your attention and let everything else fall to the wayside. You can't do everything at once. Find freedom in following the Lord; he will be faithful to direct you.

God, I want to live a quiet life. The world is so loud and demanding, and I want to be content following you. Reveal to me what my priorities should be and help me to walk confidently. I trust that you can teach me to be satisfied with the life I have.

# TRUST FOR MIRACLES

*"My God sent his angel to shut the lions' mouths so that they would not hurt me, for I have been found innocent in his sight. And I have not wronged you, Your Majesty." The king was overjoyed and ordered that Daniel be lifted from the den. Not a scratch was found on him, for he had trusted in his God.*

DANIEL 6:22-23 NLT

What impossible thing are you facing right now? God is capable of working miracles in your limitations. He is the one who can open closed doors and shut the mouths of lions. Even when everything points in one logical direction, God can interrupt the logical to make room for the miraculous. Maybe you can't imagine one more weary day of trying to get your baby to sleep. Maybe you have a broken relationship with one of your children that feels beyond repair. Maybe you have a financial need that is looming before you like a mountain.

Whatever your situation, God is capable of doing the impossible. He has done it before, and he will do it again. His intervention might not look like you expect, but his goodness and ability to transform your heart will always be miraculous. Sometimes he closes the lion's mouth and sometimes the miracle is the way he gives you peace. Today, in the stillness, give that situation to God again. Even if you've surrendered it one million times, keep trusting his goodness.

Thank you, God, that you can shut the lions' mouths and you can help me with my trial. I want my faith in you to grow and my confidence in your ability to be greater than it was yesterday. Help me to turn to you when I am in trouble. You know what is heavy on my heart and you know the burdens I carry. Help me to trust in you for miracles.

# FIND HIM

*Since the creation of the world God's invisible qualities—his eternal power and divine nature—have been clearly seen, being understood from what has been made, so that people are without excuse.*
ROMANS 1:20 NIV

If you are struggling to see God or you feel as though he is far away, take some time to look at what he has created. His eternal power and divine nature can be clearly seen in what he has made. He knows that our hearts are fickle and that we are prone to doubt, so he has literally surrounded us with reminders of who he is and what he can do. His creation speaks loudly about his intricacies and compassion.

God made delicate flowers, he paints the sky, and he causes leaves to change in the fall. He brings refreshing rains and he makes the oaks send their roots deep and their branches high. He sustains the earth, gives you air to breathe, and causes the sun to shine on your face. Instead of focusing on your own doubt, use today to search for God in his creation. He has given you an endless window into his heart. All that he has made is a reflection of his goodness.

God, your creation points to who you are! Help me to see you in the world around me. Refresh my spirit by showing me all you have done. Even if I feel far away, I know that you are close. Thank you for your creation and how it speaks of who you are.

# CHARIOTS AND HORSES

*Some trust in chariots and some in horses,
but we trust in the name of the LORD our God.*

PSALM 20:7 NIV

Where your trust lies says a lot about the state of your heart. Are you relying on the Lord for provision or are you feeling confident in your bank account? You often don't know where your loyalty truly lies until you find yourself without the security you once had. When financial trials come, are you depending on your chariots and your horses or is your trust placed firmly in the Lord? When you are experiencing security, it can be easy to assume that you are depending on God.

Today, ask him to reveal where your security lies. Then respond humbly and with thanksgiving. As you seek him, he will be faithful to move in your heart. The more you trust in him, the more he will cultivate a generous heart within you and a greater satisfaction with what you've been given. The truly generous don't give because they have a storehouse to back it up, they give because their confidence is in the provision of God. As you sit in the stillness with the Lord, let him speak to you about the state of your heart.

God, I know that trusting in my financial security is not what you want for me. Teach me how to rely upon your name more than I do my material possessions. I want to be generous because I am confident in your ability to provide for your children. Help me to humbly turn to you and accept your leading.

# THE INSIDE OUT

*"You clean the outside of the cup and dish, but inside they are full of greed and self-indulgence. You are like whitewashed tombs, which look beautiful on the outside but on the inside are full of the bones of the dead and everything unclean."*

MATTHEW 23:25, 27 NIV

You live in a world that is dominated by over-communication. Everyone is connected and has instant access to the lives of others. It can be so tempting to look at those little glimpses and feel shame or jealousy. Continuously remind yourself that what you see isn't necessarily an accurate depiction of what is happening. The same can be said about your own faith. Is what you display on the outside the same as what's inside?

Seek to be a woman who is made beautiful from the inside out. Let God be the one who dictates what your life looks like. Don't fall into the trap of making everything look picture perfect at the expense of authenticity and real change. Focus on having a heart that is devoted to God, walking in the Spirit, and humbly displaying the love of Jesus to those around you.

Help me to be authentic, Lord. Help me to focus more on the state of my heart than on the outward appearance of my life. I want to be devoted to you fully, with my eyes on you, not being distracted by fake perfection. Show me how to honor you with how I live.

# NOT FOREVER

*He was crucified because of weakness, yet He lives because of the power of God. For we also are weak in Him, yet we will live with Him because of the power of God directed toward you.*

2 CORINTHIANS 13:4 NASB

Jesus came into the world in humility and lowliness as an infant. He died painfully as a man. He was raised in power to sit on the throne next to the Father. He will return in glory as a King. Now you walk in weakness, but when he returns, you will rule and reign with him. Let the hope of what is to come and the incredible work of Jesus be your motivation today. Remember that there will be a day that you are without weakness, and you will walk fully and perfectly with Christ.

Do the hard work of looking past the mundane parts of your day and turn your eyes to the glorious story that God has laid out for humanity. Let it impact how you think, how you love, and how you behave. Let the supernatural impact the most natural parts of your day. God knows each small task laid before you, and he also knows the glory of what is to come.

Father, thank you for what you have done through you Son! Thank you for the example you've given me in him. May the gospel impact the smallest parts of my day. Draw me closer to you and teach me to love like you do. Help me to follow you closely today.

# WAIT WITH HOPE

*Wait on the LORD; be of good courage,*
*and He shall strengthen your heart;*
*wait, I say, on the LORD!*

PSALM 27:14 NKJV

Have you ever looked back on a difficult situation and been able to see clearly how God was working in the middle of it? At the time you struggled to depend on him, you were impatient, annoyed, and frustrated. Looking back now, you can see how your anxiety did nothing but make each day harder. With a clear perspective of how God moved, it's easy to see how patience, courage, and a steadfast heart would have allowed you to walk with much more peace.

Today, if you're in a difficult situation, ask the Lord for the grace to wait with courage. It is so rewarding to trust in God: to be able to look back with confidence and say that your eyes were steady on him even when it was hard. You cannot guarantee the outcome of every situation, but God does promise that he will strengthen you: that is a guarantee. Wait for him. Wait for his response to that continuously prayed prayer. Wait for him to move in your situation. Wait for him faithfully until Jesus returns to make all things new. It will be worth it.

Thank you, God, that I don't wait without hope! Not only do I trust your promises for what is to come, but I also believe that you will strengthen me in the meantime. Teach me how to trust you more. I don't want to look back with hindsight and wish I had waited with more courage.

# HE NEVER CHANGES

*Jesus Christ is the same yesterday and today and forever.*
HEBREWS 13:8 NIV

Jesus never changes. So much of the world is in conflict. Everyone is battling the unexpected and struggling to keep up with an ever-changing cultural climate. If you are feeling the weight of that, weary from trying to navigate everything, find solace in the fact that Jesus is unchanging. What he has done for humanity can never be changed. What he will do when he comes back cannot be changed.

No matter how creation groans, Jesus will return and make all things right. Not only are his actions unchanging but his character is also unchanging. He will always love, always sacrifice, and always guide. Let his consistency comfort you when the constant change of the world is mind boggling. As he becomes a steady place for you, you will have the wherewithal to point your children in that direction as well.

Thank you, Jesus, that you never change! Your character never changes, and nothing can change what you've done for all of us. Teach me how to focus on who you are when the world feels unsteady. When navigating the cultural climate is overwhelming, teach me to trust in your consistency.

# JOY IN CONSOLATION

*When anxiety was great within me,*
*your consolation brought me joy.*
PSALM 94:19 NIV

When your child comes to you with a problem, you don't respond by telling them it doesn't exist. The most compassionate response is to validate what they are feeling and help them to navigate their way through it. So it is with God. When you go to him with your anxiety, he does not respond as though your emotions are unnecessary. He consoles you unto joy. He validates you and brings healing. He doesn't respond by saying, "It's silly for you to feel that way," or "Why can't you just think differently." He is kind, compassionate and the very best teacher.

When anxiety is great within you, he will console you. He will be faithful to hold you and love you. As you experience this aspect of God's tender care, you'll find yourself responding to others in that way. The more you realize how God treats you, the more you'll find ease in validating others and holding their emotions with kindness.

Thank you, God, that you don't turn me away for feeling anxious. My anxiety is not a failure on my part, and I know that I can trust you for consolation. Help me to find joy as you console me. Help me also to treat others in the same way, with dignity and compassion.

# YOU ARE SEEN

*"Your Father,
who sees what is done in secret,
will reward you."*
MATTHEW 6:6 NIV

It's nearly impossible for anyone to know all the things you do for your family. There are countless ways you sacrifice your time, energy, and emotions for their well-being. Not everything that you do will receive a wholehearted thank you, and you likely won't be recognized for each act of kindness or love. God, however, sees all that you do.

When you feel underappreciated or taken for granted, have confidence that God knows exactly what you've done. He is aware of everything that goes unseen by man. He is the one who will reward you for what you give up. He will make sure your acts of service do not go unnoticed. When you walk through motherhood firmly rooted in this truth, you'll be less prone to experience bitterness or resentment. As you trust God for your reward, you'll look less toward others for validation. There is immense freedom to be found in being validated by God.

God, thank you that you see me. You know all that I do, and you are the one who will reward me for it. Help me to find my validation in you and not in those around me. I don't ever want to resent my family or be bitter about how I serve them. Help me to find the joy that comes from trusting you to see me.

# TOTALLY UNIQUE

*If the whole body were an eye, where would the sense of hearing be? If the whole body were an ear, where would the sense of smell be? But in fact God has placed the parts in the body, every one of them, just as he wanted them to be. If they were all one part, where would the body be?*

1 CORINTHIANS 12:17-19 NIV

You are an important part of the body of Christ. So are your children. You each have particular and important roles. It can be easy to think of your children as simply an extension of yourself but remember that God is shaping and molding them to be entirely individual. Their role is different than yours, and as you guide them and point them to Christ, he will teach you how to nurture them well.

Today, take a moment to ask the Lord to show you how and why your children are important to his body. Think about their strengths and how they might grow into them. In the midst of the monotony of motherhood, it can be refreshing to take time to dwell on who God has made your children to be. They are his delight. For a moment, set aside thoughts about laundry, your job, or schoolwork, and choose to find delight in your children's unique and beautiful qualities.

Thank you, Father, that you have designed my children purposefully. Show me who you have made them to be that I might delight in them and nurture them well. Show me the strengths you've given them and how they can bless your body as they grow in those strengths. Help me to encourage them to grow in their gifts.

# FAITHFUL AND TRUE

*God is not human, that he should lie,*
*not a human being, that he should change his mind.*
*Does he speak and then not act?*
*Does he promise and not fulfill?*
NUMBERS 23:19 NIV

As a mother you might struggle to find consistency. One minute you think you're doing enough and the next minute you're sure you are ruining your kids for life. It's a rollercoaster of emotions and constant questions about your ability to give them what they need. God, on the other hand, never changes. He is always constant, always faithful, and he always keeps his promises. It is impossible for him to go against his own Word and it is impossible for him not to fulfill something he promised.

No matter how wishy-washy you might feel, you can depend on his steadiness. He is faithful and true. While you are navigating motherhood with its ever-changing expectations and constant needs, you can find rest in the God who is always the same. His love for you never changes.

Thank you, God, that you never change. You are faithful to your Word and I can depend on the steadiness of your character. I can put my confidence in the fact that you are always good and true.

# SUSTAINED

*I lie down and sleep;*
*I wake again, because the Lord sustains me.*

PSALM 3:5 NIV

You tuck your children in at night. You brush their teeth, make sure they're warm enough, get them a glass of water, and leave them knowing that they are safe and loved. Your bedtime routine might take ten minutes or an hour, but no matter how much you do to prepare them for a good night's sleep, you are not the one who sustains them. It is God who watches over them and wakes them up in the morning. You can prepare all you like, but control does not belong to you. This is the same in all areas of your life.

Today, as you sit in the stillness, take a moment to relinquish control to the one who holds it anyway. The unexpected can change your life in a moment. If controlling, maintaining, or sustaining your life in a certain way is what brings you comfort and satisfaction, then the unexpected will uproot you with a vengeance. Remember that God is your sustainer and you can praise him as such. Rest in his power and ability to orchestrate.

God, thank you for sustaining me and my children. I want to rest in the fact that you are in control. Where I have wasted energy trying to maintain everything, teach me how to trust you. I know that it is not my power that keeps my life afloat; give me the grace to lean on you instead of myself.

# NOVEMBER

My God shall supply all your need
according to His riches in glory
by Christ Jesus.

PHILIPPIANS 4:19 NKJV

# EVER PRESENT HELP

*God is our refuge and strength,*
*an ever-present help in trouble.*
*Therefore we will not fear, though the earth give way*
*and the mountains fall into the heart of the sea,*
*though its waters roar and foam*
*and the mountains quake with their surging.*

PSALM 46:1-3 NIV

There is no force under the sun that is greater than God. Nothing can protect or help you like he can. There is no greater comfort. He is the one who is stronger than the mountains, the raging seas, and the violent wind. Why then do we turn to anything else for refuge or aid? God is invincible, mighty, and incredibly tender toward you. Not only is he infinitely powerful, his lovingkindness has no end.

No matter the storms you find yourself in, remember that God strengthens you; he is your refuge. As you sit quietly for a moment today, rest in the truth that he covers you and protects you. He is your ever-present help, never too far to hear your cries or too occupied when you are in trouble. Be blessed by his strength and the fact that he never turns away a child who is seeking him.

Father, thank you for your help when I am in trouble! May you be the one I turn to, knowing there is no greater source of help or comfort. You are the one who can protect me when the storms come. I want to run to you first without being distracted by worldly comforts.

# A LOVE GIFT

*Children are God's love-gift;*
*they are heaven's generous reward.*
PSALM 127:3 TPT

The baby is finally taking a nap after a sleepless night, the toddler is spilling milk all over the floor, and the six-year-old has just declared that you're the worst mom ever because you won't let her have ice cream for lunch. The dog is barking to go outside, you trip over a pile of dirty laundry trying to get to the door, and just at that moment the UPS man rings the doorbell, waking up the baby.

Moments like this are all too familiar as a mom. Despite how mundane motherhood can be, it can also feel chaotic and overwhelming. When struggling through the day, it can feel nearly impossible to remember what an incredible gift your children are. Right now, as you have a quiet moment with the Lord, remember that they are miracles and have been given to you by the hand of God. Let your heart soften toward them in this moment and let God remind you of his incredible love for them.

God, thank you for my children! Though I am tired and weary, I know they are a gift. No matter how overwhelming my day is, help me to remember the way you see them. May your love for them give me strength when I feel weak and stretched thin. Sustain me today and help me to love them like you do.

# SEEK FIRST

*"Seek first the kingdom of God and His righteousness, and all these things shall be added to you. Therefore do not worry about tomorrow, for tomorrow will worry about its own things."*

MATTHEW 6:33–34 NKJV

There are hundreds of parenting decisions that you make because you know what is best for your children. You can see beyond what they see. You teach them the ABCs so later they can read. You feed them well so their bodies will thrive. You make a million little decisions that ideally add up to a well loved and healthy human. This is how God sees you. As your Father, he knows what you need one hundred days from now. He knows what is best even if you don't see it. He leads you, knowing exactly how to prepare you for the future.

In Matthew, you are reminded to seek first the kingdom of God. Do that. You might be tempted to plan your own path or worry about what seems urgent. Instead, seek the kingdom. God knows that when you do this first, the rest will fall into place because you'll have put it securely in his hands. He knows the correct order of actions even if you don't. Today, rest in his leading. Do the one thing he commanded and leave the rest to him.

Thank you, God, for the ways you lead me. I can't see all of my days like you do. Teach me how to trust in your sovereignty and willingly seek your kingdom above all else. As you lead me, I know things will fall into place. I want to trust you instead of being led by worry.

# REWARDED

*Without faith it is impossible to please him,*
*for whoever would draw near to God must believe that he exists*
*and that he rewards those who seek him.*

HEBREWS 11:6 ESV

Read through that Scripture again. Let the words sink deep into your heart, *he rewards those who seek him.* As you deliberately search for the Lord, as you draw closer to him by reading the Word and meditating on his goodness, he will reward you. Each act of faith pleases him and is seen by him. It doesn't say that he rewards those who seek him all day, behave in the right way, or don't make mistakes. He rewards those who faithfully seek him. Each step you take toward God is an act of faith.

Today, as you give the time you have to him, ask him what act of faith you can move in. Ask him what you can do to seek him and listen quietly and confidently for the answer. He will be faithful to lead you. Your willingness to honor him and search for him is a delight to him.

God, thank you that you see each step I make toward you. You say that you will reward those who seek you, and I trust that you will. Teach me how to follow you more closely. How can I step out in faith today? I want to seek you with all that I have.

# A LITTLE IS BETTER

*Better the little that the righteous have
than the wealth of many wicked.*
PSALM 37:16 NIV

Once again, the values of the kingdom of God are contrary to what the world tells you. Less is more. It is better to be righteous and have a little, than to be wicked and have an abundance. In a world that is constantly reminding you that you don't have enough, it is radical to defiantly declare that you are content. It is earth shaking to refuse to be swept away by dissatisfaction and comparison. Your level of happiness with what you have not only impacts you, it also impacts your children.

As you cultivate an atmosphere of thanksgiving, they too will learn the joy of being happy with what they have. Have you ever been around someone who is never satisfied? It's exhausting. They are typically crabby, negative, and cannot be pleased. That is the fruit that waits for you when you don't practice thanksgiving that embraces humility. In a world that values more of everything, be the revolutionary type of woman who says she has enough.

Father, I want to have an attitude of thanksgiving no matter how much or how little I have. Teach me how to be content because I always have you. I have access to the riches of your kingdom and that is better than any material gain I might seek. Help me to teach my children how to have thankful hearts.

# A STURDY WALL

*Like a city whose walls are broken through
is a person who lacks self-control.*
PROVERBS 25:28 NIV

Self-control is like the fortified wall of a well-protected city. Practicing self-control is your first line of defense toward an attack. A city builds a wall not because the enemy is at their gates but because they anticipate the arrival long before. So it is with self-control. You practice self-control not because of a current struggle but because God has given you the wisdom to anticipate an attack in the future.

Don't expect to have self-control in an area where you haven't already set clear boundaries. It's really hard to build a wall while the enemy is storming your gates. You know your weaknesses, so fortify yourself by letting God tell you how to wisely face them. God will never turn you away when you ask for wisdom. If you are feeling weakened in a certain area, ask God what you can do to build up your walls. Trust that he values your protection as much as you do. He will be faithful to help you practice self-control.

God, thank you for your protection. I know that I cannot fight my battles alone. Give me the wisdom to know where I need to strengthen my walls in order to anticipate attack. I want to practice self-control. Teach me how to develop self-control in the areas where I struggle.

# TEACH AND ADMONISH

*Let the message of Christ dwell among you richly as you teach and*
*admonish one another with all wisdom through psalms, hymns, and*
*songs from the spirit, singing to God with gratitude in your hearts.*
COLOSSIANS 3:16 NIV

The body of Christ is designed to lift each other up, teaching
and admonishing each other with grace and gratitude. These are
the qualities of a healthy and thriving community. While it can
be uncomfortable, you should welcome the teaching of others.
Likewise, if someone is admonishing you, it should be done with
wisdom and kindness. Whenever Scripture describes interactions
within the body it is always defined by gentleness, selflessness,
and putting others before yourself. Seek to embody those
characteristics for the believers around you.

May your words be life-giving, and your actions display humility
and true love for your neighbor. Let the message of Christ dwell
among you richly. Let it surround you and define all that you do.
Let who Christ is and what he has done impact all your gatherings.
Today, as you seek him, ask him how you can take part in teaching
and admonishing the body.

God, thank you for your body. You have designed it to operate
in love and wisdom. May my interactions with my brothers and
sisters point them to you. I want to teach others in humility,
and I want to embrace humility as I am taught. Help me to
honor you in that way.

# PRESERVE THE GOSPEL

*Let your conversation be always full of grace, seasoned with salt,*
*so that you may know how to answer everyone.*
COLOSSIANS 4:6 NIV

Just as salt is used to preserve various foods, let your words preserve the message of Christ to all generations. Speak in such a way that you elevate the gospel and seek to bring life with all you say. Think about the incredible compassion and grace God uses when he speaks to his children and seek to address your children in that way as well.

Don't forget that the reminder in Colossians to speak with grace applies to the way you speak to your family. If your conversations with them have been less than full of grace, seek today to repent and then behave differently. Your words have great influence and what you might see as flippant can have great impact. Use your influence to lift up the name of Christ, preserving the gospel and bringing life to all who hear what you say.

Thank you for the reminder to speak in a life-giving way, God. I want to honor you with my words. Please forgive me for how I've abused my influence and have not spoken in a way that is full of grace. Teach me how to talk to my children in a way that honors you.

# FAITHFUL TO DIRECT

*I will instruct you and teach you in the way you should go;*
*I will counsel you with my loving eye on you.*
PSALM 32:8 NIV

God is an attentive father. This has been true for your entire life and will be true for all of your remaining days. There is never going to be a point or an age when you don't need his guidance. He is not like an earthly parent, stepping further back with each milestone as their child becomes more independent. God is always your Father, full of lovingkindness, wisdom, and guidance. Don't let pride, experience or busyness get in the way of listening for his counsel. If you quiet your heart, your mind, and even your schedule, you'll hear his voice. He is faithful to direct you when you turn your ear toward his voice.

In God, you have a patient teacher, wise counselor, and loving guide. He will faithfully instruct you in all of his wisdom. Like a rock climber who knows exactly where the next steady place is, God will show you exactly where you need to go. If you are overwhelmed today, ask him for the next step; you only need one direction in order to walk in obedience. Ask him what you need to do today.

God, thank you for your guidance. I know that I can trust your leading and your wisdom. Please speak to me about what you want me to do today. Give me the next step so I can be faithful. Teach me how to hear your voice and follow your directions.

# CONFIDENT IN THE CREATOR

*We do not dare to classify or compare ourselves with some who commend themselves. When they measure themselves by themselves and compare themselves with themselves, they are not wise.*

2 CORINTHIANS 10:12 NIV

Imagine your child coming to you upset, declaring that so-and-so is a better artist or is better at soccer. They're upset because all they can see is what they lack and what others have. As their mom, you are likely quick to point out the way that you see them. You easily list all that you love about them and remind them of what they bring to the table. You say that different isn't worse and you do your best to encourage them. Does this reaction come to you as easily when you are the one comparing yourself?

As you might be focusing on thanksgiving this month, remember that one of the quickest ways to ensure you aren't thankful is to compare yourself to others. Your standard isn't held by anyone but the Lord. What you bring to the table is unique and perfectly designed by God. He made you with your specific strengths and weaknesses. Today, remember that comparison to others only leaves you frustrated and without wisdom. Rest from comparison and delight in how God sees you.

Father, I know you have made me the way I am on purpose. I need your encouragement where I am weak and where I am tempted to compare myself to others. Remind me of how you see me. Teach me how to walk confidently because you are my Creator.

# ORDER OVER CHAOS

*God is not a God of disorder but of peace.*
1 CORINTHIANS 14:33 NIV

As a mother, you're familiar with disorder. That pile of shoes by the door, the never-ending dishes, the stack of mail and school papers, the piano books scattered across the bench—all of these can add up to a general feeling of chaos. More so, you can feel disorder in your heart as you strive to nurture the emotions and fulfill the needs that each of your children have.

Motherhood is not always neat and tidy; in fact, it rarely is. Yet, God is a not a God of disorder. He is a God of peace. Where there is disorder, brokenness, or things are simply not as they should be, God longs to bring peace. He isn't disorganized, chaotic, or flighty. He is peaceful, and the way he operates is peaceful. No matter how insane your life might feel, you can find peace in the presence of God. Don't let the chaos of your circumstances dictate the state of your heart. As you seek him, let God be the one to dictate the level of peace you have.

Thank you, God, that you are not a God of disorder or chaos. No matter how my life feels, I can find peace in you. Your peace does not depend on circumstances. Help me to trust you for peace when my life feels chaotic.

# LIKE A PILGRIM

*Blessed are those whose strength is in you,*
*Whose hearts are set on pilgrimage.*
PSALM 84:5 ESV

What is particular about a pilgrim? He has a specific destination and his eyes are set firmly upon it. He doesn't look to the left or the right. He isn't preoccupied by how smooth the path is because he knows that he must reach his end goal. He doesn't waver because it starts to rain or because it is difficult. He knows exactly where he is going, and he is entirely motivated by his end goal.

Blessed are you when your heart is set upon Jesus in this way, as a pilgrim on a journey. Your strength is found in the Lord, you do not waver, and you are not distracted by the journey. Your reward in Christ is so rich and sweet that you place one foot in front of the other with fortitude and commitment. Today, set your face like flint and steady your gaze. Remind yourself that you are on a pilgrimage toward eternity with God and let the end goal motivate you to keep going even when it's hard.

God, thank you for being my strength as I walk through life. Remind me today of what I am walking toward. I want to be like a pilgrim, set firmly on the path toward eternity with you. Help me to keep my eyes on you.

# ETERNAL ENCOURAGEMENT

*May our Lord Jesus Christ himself and God our Father, who loved us and
by his grace gave us eternal encouragement and good hope, encourage
your hearts and strengthen you in every good deed and word.*

2 THESSALONIANS 2:16–17 NIV

Let this be your prayer over yourself and over your children today.
God, your Father, has given you eternal encouragement through
his grace. Because of the grace that he bestows upon you, you
can be encouraged and uplifted not just today but for all eternity.
This hope is never-ending. May the hope that you have in Christ
cause you to look upward and strengthen you in every good
deed. In your discouragement, your pain, your longing, and your
disappointment, may you be held closely by the Lord who loves
you and longs to see you walking in hope and encouragement.

Isn't it delightful that the God of the entire universe wants to
strengthen you in good deeds? Of all the things that he is capable,
he uses his power to guide you through your day, lifting you up
and ensuring that you know how loved you are. It is his great
delight to shower grace upon you. He wants not only to meet your
needs but to empower you and strengthen you.

Thank you for your great encouragement, God. In the midst of
all your power, you prioritize lifting me up and strengthening
me. You encourage me when I am weak, and you give me
hope. Help me to turn to you for encouragement that is eternal.

# HE KNOWS

*"Your Father knows exactly what you need
even before you ask him!"*
MATTHEW 6:8 NLT

Much of your time as a mother is probably spent deciphering. For most of infancy and the toddler years, you are trying to figure out what your child wants or needs. Eventually, you discover what their cues are and it's almost like a second language that you speak. You intuitively know and understand the way they communicate even when others can't. You know the meanings of their poorly pronounced words and you can decode their facial expressions in a way that other adults might struggle to. Try to communicate these nuances to a babysitter or caretaker and you'll quickly realize that as their mother, you have an understanding of your child that simply can't be explained.

If in your human weakness this is the degree to which you understand the needs of your child, imagine how intricately God can anticipate your needs. Not only does he know exactly what you need, but he sees how each of your days are connected and what you need to prepare for each season of your life. As you care for those around you, feel your burden lighten as you soak in the truth that your Father is taking excellent care of you.

Father, thank you that you know what I need. Teach me how to surrender to you as I trust in your care. I don't even have to communicate to you what I need; your care for me is intricate and all encompassing.

# DAILY NEWNESS

*Blessed be the God and Father of our Lord Jesus Christ!*
*By his great mercy he has given us a new birth into a living hope*
*through the resurrection of Jesus Christ from the dead.*

1 PETER 1:3 NRSV

In the thrill of experiencing the new life of your child, you might have had a moment of sobriety when you felt the weight of bringing a baby into a broken world. You may have worried about the things they would experience or be exposed to. Reality can feel heavy in the middle of marveling at new life. All you want to do is hold them close forever and protect them from everything that lies beyond your arms.

In Christ, you too have been given new birth. You have not been birthed into brokenness and death; you have been given new birth into a living hope. Jesus saved you from death and has secured for you a life that will never fade. His death brings you the hope of being free from death forever. With his one great sacrifice, he has secured new life. Each day you can marvel at the newness that he creates. Babies grow and newness fades, but the new life you've been given in Christ can be found every day.

God, thank you that the new life I've been given can never end. In it I have hope and the joy of knowing I'll be with you forever. Help me to marvel at what you have done and how I have been made new.

# NOT A SLAVE

*No longer do I call you servants, for the servant does not know what his master is doing; but I have called you friends, for all that I have heard from my Father I have made known to you.*

Are you viewing Christ as though he is your friend or as though you are his servant? A servant feels obligated to please a master. A servant must follow rules. A servant does not seek the company of a master for comfort or companionship. A servant has a specific job and that is his highest priority. A friend, on the other hand, trusts a friend for encouragement and joy. A friend does not view the other in terms of priorities and tasks. A friend is free to express their emotions and knows they will be loved.

In your time with God, rest in the friendship that is available to you. If you find yourself viewing him like a servant views a master, ask him to reveal to you how he is your friend. Ask him to change your perspective and he will be faithful to show you who he really is.

God, thank you for your friendship. I want to see you rightly and not simply as an authority figure in my life. Help me to see you as my friend, full of love and encouragement. I am not your slave; I am your friend. In areas where I don't see our relationship rightly, change my heart.

# ENOUGH FOR YOU

*Whom have I in heaven but you?*
*And there is nothing on earth that I desire other than you.*
*My flesh and my heart may fail,*
*but God is the strength of my heart and my portion forever.*
PSALM 73:25-26 NRSV

He is enough for you. No matter what you are lacking or what the world says you need for a complete life, God is enough. There are so many voices telling you what you need to be happy and successful. It can be exhausting to constantly feel like you can't measure up. It's a losing battle to try and stay afloat in a culture that is never satisfied. Drowning in want doesn't take long. Waters of jealousy and dissatisfaction can swallow you up like the sea, waves of discontent crashing all around.

He is the one who can truly satisfy your soul. You were designed to live in communion with him and you won't find true rest until you find it in him. If you are feeling anxious or unsettled, he is with you, steadfast and able to quiet all the noise inside your heart. He is your greatest comfort, your kindest advocate, and your truest strength.

You are enough for me, God! Teach me how to find my satisfaction in you. Today, strengthen me and teach me how to depend on you in my weakness. Help me to turn away from the voices that tell me I always need more. You are my portion and my greatest reward.

# PEACE AT ALL TIMES

*May the Lord of peace himself*
*give you peace at all times*
*and in every way.*
2 THESSALONIANS 3:16 NIV

God is capable of giving you peace at all times and in all ways. He can calm your heart in whatever way is personal to you. He can help you breathe deep and make your heart beat slower. He can steady your gaze and calm the most frantic spirit. When you feel like you're running in circles or you're walking through something particularly painful, turn to him for peace. It's possible to be in pain and at peace. It's possible to be broken and at peace. As you ask him for healing, he can give you peace in the waiting.

Peace is not a lack of emotion or a denial of circumstances, it's a lack of anxiety and a steady trust in the Lord. In your deepest darkness, God can bring you peace. In your most painful moments, God can bring you peace. Let him hold your heart no matter your circumstances. Let him comfort you and keep you steady especially when everything around you is frantic.

God, thank you for your peace! It's a gift and I want to walk in it fully, no matter what is happening around me. Teach me how to receive peace from you in all circumstances. Your peace is bigger than my emotions, so help me to turn my eyes to you when things are difficult.

# SEEK TOGETHER

*"Where two or three gather in my name,*
*there am I with them."*

MATTHEW 18:20 NIV

If you are feeling as though God is far away, gather with others in his name. He promises that he will be with you. This Scripture can be an incredible blessing because of the clarity of direction found in it. It's a direct and simple promise, where two are more are gathered, God is there. There isn't an age stipulation here, so remember that this can apply to your children! You can seek the Lord together and he promises to show up. It might not be neat or quiet, but God will be there. Sit with them, pray with them, read the Word, and you will meet God.

You might feel as though the busyness and exhaustion of motherhood has kept you from seeking God. You can change that today. Take what you have and give it to the Lord. Gather in his name with your family, and trust that he will be true to his Word.

I need you, Lord! I need your nearness and your mercy. I can gather in your name with my family and you will be there. You promise that you will meet us, so I trust that you will be true to your Word. Help me to remember I can seek you just as much with my kids as I did before.

# OVER PRODUCTIVITY

*Give thanks to the Lord over all Lords!*
*His tender love for us continues on forever!*
*Give thanks to the only miracle working God!*
*His tender love for us continues on forever!*

PSALM 136:3-4 TPT

Take a moment to praise God. If you have a lot going on today, it can feel counterproductive to stop everything. It is difficult to move your attention from your task list onto God and his many praiseworthy attributes. Embrace that feeling of difficulty and recognize that your mental change in direction is actually the most productive thing you can do. The more you praise him, the more your heart will be turned toward him in tenderness and affection.

Praise can change your heart, your mindset, and your perspective. As you focus on his greatness, you'll also find the peace you need to move through your day. Let these few moments of praise be the foundation from which you start your day. As you turn your heart toward him, let it set a posture of thanksgiving that influences all you do.

I am so thankful for you, Father! You love me fully and you deserve all of my praise. Help me to turn to you now in praise that I might honor you throughout my day. I know you have done great things for me. Turn my heart to you in thanksgiving and praise that I might not be consumed by busyness and productivity.

# REFLECTED HEART

*"A good man brings good things out of the good stored up in his heart,
and an evil man brings evil things out of the evil stored up in his heart.
For the mouth speaks what the heart is full of."*

LUKE 6:45 NIV

What comes out of your mouth is directly related to the state of your heart. As uncomfortable as it can be, it's helpful to take inventory of the things you find yourself saying. According to the Word, what you say is a reflection of your heart. There isn't a "might," a "maybe," or a "sometimes" in this Scripture. What you say defines who you are. In humility, realize that if your words are primarily complaining, negative, crude, or angry, then that is the state of your heart as well.

If you realize there is a disparity between what you say and who you think you are, humbly ask for forgiveness. Where Christ brings conviction, he always brings redemption. You are never meant to sit and dwell in sin. There is always the possibility of healing and hope. If he has brought a habit of speech to mind, he will also empower you to repent and change.

God, thank you for the reminder that the words I say reflect the state of my heart. I want the things I say to reflect you. Help me to speak in a way that honors you and is life-giving. Forgive me for habits that I've developed that don't exemplify you and your character.

# GIVER OF GIFTS

*Every good gift and every perfect gift is from above,*
*and comes down from the Father of lights,*
*with whom there is no variation or shadow of turning.*
JAMES 1:17 NKJV

The steady beat of your heart, the breath in your lungs, the painted sky, the colors of fall, and the roof over your head are all gifts from your Father. He is the Creator and sustainer of life. He is the one who has given you every good thing you have. The love of a friend, the last meal you ate, the cool breeze on a warm day, and the flicker of a candle on a fall evening are all from him. All good things come from him. The weariness and busyness of motherhood can leave you forgetting about the million little ways that God has shown you his love. Each good gift comes from his abundant love for you.

Today, even if you can only muster up one thing, thank God for something good in your life. He has showered you with goodness; ask him to open your eyes to see it. The good things in your life might not look like your neighbor's but that doesn't make them any less good. Focus on what he has done for you and let thanksgiving draw you closer to him.

Father, you have given me so many good things! I know that you have blessed me in ways that I don't even see. Open my eyes to see the gifts you've given, big and small. I want to walk in thanksgiving and praise rather than comparison and frustration. Thank you for all you've given me.

# ALWAYS THANKFUL

*I will give thanks to the LORD with my whole heart;*
*I will recount all of your wonderful deeds.*
*I will be glad and exult in you;*
*I will sing praise to your name, O Most High.*

PSALM 9:1-2 ESV

While thankfulness is an easy and obvious topic to focus on this month, don't forget that it should be a year-round state of your heart. It's good to feel extra thankful now but seek to carry that habit into the rest of your year. Seeing all that has been done for you and all that you have will draw you closer to God. The more you are aware of God's wonderful deeds and eternally good character, the more you will delight in what you have, leaving less room for comparison and dissatisfaction.

You live in a culture that tells you it's okay to never be satisfied: that you should always be searching for more. Deliberately fight against that by walking in thanksgiving. It's difficult to be dissatisfied when you are walking in gratitude. Today, ask the Lord to show you what you have to be thankful for. Then, praise him for it! Praise him for all that he's done and all that he will do. He is always at work and he is always good.

God, teach me to walk in constant thanksgiving! Your name is great, and your works are good. I want to see how you have moved in my life and be thankful for it. I want to see your works and praise you for them. Open my eyes more to what you've done and who you are.

# A RICH GOSPEL

*Always be thankful.*
*Let the message about Christ,*
*in all its richness,*
*fill your lives.*

COLOSSIANS 3:15 NLT

The gospel makes the poor man rich. It fills empty spaces and brings joy to the broken. It makes the lame man walk and the blind man see. In your desire to walk in thanksgiving, don't forget the beautiful miracle of Christ. As you think of all that God has blessed you with, remember the incredible gift that you've been given in Jesus. As you walk forward in faith, following Jesus all your days, it is good to dwell on the miracle of his life and death.

The cross is your foundation and your strength. You will never be a mature enough Christian that the foundational message of the cross will be any less important. The gospel is never mundane, never irrelevant, and never repeated too many times. Today, take a moment to kneel at the foot of the cross and remember all that Jesus has done. Let the richness of the gospel fill your life. Let it stir thanksgiving and praise in your heart. Let it push you toward worship and exaltation.

God, you have been so good to me! Thank you for what you have done through Jesus. Open my eyes to the miracle of the gospel. May my heart be stirred in tenderness and thanksgiving. Help me always to be moved by the miracle of the gospel.

# UTILIZE THE WORD

*All Scripture is inspired by God and profitable for teaching,
for reproof, for correction, for training in righteousness.*
2 TIMOTHY 3:16 NASB

Have you ever provided your children with a resource only to see them completely ignore it and struggle through whatever task they have? Maybe you have a tumultuous relationship with your preteen and even though you have a math degree, they refuse to let you help them with algebra homework. You watch them stubbornly muddle through it, knowing that your help would make all the difference.

Likewise, don't forsake the gift that you've been given in the Word. Though it might sound cliché, you truly have been given a manual to live by. When you find yourself unsure of something, lost, or discouraged, read the Word. In all circumstances, read the Word of God. It is full of life and always profitable for you. The more you fill your heart with Scripture, the more you'll be able to quickly decipher between truth and lies. As you become familiar with what God has said, you'll find yourself wasting less time worrying about things that he didn't say.

God, thank you for the gift that you've given me in the Word. Help me to utilize it well. I want to be so familiar with your Word that I can quickly decipher what is true and what is not. As I read it, with whatever amount of time I have, help it to sink deep into my heart.

# GIVEN EVERYTHING

*I say to the Lord, "You are my Lord;*
*apart from you I have no good thing."*

PSALM 16:2 NIV

As you seek the Lord today, remember that he is the true source of goodness. The blessings that you have in him will outshine, outlast, and bring more satisfaction than any earthly thing you could find for yourself. The healthiest relationship, the best vacation, the most perfect meal still cannot compare to his goodness. When you begin to see him as the true source of all that is good, your heart will grow in humility and in thanksgiving. It is he who sustains you and blesses you.

No striving on your own part has brought goodness to your life. Understanding this will also open your eyes to see those around you in the same way that Christ sees you—with grace and mercy. In his mercy, he has held you all of your days and will continue to do so. Today, when you thank him for the life you have, do it earnestly and with the kind of humility that shows you understand his hand on your life. Truly, without him, you have nothing.

Father, thank you for all you've given me. Any good thing in my life comes from you. Help me to see that with humility. I want to have a heart that overflows with thanksgiving, constantly praising you and uplifting you above myself. Without you, I have nothing. Thank you for sustaining me and blessing me with your presence.

# REFUGE BRINGS HAPPINESS

*O taste and see that the LORD is good;*
*happy are those who take refuge in him.*
PSALM 34:8 NRSV

Happy are those who get what they want. Happy are those whose lives are trouble free. Happy are those who reach their goals. None of these are found in the Word. None of these will bring lasting satisfaction or true happiness. The truth is this: happy are those who take refuge in God. True satisfaction and joy come only from his presence. Anything else you might try as a substitute will leave you wanting.

As you spend your days caring for others, it can be easy to daydream about all the things that might make you happy. If only you could sleep more, your home was prettier, or you were more organized. If only you had more time to yourself or your children behaved differently. Today, quiet that list and remember that true happiness comes from taking refuge in God. From that place you'll begin to see the rest of your life with the thanksgiving and humility that comes from seeking him above all else.

God, you alone are my refuge. You are the only place I can find true happiness and joy. You are always faithful to protect and shelter me. Teach me how to see your goodness more clearly and to take refuge in you instead of dwelling on what I wish were different about my life.

# ALL NATIONS

*After this I looked, and behold, a great multitude that no one could number, from every nation, from all tribes and peoples and languages, standing before the throne and before the Lamb, clothed in white robes, with palm branches in their hands, and crying out with a loud voice, "Salvation belongs to our God who sits on the throne, and to the Lamb."*

REVELATION 7: 9-12 ESV

This image (all nations, tribes, and people worshipping together) is what you were designed for. This is the glory that is to come. This is what you have to look forward to as a follower of Jesus. You'll be able to worship him, all together, unhindered by earthly troubles and broken humanity. This is the type of communion you were made for. When you feel the lack of this poignantly, let it stir up hope that strengthens you to patiently endure.

No matter your current struggles, there will be a day when you are fully at home and fully alive, worshiping God in front of his very throne. Your tears will be tenderly wiped away and your broken body will be made new. Today, as you seek God in the stillness, be blessed by what he has given you to look forward to.

Father, thank you for the beautiful picture of what is to come. I can't even imagine what it will be like to be surrounded by people who are all worshipping you. Teach me how to patiently endure what is hard right now because what is to come is so great. Keep my eyes focused on you when I get tired and teach me what it looks like to have my hope securely placed in what you've promised.

# TRUE NEWNESS

*You were taught, with regard to your former way of life, to put off your old self, which is being corrupted by its deceitful desires; to be made new in the attitude of your minds; and to put on the new self, created to be like God in true righteousness and holiness.*

EPHESIANS 4:22-24 NIV

Are there parts of your former self that you still carry around? Do you truly believe that you have been made new in Christ? Your new self, created to be like God, is alive because of what Christ did on the cross. God desires freedom for you. If you are still holding burdens from your past, know that you can place them in God's hands and trust him for healing. God's ability to make you new is not incomplete. He takes every part of you into account and he still declares that you are new in Jesus. Your deepest pain is not too much for him. Your worst trauma is not ignored. He wants to see you walk in wholeness and fullness of life.

As a mom, you are often focusing on the needs of everyone around you. Remember that God sees what you need. He has not put you on hold while you raise your children. As much as before, and as much as he will in the future, he desires to bring healing and wholeness to your life. Be blessed by the truth that as you put off your old self, God meets you.

God, I believe that I am alive in you and made new. I want this to impact every area of my life. Teach me how to walk as a new creation. Show me where I have held onto my former self and help me to surrender that fully to you. You see me and you know what I need.

# END GOAL

*You make known to me the path of life;*
*you will fill me with joy in your presence,*
*with eternal pleasures at your right hand.*

PSALM 16:11 NIV

Having a clear destination makes your path easier to navigate. If you know what your end goal is, you can keep it in mind when difficulty arises. Without the motivation of a clear purpose, it can be easy to stray from the right path. If your main goal as a mother is for your children to be healthy and well educated, then this will dictate the life of your family. If your main goal is for them to be well behaved or self-sufficient, this will also dictate how you interact with them. For better or worse, your values have power over your everyday life.

The same is true when it comes to your relationship with God. What is your end goal? The Psalmist says that joy in God's presence and eternal pleasures at his right hand are what is to come. Let this impact the way you live today. His highest goal for you is joy in his presence and an eternity together.

Father, thank you that your plans for me are not a mystery. I don't have to fret that I'm not on the right path because you have made it clear. Help me to value joy in your presence above all else. Teach me how to keep my eyes steady on an eternity in your presence and let that dictate how I live and love now.

# DECEMBER

Faith is the confidence that what we
hope for will actually happen; it gives us
assurance about things we cannot see.

Hebrews 11:1 nlt

# WONDERFUL COUNSELOR

*To a us a child is born, to us a son is given; and the government shall be*
*upon his shoulder, and his name shall be called Wonderful Counselor,*
*Mighty God, Everlasting Father, Prince of Peace.*

ISAIAH 9:6 NIV

As the days get shorter and the world around you begins to quietly settle into winter, let the physical darkness of this season draw you toward the great light of Christ. Let your heart sit in wonder at who he was to a waiting and anxious world. Imagine the great hope that he brought: a prophecy fulfilled and an awaited promise brought to fruition. He came as a baby, humbly to save you from death.

As you remember the Messiah and his birth, remember also who he was promised to be. In Christ Jesus, you have not only a Savior but a wonderful counselor. He is the one you can lean on in times of uncertainty. He is the one you can lean on for guidance. He is the one you can process with and depend on for counsel. He cannot and will not steer you down the wrong path. He will always faithfully draw you to truth and to the presence of the Father.

Father, thank you for the gift of Jesus. He came to save me from sin but he also is my counselor, friend, and advocate. Today, as I dwell on the gift of who Jesus is, may it draw me closer to you in thanksgiving and praise.

# LIFE FROM DEATH

*By this we know love,*
*because He laid down His life for us.*
1 JOHN 3:16 NKJV

As you focus on the birth of Jesus this month, remember that he was born to die, and he died to bring new life. His miraculous birth was the start of an earthly life that would lead him to defeating death and bringing redemption for all. You know that his love for you is great because he gave up everything to redeem you. He left the glory of the Father to come to earth and make a way for you to come to God. He knew precisely how difficult his life on earth would be and he willingly chose to do it anyway.

When you struggle to love others, you can simply look to Christ as example. In what ways can you lay down your life? Despite how difficult it might be, God urges you to show love to others in the same way that Christ displayed his love for you.

Jesus, as I dwell on your birth, help me to remember your death as well. Thank you for the example that I have in you. Teach me how to lay my life down for others. Teach me how to love like you love.

# WHAT I WANT

*I don't really understand myself,*
*for I want to do what is right, but I don't do it.*
*Instead, I do what I hate.*

ROMANS 7:15 NLT

God knows precisely the struggles you face. He knows your weaknesses and your intentions. The Bible is full of examples of how people just don't measure up. You aren't alone in your shortcomings. You are not alone in your struggle against sin. Paul goes so far as to say he knows what he should do but he doesn't do it. Instead, he knowingly does the wrong thing. Have you ever said to your children, "You know better!"?

The knowledge of right and wrong is not what empowers us to behave a certain way, to follow the right path and keep ourselves in check. The work of the Holy Spirit within you, bringing conviction and then reminding of you the grace that is bestowed upon you is what empowers you to say no to sin. Today, remember that is not your own striving that will lead you to holiness. The power that raised Christ from the dead is what leads you to sanctification.

Thank you for what you did for me, Jesus. I can't say no to sin in my own power and with my own ability. Help me to humbly turn to you, Lord, depending wildly on your grace. Help me to realize that my strength comes only from you and not my own striving.

# NOT DISAPPOINTED

*This hope will not lead to disappointment.*
*For we know how dearly God loves us,*
*because he has given us the Holy Spirit*
*to fill our hearts with his love.*

ROMANS 5:5 NLT

If you find yourself feeling insecure about the love God has for you, ask the Holy Spirit to fill your heart with his love. You have been given the gift of the Holy Spirit so that while Christ cannot be with you in the flesh pointing you the Father, you have an advocate who can. It is the Holy Spirit's joy and delight to remind you of the unfailing love of God.

If God expected you to have consistent confidence in him, he would not have felt the need to leave you with a counselor, teacher, and guide. He knew exactly how prone to wander and doubt you would be, and he equipped you in advance. No one knows you better than God. He sees you clearly and loves to strengthen you in your understanding of his character. If the thought of God as loving, kind, gentle, and tender leaves you feeling doubtful, ask him to show you who he is. Ask him to build your confidence in his love. God will be faithful to reveal himself to you.

Father, thank you for the Holy Spirit who reminds me of how much you love me. My doubts and wanderings don't surprise you or cause you to be disappointed in me. Instead you have equipped me, teaching me gently and guiding me toward you.

# INWARD BEAUTY

*Don't be concerned about the outward beauty of fancy hairstyles,
expensive jewelry, or beautiful clothes. You should clothe yourselves
instead with the beauty that comes from within, the unfading beauty
of a gentle and quiet spirit, which is so precious to God.*

1 Peter 3:3-4 nlt

Motherhood has a way of stripping you down. Your body is a map of who you are. It might bear the scars of pregnancy and childbirth or your heart might bear them from loving a child you didn't physically carry. Your eyes might be dark and heavy, hinting of the sleepless nights you've spent caring for little ones. Your hands may be more wrinkled, showing you've cradled, caressed, and worked hard to serve your children. Your back might be sore from carrying the child who just wants to be close. Motherhood can be rough.

Today, let God gently hold you where you are worn and remind you that no matter your physical weariness, he is cultivating within you the unfading beauty of a quiet and gentle spirit. Don't look at yesterday and long for how your body was. Instead, look at how far you have come. Look at how this body has served you and remember that what is most precious to God is the beauty that comes from within. His work in your heart is far more valuable than anything outward could ever be.

Thank you that you look at my heart, God. You are cultivating within me a quiet and gentle spirit. Where my body is fading as I serve my family, my spirit can thrive in you. Help me to keep my eyes focused not on outward beauty but on you and what you are doing. Today, teach me to value what you value.

# BOASTING

*What, after all, is Apollos? And what is Paul? Only servants, through whom you came to believe—as the Lord has assigned to each his task. I planted the seed, Apollos watered it, but God has been making it grow. So neither the one who plants nor the one who waters is anything, but only God, who makes things grow. The one who plants and the one who waters have one purpose, and they will each be rewarded according to their own labor.*

1 CORINTHIANS 3:5-8 NIV

Depending on their age, your child might still look at you like you make the sun rise. For a season, you are everything to them. They think you are invincible. You are their entire world. In their innocence it is good and right that they see you this way, but ultimately it is your job to point them to Christ. They can't possibly see you in that light for their entire lives. Likewise, it is good to have mentors and those you look up to. It is good for you to be encouraged by the lives of other believers.

You might have a favorite author, social media influencer, or pastor. There isn't anything inherently wrong with that. In your admiration, it is paramount that you ascribe glory where it is due. God is the one who is truly at work. If your worship of another person has surpassed your worship for God, then you need to rearrange your focus. It's easy to be wrapped up in passionate discussion about particular beliefs but remember that God is the one you should be boasting about. No human words, platforms, or songs can surpass who God is and what he has done.

God, thank you for the people in my life who have spoken wisdom over me. I am thankful for their examples and encouragement, but I don't want to value them over you. Help me to always see your hand at work.

# GLORY AND GRACE

*The LORD God is our sun and our shield.*
*He gives us grace and glory.*
*The LORD will withhold no good thing*
*from those who do what is right.*

PSALM 84:11 NLT

How beautiful that you serve a God who gives you grace and glory. Not only does he empower you to live rightly but then he rewards you for it, even though it is his work within you that has made you holy. He is the God who delights in providing for you, protecting you, and encouraging you. He is your sun, the source of your life, and the one who sustains you. He gives you abundant grace whenever you need it and longs to have compassion on you. When you follow him, he says that he will withhold no good thing from you.

As you follow him, he will open your eyes to his goodness, heal your heart, and equip you to persevere until the day Jesus comes back. Praise him today for all he has done in your life and in your heart.

Thank you for your protection in being my shield, God. Thank you for your sustaining grace in being my sun. You give me glory and withhold no good thing from me. Teach me how to do what is right, so I might honor you all of my days.

# BE CONTENT

*Be content with what you have, because God has said,*
*"Never will I leave you; never will I forsake you."*
HEBREWS 13:5 NIV

During the holiday season it's easy to become bombarded with all the things you don't have. As the world seeks material gain, it can be easy to feel overwhelmed that you have to provide everyone with the perfect Christmas experience. You need to buy the perfect gifts, make the perfect meal, plan the perfect memories, and decorate beautifully on top of everything else.

This year take a deep breath, let all of that go, and find the freedom in being content with what you have. Truly, this time of year you can be content because God is near. Let that draw you closer to him in thanksgiving while the rest of the world is constantly striving for more. Celebrate the simple and miraculous gift of Christ's birth with a quiet heart and a thankful spirit. Instead of drowning in comparison, dwell today on what is truly valuable and eternal—the lovingkindness of Christ and his ability to redeem all that is lost.

God, if I'm being honest, it's really hard to be content. I need your help not to compare my life to everyone around me. Teach me how to be content with what I have because what I truly have is miraculous and eternal. I want to value your presence above all the other things that tug at my affection.

# OVERLOOKING OFFENSE

*A person's wisdom yields patience;*
*it is to one's glory to overlook an offense.*
PROVERBS 19:11 NIV

When someone offends you, it is not easy to overlook it. Your natural tendency is to protect yourself and hold onto hurt. Know that it is possible to acknowledge your pain, find healing, and still overlook an offense. Overlooking doesn't mean ignoring it or getting over it. It means looking past it. Overlooking an offense means acknowledging the other person's humanity as well as your own. This can only be done when you see Christ rightly in his miraculous ability to cover all sins and redeem you when you least deserve it.

In understanding that you don't deserve the mercy of Christ, you'll find it easier to extend mercy to those around you even when wronged. You, a sinner, are surrounded by sinners. We all fall short of the glory of God, but we are all given access to his great mercy in an equal measure. Today, ask the Lord to soften your heart toward those who have wronged you. Let him lead you in whatever reconciliation and healing is necessary.

Father, it's so hard to overlook offenses but I know that you have covered my sins even when I didn't deserve it. Teach me how to see others the way you see them and to have mercy for them.

# ELEVATE OTHERS

*"I have the right to do anything," you say—
but not everything is beneficial. "I have the right to do anything"—
but not everything is constructive. No one should seek their own good,
but the good of others.*

1 CORINTHIANS 10:23-24 NIV

As a mother, you know exactly what it means to put the needs of others before your own. You are constantly making sure that your children are well cared for before you think about yourself. Each little way you seek their good over your own is an act of faith, trusting the Lord that he will care for you. Notice that there aren't any precursors to this Scripture.

It feels natural to put the needs of your children before your own, but what about your neighbor? Or your enemy? The call to seek the good of others over your own isn't limited to areas that make you comfortable. In every area of your life—relationships, education, politics, the workplace—seek the good of others. As you do this, being more concerned with injustice toward others than yourself, you can trust God to be the one to fight for you. He will faithfully care for you as you seek to value others above yourself.

Thank you, God, for the reminder to seek the good of others. I'm sorry for the areas where I have selfishly elevated my own well-being. Help me to selflessly care for others and trust you for my own needs.

# PERFECTLY MADE

*O Lord, you are our Father;*
*we are the clay, and you are our potter;*
*we are all the work of your hand.*
Isaiah 64:8 esv

Who you are as a mother, a woman, a sister, or a daughter is not an accident. You've been handcrafted to fit intricately into the lives of the people around you. Feelings of inadequacy can overwhelm you as you find yourself faced with tasks you don't feel equipped for. On any given day, you need to instill kindness, ensure your home is peaceful, manage the laundry, counsel the children, maintain the schedule, or do your job well. You might feel entirely unfit for the job you've been given.

Does the clay say to the potter, "What have you made"? Does the clay question the potter's ability to form it into a perfectly functional and beautiful vessel? You are the work of a master potter, with perfect skills and unlimited resources. He has made you specifically for this job, at this time. You are the work of his hands. When you feel inadequate, you can place your confidence in the fact that he created you perfectly. He knew what your life would look like and he knew what you would need to walk through your days.

Thank you, God, for your work in my life. Teach me to depend on you where I am weak. Renew my confidence in your ability as the potter. When I feel inadequate, remind me of who you are and what you have done. Today, help me walk in the freedom that comes from knowing you are my Creator and you don't make mistakes.

# FAITHFUL ENCOURAGER

*The God of all grace, who called you to his eternal glory in Christ,*
*after you have suffered a little while, will himself restore you*
*and make you strong, firm and steadfast.*
1 PETER 5:10 NIV

Imagine yourself curled up in the arms of your loving Father. You feel broken, tired, and overwhelmed. You've had an exceptionally hard day, and as you seek comfort from the Lord, he acknowledges your suffering, and he reminds you of what he has planned. "I will make you strong," he says. "I will restore you." "I will make you firm and steadfast." Can you hear him saying these things to you? In the midst of your pain, his words are steady and reassuring—a balm to your soul.

You believe what God says because you have a relationship that speaks of his faithfulness and the reliability of his character. His promises give you strength to walk through another day. His truth washes over you and covers you. It gives you confidence and motivates you to keep walking. Let this image be on your heart today: that you can always run to your Father in your suffering. He will be faithful to encourage you. He will be faithful to speak truth over you if you let him.

God, thank you for your reminders of what is to come! When I am overwhelmed, give me the grace to run to you and be reminded of what you've promised. You say you will make me strong, firm, and steadfast, so I believe you will. You are true to your Word and I am thankful.

# A SOFT HEART

*"Rend your heart and not your garments. Return to the Lord your God, for he is gracious and compassionate, slow to anger, and abounding in love, and he relents from sending calamity."*

JOEL 2:13 NIV

As you teach and guide your children, you can see the difference between when their hearts are soft and when they're stubborn. Even in obedience, a soft heart looks very different from one that is going about the actions but holding onto frustration and bitterness. You need to win their hearts because the state of their heart matters more than walking through the motions.

When you find yourself in trouble, rend your heart and not your garments. It might feel counterproductive, but if your actions don't stem from a heart that is devoted to the Lord, then they are empty. While you might want to make a plan, create a list, or execute a solution, your first order of business should always be to examine the state of your heart. Before you plan, ask yourself if your heart is contrite before God. Turn to him in humility and let him heal what is broken, then let your actions reflect what he has done internally.

God, you are more concerned with my heart than my actions. You value true healing and a heart that is contrite before you. Let my outward actions reflect what you've done in my heart.

# YOU ARE UNDERSTOOD

*The Lord looks down from heaven
and sees the whole human race.
From his throne he observes
all who live on the earth.
He made their hearts,
so he understands everything they do.*

PSALM 33:13-15 NLT

Have you ever seen your child act impulsively and then be confused about the entire scenario? You look at them bewildered saying, "Why would you do that?" and their honest and innocent response is that they don't know. Their developing minds aren't always capable of understanding how something will play out or what the consequences for their actions could be. You can see it clearly, so you do your best to tenderly educate them and guide them through the circumstances.

God clearly sees your heart even when you don't understand it. Even when you can't seem to conquer an incorrect mindset or resist temptation, God sees you and understands you. If you are feeling frustrated with your own heart, turn to him: the one who looks at you with a perfectly right perspective. Instead of looking inward in shame or frustration, look upward in the stillness, asking him for wisdom and direction. He will be faithful to pour out mercy on you and equip you with whatever you need.

God, thank you for seeing me! Even when my heart deceives me, you see it clearly and you understand me. Teach me how to look to you for help instead of looking at myself. The more I look inward, the more focused I am on shame and frustration. Help me instead to look to you in humility and thanksgiving.

# BY THE SPIRIT

*"Let me ask you only this: Did you receive the Spirit by works of the law or by hearing with faith? Are you so foolish? Having begun by the Spirit, are you now being perfected by the flesh?"*

GALATIANS 3:2-3 ESV

As a mom, you have to operate in some level of efficiency and productivity. Even if it's not your natural tendency to live by a schedule or make a list, it's kind of unavoidable with children. They need to be certain places at certain times and tasks need to be completed. Motherhood is full of work. Don't let this work be what makes you feel successful. Don't let it roll over into your relationship with God. If you find yourself checking your quiet time off a list of daily tasks, it's time to re-evaluate the state of your heart. When you first chose to follow Jesus, you made that decision in faith. You knew all that you were lacking, and his promises gave you hope and a future.

If the backbone of your current faith is a successful pattern of works, then what you need is to humbly repent and remember that your trust should lie in the Spirit. Maybe you feel like you've become proficient at following Jesus, so you've stopped desperately depending on him for what you need. Today, remember that your great need for him is never diminished. No matter how many quiet times you have, no matter how much Scripture you read, your need for Christ remains the same for all of your days.

I need you, Jesus. I want to depend on you for my salvation. It can be easy to be distracted by a task list, so please soften my heart toward the work of your Spirit in my life. Forgive me for acting as though my good habits bring redemption.

# REST IS PRODUCTIVE

*It is useless for you to work so hard*
*from early morning until late at night,*
*anxiously working for food to eat;*
*for God gives rest to his loved ones.*
PSALM 127:2 NLT

If you try to maintain productivity from morning until night, you will wear yourself out. You aren't designed to operate at a level ten at all times. You were designed to rest when you need it. Remember that it's not only your body that needs rest. Your heart, mind, and emotions need rest as well. If you wait until you are physically tired, you may have already pushed yourself too hard. Certain tasks can be emotionally tiring, and it's okay to need to recover from those. Give yourself the space you need to navigate your day in a healthy way.

If you feel guilty for slowing down, ask yourself what defines your opinion. Do you feel like you are only valuable if you are productive? Does your emotional or mental strength make you feel like you are worthy? Remember that your value and worth come from the Lord and anything else is simply idolatry. Slow down, take a deep breath, remember how God sees you, and find rest.

Thank you, God, that you designed me to need rest. Sometimes I struggle to choose rest. I need the Holy Spirit to remind me that it is good to take a break. Teach me how to slow down and find my rest in you.

# HE UNDERSTANDS WEEPING

*When Jesus saw her weeping, and the Jews who had come with her also weeping, he was deeply moved in his spirit and greatly troubled. And he said, "Where have you laid him?" They said to him, "Lord, come and see." Jesus wept.*

JOHN 11:33-35 ESV

Jesus is not unfamiliar with emotion and grief. He wept, and he felt things deeply and strongly just like you do. As the world around you is celebrating the holidays, you might find yourself lost in pain. Maybe the holidays hold difficult memories for you or have been a source of stress. This can be compounded by the fact that as a mom you might feel pressure to make the holidays magical for your children.

Today, go to Jesus in your pain and know that he is familiar with your weeping. He is a friend to the broken. He came to the world in humility, as a baby, to do the very thing you need right now. There is nothing greater that you can do in celebration of his birth than to honor him by running to him in your need and in your pain. He came that you might have redemption from sin and abundant life. Let go of everyone else's expectations for a moment and celebrate Christ by letting him hold you close.

Father, thank you that you created my emotions and you are not intimidated by them. When I am hurting, you understand. Help me to run to you and be comforted by you. You aren't a stranger to weeping and when I am struggling, you hold me close.

# TRUE GOODNESS

*We know that in all things God works for the good of those*
*who love him, who have been called according to his purpose.*

ROMANS 8:28 NIV

God's plans for you are good. This can be hard to believe in pain, disappointment, and brokenness. If you read this Scripture and feel a catch in your heart or that you don't quite believe it, maybe you need to adjust your definition of *good*. God's version is likely different than your own. He is constantly drawing you closer to himself and teaching you how to reflect Jesus. He redeems you through Christ and reminds you of his character.

If your definition of good is a laundry list of physical or monetary things, you might be left wanting. The greatest good you will ever experience hasn't yet occurred. On the day that Christ returns and you are fully alive, you'll understand true goodness. Until then, God gives you what you need to patiently endure. Today, seek to adjust your perspective and ask him to show you the good plans he has for you.

God, thank you that your definition of good is infinitely better than my own. When I am discouraged, remind me of what you have planned for those who love you. When I don't see your goodness, show me all that you've done.

# TRUE LOVE

*This is love: not that we loved God, but that he loved us
and sent his son as an atoning sacrifice for our sins.*
1 JOHN 4:10 NIV

As you seek the Lord, remember once again that your salvation has nothing to do with you. There is nothing that you could bring to the table that would give you right standing before the Lord. It is not your love for God that saves you but his love for you. This is true for all of your days. You will never reach a point where God says to you, "Good job! Your love is good enough now!" No matter how many days you've been walking with Christ, you will always be in desperate need of his atoning sacrifice for your sins.

Let this be your heart's cry as a mother. If you are unsure of how to lead your children in the ways of the Lord, start here. Tell them of their need for Jesus. Over and over, tell them of your collective need for Jesus. Show them that he is merciful and that it is his joy to redeem. As they see you display your humble and consistent need for the love of God, they too will turn to him in their need.

Thank you, God, that your love is what sent Jesus to redeem us from our sins. My salvation isn't dependent upon my love. Even at my best, my love is not enough. Help me to see you rightly.

# LOOK OUT FOR OTHERS

*Make me truly happy by agreeing wholeheartedly with each other, loving one another, and working together with one mind and purpose. Don't be selfish; don't try to impress others. Be humble, thinking of others as better than yourselves. Don't look out only for your own interests, but take an interest in others, too.*

PHILIPPIANS 2:2-4 NLT

The reminder to look beyond your own interests and prioritize the interests of others feels especially poignant at this time in history. It can be tiring to trying and navigate the division that the world is sitting in. Opinions are loud and debates are haughty. When you feel unsure of how to deal with all that is happening, remember this portion of Philippians. Your priority is not to be right or to be heard, but to love one another, to work together, and to assume that others are better than yourself. Imagine what the body of Christ would look like if each person assumed that their neighbor was better than them.

If you feel emotionally exhausted in today's culture and climate, maybe it is because the instructions in this verse are not a priority in your interactions. If that's the case, humbly repent and ask the Lord to change your perspective. He is faithful to bring transformation especially when the end goal is to love his children better. As you humbly seek to love like Jesus, your children will learn the value of elevating others above yourself as well.

Father, thank you for the reminder to love others more than myself. It's so easy to get caught up in haughtiness and debate. I want to honor you with my words and my actions. Teach me to love like you love. I want to teach my children how to love well, without selfishness. I need your help to do that.

# HELP THE WEAK

*"You yourselves know that these hands of mine have supplied my own needs and the needs of my companions. In everything I did, I showed you that by this kind of hard work we must help the weak, remembering the words the Lord Jesus himself said: 'It is more blessed to give than to receive.'"*

ACTS 20:34-35 NIV

What might the world look like if every day each person prioritized helping someone weaker than themselves? Can you even imagine a society that functions that way? So many people are tired and desperate for a hand to reach out and love them where they are. Instead of insisting that those weaker than you strengthen themselves in order to find success, try to see them the way Christ does—the way he sees you. He didn't hesitate to redeem you in the midst of your sin. He doesn't require you to better yourself before you receive the love that he has for you.

As he generously pours his love and mercy on you, let it overflow and be what you express to others. You have been given much, so you have much to give no matter what your financial status or material wealth looks like. Seek to love like Jesus did, and you'll find the joy that comes from a generous heart that loves without condition.

God, thank you for the reminder to help the weak. It can be easy to look down on them but you have never looked down on me in my weakness. Teach me how to love like you have loved and to give whatever I have to help others. I want to honor you in the way that I treat those around me.

# NOT YOUR HOME

*Our citizenship is in heaven.*
*And we eagerly await a Savior from there,*
*the Lord Jesus Christ.*
PHILIPPIANS 3:20 NIV

As a mom, you spend nearly two decades preparing your children as best you can. You love them, teach them, correct them, and build a life together, all while knowing that they're home isn't truly with you. The end goal is to see them thriving as adults, making their own choices wisely, and living successfully apart from you. Likewise, your time here on earth will not last forever. This place is not your forever home. You don't truly belong here.

For all eternity you will dwell in perfection with God; this is but a drop in time. It can be easy to be discouraged and overwhelmed by how the world is operating around you but remember that this is not your home. You've been asked to live as Jesus did, to love justice, to act with mercy and to walk humbly before the Lord. As you navigate your days in that way, your truest hope should not be in the powers and principalities of earth but in the kingdom of heaven that is waiting for you.

Father, when nothing feels right and the world around me seems chaotic, help me to remember that this is not my true home. When politics and culture are discouraging at best, renew my hope in eternity with you. I want to live on earth as Jesus did, with my eyes firmly on eternity with you.

# CLOSE TO THE BROKEN

*The LORD is close to the brokenhearted*
*and saves those who are crushed in spirit.*

PSALM 34:18 NIV

As the body of Christ joyfully celebrates the birth of Jesus, maybe this season is more painful for you than it is light and celebratory. Maybe you're walking through loss, or perhaps the memories you have of this time are just not very heartwarming. Wherever you find yourself, know that God is near you. He is close to the brokenhearted. He doesn't ask you to get yourself together; he reminds you that he delights in meeting you where you are. He wants to comfort you and save you.

If you don't relate to the hurt that can come rushing in during holidays, reach out to a friend who does. If God is close to the brokenhearted then you know that it is godly to reflect his character and do the same. He is near to you; he is near to those around you. Reach out and be a comfort to the hurting. Encourage the body to take refuge in God who is gentle and kind.

Thank you that you are near to me, God. You see the state of my heart, and you bring comfort. Help me to turn to you in my brokenness. Teach me how to encourage others about who you are. Give me opportunities to comfort the hurting.

# HE GIVES RIGHTLY

*"You parents—if your children ask for a loaf of bread, do you give them a stone instead? Or if they ask for a fish, do you give them a snake? Of course not! So if you sinful people know how to give good gifts to your children, how much more will your heavenly Father give good gifts to those who ask him."*

MATTHEW 7:9-11 NLT

As a mother, your desire is to provide for your children—security, love, empowerment. The list of what you want to bestow on them is limitless. You want to provide them with their needs but also with their wants. While our intentions are good, our resources are finite. This is not the case with God. He provides graciously, abundantly, and generously. There is no gift that he cannot give. In his goodness, he gives to his children just like you desire to give to yours. The difference is that his resources have no bounds and his perspective is always right. He gives perfectly.

As your Father, he loves you abundantly and wants to give you good gifts. Bring your needs to him confidently and trust that he sees you and answers you. You are his child. You can go to him as such and put your confidence in his goodness. Today, as you go about your day, ask for what you need. Remember that your Father has unlimited resources and is kind and generous.

Thank you, God, that you are a good father. You are kind and generous and you love for me to come to you with what I need. Teach me to ask you for good gifts. Align my heart with yours that my desires would line up too.

# REJOICE IN PERFECTION

*"God did not send his Son into the world to condemn the world,
but to save the world through him."*

JOHN 3:17 NIV

Today you can rejoice in the perfection and wonder of God's redemptive plan! Jesus was sent to save the world in humility and meekness. As you gather your loved ones near, remember that Jesus could have arrived in splendor and majesty, but instead he left his Father's side and was brought low. God knew that we needed to be able to see and feel and relate to the one who would save us, so he sent a man, a baby, to save the world. He came not to condemn you but to bring you close to the Father. In his lowliness, Jesus draws you near to the Creator of the universe. This is such a delightful and life-giving paradox.

This Christmas, marvel at what God has done. He used what was foreign to the world to save it. He used humility and sacrifice to accomplish what could have been done in power and condemnation. We don't deserve the gift of Christ, and we don't deserve his return as King. Today, put your confidence in what God has done, and place your hope in what is to come.

Thank you, God, that you sent a baby when we deserved a tyrant. Thank you for the merciful gift of the birth of Christ. Teach me to marvel at what you have done. Help me to place my hope in Christ's return. As he embraced humility and servanthood, give me the grace to do the same.

# MORE THAN DESERVED

*The wages of sin is death,*
*but the gift of God is eternal life*
*in Christ Jesus our Lord.*
ROMANS 6:23 NIV

What you've been given is not what you deserve. You've been treated with mercy and grace when death was the appropriate path. Instead of looking at your transgressions, God looks at the sacrifice of Christ. Let this redefine your day. Let the miracle of God's mercy change the way you view your children and the people around you. May you bestow upon them the same radical mercy that's been given to you. Together, delight in the nearness of God that is available to you through Jesus.

As you've spent time relishing in what God did by sending the baby Jesus as the Messiah, remember that his death is what has redeemed you. The miracle of his birth is made even more incredible by what it points to. Everything that Christ has done, from his birth to his death to his rising again is immensely more than we deserve. Let this draw you closer to him in thanksgiving and praise.

As we revel in the peace and glory of your birth, Jesus, help me also to remember that it led to your death. I am undeserving of your mercy, but you've given it to me abundantly. Help me to remember that what I deserve was taken on by Jesus and instead I have been redeemed.

# LOVE AND FAITHFULNESS

*Let love and faithfulness never leave you;*
*bind them around your neck,*
*write them on the tablet of your heart.*
PROVERBS 3:3 NIV

No matter the path you find yourself on, covered in weeds and difficult to navigate or speckled with wildflowers and incredible views, let love and faithfulness never leave you. Whether you feel confident in your relationship with God, or you are struggling to remember the truth, let love and faithfulness never leave you. No matter if you are heavy with brokenness or feeling content and satisfied, let love and faithfulness never leave you.

This is called a fortitude: a deliberate refusal to let go of what you have no matter your circumstances. When love and faithfulness are written on your heart, you cannot be separated from them. In all things, love the Lord. In all things, remember his faithfulness. Ask the Lord to develop fortitude within you and he will hold you steady in his love and faithfulness.

Thank you, God, for the way you love me and the way you are faithful to me. Develop fortitude within me that no matter my circumstances I will always return to your love and faithfulness. Let these two things define my life and the way I walk through my days.

# APPROACH CONFIDENTLY

*Let us then approach God's throne of grace with confidence, so that we may receive mercy and find grace to help us in our time of need.*

HEBREWS 4:16 NIV

Has your child ever approached you sheepishly, afraid of what your answer might be or nervous about how you might respond? Have you ever analyzed a situation or imagined how a conversation might go before it's even happened? These types of anxieties are needless with God. He has proven his character in such a way that we can approach him without fear of repercussion. He is not intimidated by your questions or overwhelmed by your emotions, no matter how big they might be. You cannot have doubts big enough to change God's love for you.

No matter what your needs are, you can approach God's throne of grace with confidence. Your confidence shows that you have a right understanding of who he is. Knowing his character and believing in his goodness allows you to approach him as a child, fully trusting that he will respond to you with mercy and grace in your time of need. Today, pay attention to how you approach God. Bring your needs to him, confident that he sees you through eyes of mercy.

Thank you that you are approachable, God. You are not far off or too lofty for me to ask you for help. When I need it, you give me grace. Thank you for your mercy, that you help me even when I don't deserve it. Remind me of your character and help me to come to you as a trusting child.

# TREASURE LOCATION

*"Where your treasure is,
there your heart will be also."*
LUKE 12:34 NIV

If you are unsure of where your priorities lie, look for your treasure. Where you spend your resources is where you heart will be. Look at how you spend your time, energy, and money. Those reveal what you value most. Ask for wisdom and discernment to honestly evaluate. Let the Holy Spirit lovingly lead you to areas that need adjusting.

If you discover that something is out of line, seek the Lord for the grace to change it. It is never too late. It doesn't have to be a Monday, a new year, or the first of the month to make adjustments in your life. God will be faithful to empower you when you are seeking to align your life with his heart. As you ask him for guidance and lean upon his strength, God gives abundant grace and mercy.

Thank you for your guidance, Lord. Help me to turn to you when evaluating my life. As you lead me, help me walk in humility. Help me also trust in your grace to make changes where I need to. I trust you with my priorities and my resources. I want to hold all that I have with an open hand and a generous heart.

# LOVE DEFINED

*God so loved the world that he gave his one and only Son,
that whoever believes in him shall not perish but have eternal life.*

JOHN 3:16 NIV

As you prepare for a new year, let the simple truth of the gospel
be what defines you. As you wrap up celebrating Christmas,
remember why he came to earth as an innocent baby. Set your
eyes firmly on the cross. What Jesus did was more than enough
and beyond what anyone deserves. His body, broken for you,
displays the infinite love of God. We cannot even begin to fathom
the kind of love that God has for humanity. It goes beyond our
understanding and our instinct. He gave his one and only Son so
you would have eternal life.

Let this incredible love be what you rest in as you move into a new
year. Let it cover disappointments and sorrow. Let it be what defines
you instead of picking a list of goals that might leave you in shame
or frustration. When you think about what you want the next year of
your life to look like, start with the foundation of being defined by
the sacrificial and eternal love that God has for the world.

I can't understand the love you have for us, Father. I can't
understand giving up my child for the salvation of others. I
want your incredible love to be what defines my life. Let it be
my foundation and my starting point.

# 365 DAYS

*"Give thanks to the Lord*
*for his love endures forever."*
2 CHRONICLES 20:21 NIV

Today, look back. Find a moment, no matter how brief, and think about who you were a year ago. 365 days have passed, and without a doubt, God has been at work in that time. Don't think about what you've accomplished. Though those things are notable, think about the ways that God has been faithful to you. The fact that you are here, breathing, reading these words, means that he sustained you. Maybe some of those days were wonderful, maybe a lot were normal, maybe some were so painful you didn't think you would make it. Give thanks to the Lord. His love endures forever and it has carried you over the last year.

Too often we base our success on how we've changed or what we've done. Instead, turn your eyes to how he has remained the same and all that he has done. You are here, at the end of an entire year, seeking to fill your heart with truth, giving a moment to God, focusing on him instead of yourself. Praise the Lord! By his grace and mercy, you are still following him.

Thank you, God, that you have sustained me over the last year! Show me the ways you have been faithful. Help me not to look at what I have done but at who you are. Thank you for your enduring love—love that covers me on my best and worst days. Help me to walk into this next year leaning on you.